Language, Identity and
Symbolic Culture

Also available from Bloomsbury:

Language and Identity, edited by David Evans
Language, Culture and Identity, Philip Riley
Second Language Identities, David Block

Language, Identity and Symbolic Culture

Edited by
David Evans

BLOOMSBURY ACADEMIC
LONDON • NEW YORK • OXFORD • NEW DELHI • SYDNEY

BLOOMSBURY ACADEMIC
Bloomsbury Publishing Plc
50 Bedford Square, London, WC1B 3DP, UK
1385 Broadway, New York, NY 10018, USA

BLOOMSBURY, BLOOMSBURY ACADEMIC and the Diana logo
are trademarks of Bloomsbury Publishing Plc

First published in Great Britain 2018
Paperback edition first published 2020

ISBN: HB: 978-1-3500-2301-7
      PB: 978-1-3501-4162-9
      ePDF: 978-1-3500-2302-4
      eBook: 978-1-3500-2300-0

Typeset by Newgen KnowledgeWorks Pvt. Ltd., Chennai, India

To find out more about our authors and books visit
www.bloomsbury.com and sign up for our newsletters.

Contents

List of Illustrations

Figures

Tables

Acknowledgements

I would like to acknowledge the support and encouragement provided for this book by the Rev. Canon Professor Kenneth Newport, pro vice chancellor (academic) and dean of education at Liverpool Hope University, as well as to the University more generally

Furthermore, I would like to acknowledge, over the course of the project, the support of Andrew Wardell, linguistics editor at Bloomsbury Publishers.

I also acknowledge all the chapter contributors, without whom our book *Language, Identity and Symbolic Culture* would not have become a reality. My thanks to all those contributing academics.

Deo Gratias
Dr David Evans

Part One

Language and Identity: A Theoretical Perspective

Editor's introduction

This is a theoretical section, consisting of two chapters following on from the introduction to the book as a whole in Chapter 1.

Chapter 2 charts a journey from a traditional Cartesian view of language reflecting individual rational mind, characterized by the linguistics of Chomsky and going towards a more social view of language and identity. The chapter progresses to a view of language, meaning and identity as intersubjectively constructed; then to a post-structural view of meanings and therefore identities as multiple, fluid, located and subject to interpretation in the social world rather than the mind of the individual. Chapter 3 focuses on the formation of discourse as language use in social action reflecting the ideologies of speakers and texts from their positions of sociocultural positions of power. It examines the extent to which the individual is located inside or outside of discourse and with this the extent of the power.

1

Introduction

David Evans

The rationale of this book is to explore the interwoven connections between language, identity and symbolic culture. The purpose for this rationale is the analysis of the power of language, not only power occasioned by the application of words and signs in language use or discourse, but also the ideologies that lie within language and discourse. We see in the book how language and its social use or discourse can be viewed as a 'symbolic capital' analogous to economic currency where some languages and language types are more valued than others. The book's aim in the final section moves to ways of achieving linguistic and therefore cultural equity as expressions of social justice through a much more critical pedagogy where all languages and cultures of participants in education are equally valued.

The book is organized over four sections: Part I is theoretical examining the dual function of language as constructing reality subjectively and intersubjectively and /or describing a pre-existent reality; therefore language as creative or referential. This theoretical section also explores the connection between language as internal in terms of its components such as lexis and grammar and language as externally facing in its social usage, or in other words discourse.

Part II is a research section on urban discourses examining power, marginalization and resistance in language and discourse. It examines some current debates occurring in the interface and interrelationship between local and metropolitan discourses in one instance and youth discourses in the formation of identity in another. This involves looking at cultural issues of marginalization by dominant discourses and the corollary of resistant discourse.

Part III broadens themes of language, cultural marginalization and resistance from locations in the United Kingdom to case studies around the world in Africa, India, China and migrant journeys across national borders.

The case study in Africa explores the relationship between linguistic marginalization and opportunity in Cameroon where French is the language of opportunity and privilege, especially in the area of access to educational resources. Unfortunately this linguistic dominance marginalizes both tribal languages and the nationally understood and spoken Pidgin English which is regarded as non-standard and prohibited from use in educational institutions. Clearly here language use impacts on social justice in the discrimination between language types resulting in the restriction of access to cultural and educational resources. Chapter 7 narrates and analyses the geopolitical and sociocultural live topic in the world today concerning the loss of refugee voice as refugees cross national borders and struggle to gain acceptance in host countries. This chapter narrates and analyses their shifting identities as they journey across geographical, sociocultural and economic boundaries to unknown destinations. We see how their identities are marginalized as they become depersonalized objects of debate by the political media and framed within a negative and menacing discourse. The consequence of this is the disappearance of their own voices.

The case study in India examines in particular the role of dalit literature as a resistant language and discourse to the dominant Indian mainstream culture. Dalits were historically regarded as 'untouchables' without voice but have now made their voice heard through dalit literature. This literature is written in the languages of Marathi, Tamil and Telugu and is expressed as poetry, ballads, short stories and novels.

Chapter 9, which concludes Part III, is a case study set in the Uyghur province of northwest China. It follows the struggles of the Uyghurs as they strive to preserve their language and culture in the face of an encroaching Chinese Mandarin language culture.

The interconnecting characteristic between Parts II and III is the notion of language and discourse constituting a symbolic culture and the ideas of Bourdieu (1977, 1982, 1989, 2013) figure strongly where language is a symbolic capital analogous to economic currency. We further evidence this in Chapter 10 in the pedagogical Part IV, in terms of foreign language education in UK secondary schools where clearly the decision on which languages are taught in schools is based in large part on sociocultural and therefore economic power. For instance, most secondary schools teach French and many teach Spanish and German based on their current global and European economic reach and also on the cultural historic legacy of these countries. In the past few years Mandarin Chinese has been introduced into many secondary schools due to the emergence of China as an economic superpower offering possibilities of extensive trading links with the United Kingdom. Contrast this with European languages such as Lithuanian, Hungarian, Serbo-Croat, Polish and Czech which are not taught in schools nor are UK community languages because they lack the socio-economic capital of French, German, Spanish and now Mandarin Chinese.

Moreover, in Part II, we see that linguistic capital also pertains to urban discourse where some ways of speaking are more highly regarded than others and therefore set in train resistant and alternative creative discourses.

The main lessons from the first three sections of the book are the notions of language as ideological, constituting and expressing power and that the consequences of this impact on identity. However the other lesson is that identity and power are not unitary and monolithic imposed from above but diverse and diffuse, negotiated situationally. We can then talk about identities in the plural since language and power exist at many different social levels. So, for instance, locally a particular urban or regional dialect may well carry more social capital than the standard language. There may then well ensue a situation of conflict between the local and the standard as we see in Chapter 4.

Part IV is a pedagogical section which explores the possibilities for the valorization of marginalized language-culture. This section focuses on education as a force for social justice and therefore foregrounding of marginalized culture.

The chapters in this section are research chapters which explore a more critical view of education, challenging existing traditional power relations in the development of teacher identity in Chapter 11 and the 'banking system' in foreign language teaching in Chapter 10, which often overlooks cultural understanding to focus on the economic outcomes of language learning.

In the concluding Chapter 12, Freire (1972, 1989) has much to say with regard to democratizing the power differentials in education between teachers and students. This can be achieved by viewing language, culture and knowledge as processes which are co-constructed socially rather than imposed as finished definitive products. Students and their teachers can then valorize or re-valorize marginalized language by using it to learn knowledge and skill not just at primary school but throughout the educational system. At the same time social justice also includes economic opportunity and students should learn dominant lingua francas such as Standard English alongside their own languages of local community identity. This chapter therefore proposes a co-construction of knowledge and skill through bilingual education where all students are open to at least another language and culture. In the United Kingdom, the current Brexit (British exit of the European Union) polemic, in 2017, should not close down foreign language learning to favour the hegemony of the English lingua franca, nor should the only argument for learning a foreign language be for economic outcomes but rather to engage in foreign language learning to understand the alterity of otherness in language-culture and explore therein the possibilities for identity.

Finally, education should not just address performance unquestioningly as in Freire's (1972) 'banking system' but critically question the status quo of socio-economic distribution of cultural and linguistic resources so that they may be more equitably allocated in the interest of social justice. In this respect we hope that readers of this book will see that education, with an equitable access to sociocultural resources through language in particular, can remain an agent for social change.

References

Bourdieu, P. (1977). *Outline of a Theory of Practice*. Cambridge. Cambridge University Press.

Bourdieu, P. (1982). *Langage et pouvoir symbolique*. Editions Fayard.

Bourdieu, P. (1989). 'Social Space and Symbolic Power'. *Sociological Theory* 7.1: 14–25.

Bourdieu, P. (2013). 'Symbolic Capital and Social Classes'. *Journal of Classical Sociology* 13.2: 292–302.

Freire, P. (1972). *Pedagogy of the Oppressed*. London: Penguin Books.

Freire, P., & Faundez, A. (1989). *Learning to Question: A Pedagogy of Liberation*. Geneva: WCC Publications.

2

Meaning: From Inner Structure to Post-structure

David Evans

Introduction

Language in this book is conceived as closely and inseparably entwined with the nature of being. Identity, as the nature of being, can be viewed differently as, for example, unitary, continuous and located in the mind, or created socially, communal and systemic or intersubjectively between subjects or alternatively as fragmented into multiple levels and facets, all according to the philosophical approach we take to language. The rationale of the book in the title *Language, Identity and Symbolic Culture*, as explained in the introduction, is to explore the relationships between the three elements of the title. This chapter will focus on a progressive range of interrelations between language and identity, starting from individual subjective identity of rational language as mind based, then towards more social intersubjective accounts of language and identity, then systemic explanations in structuralism and finally post-structural accounts of multiple and continually developing identities. The next chapter will focus on the third element of the title in terms of how language becomes discourse, invested with symbolic power to promote some languages and forms of language while marginalizing others.

Hardcastle (2009) narrates historical philosophical approaches to language from the European Enlightenment era of the seventeenth century onwards starting with the English philosopher Locke and referring to the ideas of Herder and von Humboldt. This reveals fundamental questions as to whether the individual stands inside or outside of language. In other words, does individual identity preexist language or is it constituted by and within language? Hardcastle states Locke's position for language as the transmission of preexisting ideas and the vehicle of thought. Succinctly Hardcastle (2009: 186) states this position as, 'Ideas come first: words follow.' Condillac in the 1700s placed language in a much more forward position as a tool for gaining mastery over thoughts. Here, thoughts could only be organized and cohere through signs and symbols. Condillac argued that psychology needs language to produce a psychologized self, by opening up a space for consciousness and reflection, 'unconstrained by immediate circumstances' (Hardcastle 2009; 187). Herder took Condillac's view of language much further by considering it to be more dynamic in constituting identity itself. Hardcastle (2009; 189) states, 'On this view, expression is the process by which people make themselves.' Von Humboldt in the nineteenth century follows a similar line as Herder in viewing language as self-constitutive of identity but differs from Herder in the notion that intellectually developed identity is formed intersubjectively and communally with others. Hardcastle (2009: 190) sums up Von Humboldt's thinking, stating that '[t]he significant point for von Humboldt was the shaping and ordering influences of languages on the development of the mentalities of the peoples that speak them-their whole orientation towards the world'.

We can see therefore that historically, philosophers viewed individual identity shaped differently by different 'takes' on the nature of the relationship between language and the individual. We will see the Cartesian view also in the chapter where Descartes (2008) views language as a rational expression of the individual's preexisting rationality.

Consequently, following on from this historical perspective, this chapter's thesis is that different paradigms of linguistics can account for different narratives of being in the world and to see identity not only as individual, rational and located entirely in the head but also as progressively becoming social and intersubjective. This progressive direction is important in terms of the rationale of this book which aims to foreground the links between language, its use and how this affects identities of individuals and groups concerning their opportunities on the one hand and marginalization and cultural resistance on the other. The chapter will outline movement and progression across paradigms and to assist this dynamic, I argue that it is necessary to explore more fully the earlier philosophical accounts already briefly outlined to provide this progressive range of accounts for narratives of language and identity.

Historical philosophical accounts of language-identity

Two opposing Enlightenment philosophers proposed very different models of the individual and subsequently how notions of identity would unfold over time.

Descartes's view (*Meditations*; Moriarty 2008) was of the individual's innate rationality containing inner structures corresponding to the structures of knowledge in the outside world. This is very much a metaphysical philosophy where Descartes argues that God guarantees the individual's epistemological connection to the outside world. So the structures for all knowledge are contained in individual rationality, meaning that the individual acquires knowledge in the sense that he/she learns what he/she already knows. Knowledge is not actively constructed by the individual but is simply out there awaiting discovery by corresponding mental structures in the fullness of time. As it will be discussed later in this chapter, Chomsky (2009) takes up the baton of Cartesian linguistics in his notion of Universal Grammar where children in particular acquire language rather than actively learn it. However Chomsky does not mention any reference to a divine guarantor of subject-object interconnection although neither does he lean towards linguistic evolution, referring instead to the origin of language arising out of a chance mutation early on in human history.

Opposed to Cartesian views of epistemology is Locke's (2010–15) view of human knowledge which conceives of the individual as a 'blank slate'. He states his position as follows:

> Let us then suppose the mind to have no ideas in it, to be like white paper with nothing written on it. How then does it come to be written on? From where does it get that vast store which the busy and boundless imagination of man has painted on it – all the materials of reason and knowledge? To this I answer, in one word, from *experience*. (18)

For Locke, knowledge is generated by a combination of experience of the world and also reflection, being the ability to turn inwards to view the contents of mind and reflect upon what the senses have experienced. Nevertheless the raw material for knowledge is experience of the outside world as opposed to Cartesian innate structures for knowledge. Therefore all knowledge including language is empirical and not derived from innate structures beyond the ability to reflect.

The two opposed positions of Descartes on the one hand and Locke on the other give rise to the linguistic positions of Chomsky and Vygotsky respectively. Chomsky, on the one hand, talks about language being generated by innate structures within mind which correspond to the structures of language just in the same way that Descartes talked about structures for knowledge residing innately in mental structures. Vygotsky, on the other hand, talks about language being learned from experience of the outer world in the same way that Locke referred to all learning being based on the raw material of experience of the outer world. The production of language, whether it is simply acquired as in Cartesian linguistics or actively learned through the social world, reflects a philosophical dichotomy between rationalism and empiricism.

Chomsky's Cartesian linguistics

The key to Descartes's philosophy and to subsequent Cartesian linguistics is rationality based upon mind-body dualism. Descartes's statement 'Cogito ergo sum' 'I think therefore I am' (*Second Meditation*; Moriarty 2008) is derived from the human mind or Descartes's mind affirming its own existence and subsequently affirming the existence of the body and the outside world. However this is very much about the lone individual mind affirming its own existence in original isolation. Therefore mental contents are rationally located inside the mind rather than within any notion of the social world, because language is conceived as a rational item of knowledge that the mind deploys to express inner rationality.

This rational based linguistics is taken up by the Port Royal grammarians in the 1600s. Their book entitled *The General and Reasoned Grammar* is described by Roy (1999) as not being about the grammar of a particular language but about the relation of languages in general to Cartesian ideas. Roy maintains that for the Port Royal grammarians 'language and ideas are correlative and, as such, are really inseparable. That the "art of speaking" lives and dies with the "art of thinking" holds as true as the converse' (132). Here there is no mention of language as a means of communication or as relational but simply as a tool for rational thought.

Similarly Chomskyan linguistics conceives the individual as a rational person with language as the tool for expressing this rationality in thought without regard for social communication or social identity. Language is therefore a rational adjunct to the mind and as such idealized as an expression of logic.

This has implications for meaning because meaning is generated within the inner structures of language and mind rather than socially.

Universal Grammar

The Port Royal grammarians of the seventeenth century used a notion of universal grammar as mentioned above to apply linguistics to Cartesian ideas of mind and Chomsky takes up this concept to explain the ease with which individuals know and speak a language. Chomsky's Universal Grammar is not the grammar of any particular language but the blueprint for all languages. It is an innate structure for language that exists within all humans so that, given normal everyday circumstances of human contact, children will learn to speak and know a language or languages, even if the linguistic content surrounding them is limited or of a non-standard variety. For Chomsky and Lenneburg (1967), his colleague, there is an optimum age for this which is infancy. This means that if children are deprived of all human linguistic contact, they will have missed the moment and grow up without a full linguistic facility.

Chomsky (2009) divides language into 'deep structure' and 'surface structure'. As we see in the following statement, it is the deep structure that contains the universal grammar which is the rational facility for the construction of thought across all languages, that which separates us from the superficial and instinctive physicality of surface structure. It is therefore the deep structure which accounts for our rational identity as human beings. Chomsky points out as follows: '[W]e can distinguish the "deep structure" of a sentence from its "surface structure". The former is the underlying abstract structure that determines its semantic interpretation; the latter, the superficial organization of units which determines the phonetic interpretation and which relates to the physical form of the actual utterance, to its perceived or intended form' (79).

According to Chomsky language has a mind-body duality corresponding respectively to semantics and phonetics. However the meaning of a sentence is in the mind or the deep structures and this is the domain of semantics whereas the surface structure is only the local expression of the deeper meaning. Chomsky (2009: 83) goes on to reinforce the relations between deep and surface structures as follows: 'The deep structure that expresses the meaning is common to all languages, so it is claimed, being a simple reflection of forms of thought. The transformational rules that convert deep to surface structure may differ from language to language'.

Chomsky (2006) argues for language study to form a central part of general psychology because universal grammar or language universals are integral to mental functioning. This would imply that mental processes can be understood through language use. This is justified by Chomsky in the following statement, '[I]t is natural to expect a close relation between innate properties of the mind and features of linguistic structure; for language, after all, has no existence apart from its mental representation. Whatever properties it has must be those that are given to it by the innate mental processes of the organism that invented it' (83). Here Chomsky is arguing that there is little to distinguish universal grammar from mind and so language is not something learned by repetition by a learning mind alongside everything else. The young child internalizes external linguistic data from the social world which corresponds to language shaped innate mental structures. This innate approach should then be distinguished from language learning as part of general learning strategies where one could argue that learning any skill is much more easily done in childhood because of a heightened general capacity of learning.

The innateness of the Chomskyan approach to the nature of language and identity and concomitant language learning has its critics due to a perceived lack of evidence concerning the internal mental structures of Universal Grammar. Dabrowska (2015) criticizes Chomsky's notion of universal grammar by arguing that Chomsky has no empirical evidence for this, that he does not specify or empirically verify what exactly universal grammar is, or in what it consists. Dabrowska is a constructivist linguist and justifiably argues that universal grammar as a concept should be fully justified through empirical evidence and then posited as a conclusion rather than as an a priori principle or precept. Within a paradigm of evidence based social science, Dabrowska is undoubtedly right in stating that universal grammar is a hypothesis to be tested against rather than an a priori principle. It needs the chance to be challenged by the evidence in order to be falsified like any other scientific data. However Chomsky is a linguistic philosopher rather than an empirical scientist and comes to his a priori precept by logical inference. Universal Grammar can be framed as a specific structure of mind which corresponds to language and serves as a body of organizing principles. This logical inference is based on the notion of 'necessary conditions'. What are the necessary conditions for language to take place, for a child to learn the basic forms of language in so short a time with only a minimum of exposure and with even non-standard or incorrect grammar? Given frequently unfavourable circumstances, universal grammar, generating meaning from inner organizing principles via surface structures, would seem more plausible to rationalists than the notion of learning a language by quantitative increments. The rationalist method starts with innate organizing principles but then states that the creative use of grammar can generate completely new sentences which have not necessarily ever been heard, learned and repeated. Therefore, for Chomsky, innate grammar accounts for the idea that we use language creatively from a comparatively small strategic base.

However the social constructivist model is that we learn language by exposure and repetition and then, by constant use, we learn which parts of the lexis or vocabulary can serve as functional grammar to control and generate new sentences. The former therefore works from the inside going outwards and the latter model works from the outer sociocultural going inwards.

An argument running through this chapter is that the two opposing paradigms of language represent two differing views of human identity-rational individual on the one hand and sociocultural on the other. We proceed now to a sociocultural model for language learning.

Social constructivism: language as a social phenomenon

For Vygotsky (1962) all meaning is at first social and meanings attach themselves to word sounds before becoming individual through inner speech within thought processes. Word and object are separate entities and not intrinsically connected but nevertheless enter into each other by close sociocultural association. It is possible for a child or even an adult to use a word by repetition without being fully aware of its meaning. It is also possible for the word to change meaning over time. The mechanism for the arbitrary nature of word sounds and spellings will become clearer later on when the chapter comes to focus on the work of Ferdinand de Saussure, the founder of modern linguistics.

For Vygotsky the origins of the thinking process and language start in different places but then come together in the human mind around the age of two years. It is at this stage that word sounds start to take on the social meanings from the outside world in the minds of young children. Before this time, basic instinctive word sounds can exist in the young child without thought but rather as prelinguistic emotion. Equally, thought in terms of basic instincts can exist without language much as it does in mammals such as apes. It is only when social language and the thought processes in the child intersect that thought itself begins to develop and is able, in thought-language interaction, to attain higher-order rational thinking. Higher-order thinking would not exist without language and there is something of a consensus over this across the linguistic paradigms of both Chomsky and Vygotsky.

The internalization of word sound social meanings and their intersection with thought processes have implications for the construction of personal identity. This is because the words that children encounter come with preexisting meanings which they internalize and such preexisting meanings contain ideologies which children are not yet in a position of sufficiently fully conscious thought to analyse and investigate. Vygotsky argues that children internalize meanings by narrating actions to themselves in egocentric speech during play. The meanings of particular words are therefore only understood in particular situations of narrated play or sociocultural action. A full impact of all the possible meanings of words may only 'sink in' at a later stage when the thought-language interaction is more fully developed. Obviously the degree to which this development occurs is a matter of personal education and development.

Vygotsky (1962) argues that language and linguistic interaction between individuals are a major tool in the construction of thought and understanding. He formulates the notion of the Zone of Proximal Development (ZDP) where the higher level of linguistic and communicative ability of a capable peer can help less experienced learners to reach out beyond their current understanding to the more advanced concepts that would otherwise be beyond them. Therefore much in line with the Lockean notion of the 'blank slate' and learning from experience, Vygotsky's view of learning is that it is active and social leading to pedagogical strategies of group and pair work learning where students learn from each other. The identity of the individual and learner here is social and not individual and certainly not, as perhaps Chomsky and also Piaget would argue, based on maturational levels of inner development. Again the identity of the individual in the Locke, Vygotsky line of thinking is outer and not inner, social and not innate.

Cole (1996) regards language as an artefact used by the individual to mediate the world. Language is then a highly developed means by which the world is presented or re-presented to us. We are then able to use these linguistic representations as intellectual tools to further construct the world. Social constructivism argues that we construct ourselves, each other and the social and technical world through linguistic interaction. Space rockets, jet airplanes, high performance motor cars or highly sophisticated scientific and medical equipment could never have been developed if we had not first engaged in thought-language interaction through education and secondly had never interacted with each other. The implication of this is that if linguistic capability is underdeveloped, then so is our intellectual and cultural identity.

If Vygotsky's perspective of language and identity may seem socioculturally deterministic and lacking in agency, then we should look to Bakhtin to restore a sense of individual and group agency to language where individuals and groups are able to appropriate preexisting meanings and change them according to particular need and ideology.

An ideological view of language: notions of discourse

Bakhtin (1981) focuses on the internalization of social language, as does Vygotsky, with the principal difference between them being the emphasis by Bakhtin on dialogue and the presence of the Other within inner voice. Bakhtin views inner identity being permeated by the voices of others within individuals since, in the social world, they live in constant dialogue with others. Bakhtin refers to this as dialogized heteroglossia where, in terms of language and communication, the individual resides within the interactions at the intersection between him/herself and others. Identity therefore is ongoing and constantly being shaped within intersubjectivity. Along with Wertsch (1991), Bakhtin maintains that words are half the property of others in that they are borrowed with their pre-existent meanings but then adapted by individuals and groups to their own situations. Therefore one appropriates the words of others and personalizes them with one's own meanings and ideologies. The voices of others however still persist, in Bakhtin's dialogism, as opposed to any notion of dialectic that would imply synthesis of meanings. Bakhtin (1981: 341) states this as follows, '[T]he ideological becoming of a human being . . . is the process of selectively assimilating the words of others'. There is therefore always a tension within the individual due to a struggle for meaning between the individual and the other. This tension will remain and Rule (2011: 940) points out, Bakhtin always views individuals as inter-relating within a 'tense dialogic struggle that each individual experiences on the boundary of his own and others' words' and that this 'is a learning process of 'selecting and assimilating the words of others' (940).

Bakhtin's view of identity is then a 'far cry' from the idealized individual identity proposed by Descartes and taken up by Chomsky in his rational linguistics. Rule (2011: 934) maintains that Bakhtin (along with the educational philosopher Paolo Freire) proposes the individual as a 'social being, it is being-with-others and being- in-the-world. Both Bakhtin and Freire reject the notion of the isolated and divided individual human subject of Cartesian philosophy. Humans become through a process that is with and through others'.

Consequently when the individual speaks, it is to take into account the response of others and so the utterances become populated with the views and voices of others and the sense of 'I' is shaped by how others might or do respond to us. Therefore even when alone, the absent other is present in our own sense of being. In this way the unitary notion of single identity is problematized where it is difficult or impossible to separate out the 'I' from the other and where the 'I' is defined by both its otherness and connectedness to the 'you'. Identity is therefore not isolated but both differentiated and connected.

The notion of identity as 'becoming' is a feature of Bakhtin's philosophy and also of Derrida (1967) whom we shall encounter later on in this chapter. It is the notion of all human identity being unfinished and always becoming rather than any state of fixed being. Given Bakhtinian philosophy of the individual as being always in dialogue, individual identity is seen as continually emerging from dialogical interaction continuing through time. Individuals' identities remain always incomplete because time is as yet unfinished and ongoing. Therefore for Bakhtin, 'human existence, like language and meaning, is open-ended, always "yet-to-be"' (Rule 2011: 934);. The open-endedness of identity depends on its location in time and place, because identity, firstly, can be multiple according to social context; therefore identities can exist as a plural rather than a singular unitary concept. Secondly, identities can change over time. This second view of identity depends on the concept of deferred meanings or deferral which is a central plank of Derrida's post-structural linguistic philosophy.

Bakhtin's view of language is that it is at the same time the property of the supposed linguistic system and also the property of the individual. Words are borrowed from the common pool and instantiated by the individual within his/ her social group to locate a particular meaning appropriate to his/her context. Bakhtin therefore places a strong emphasis on the identity of individual agency where the individual is constituted by his/her own dialect or genre and by the otherness of a supposed system.

Price (2014) proposes that Bakhtin's system is really grounded on language use which solidifies over time to appear objective. As such grammar is simply the historical manner in which language has been arranged over time. Beyond this, the language system and grammar are groundless and the only guarantee of meaning is the potential interpretation of the addressee. Linguistic meaning then is horizontal between social participants and not vertically grounded in any system. Therefore identities in language are forged intersubjectively through and by spoken utterances. Meanings fluctuate because individual utterances are part of a continuous chain of utterances which precede and succeed the individual utterance. Price points out that language has no real independent existence and only exists through mutual participation. Price quotes Bakhtin as follows: 'An utterance is always a response to prior utterances' and 'any utterance is a link in a very complexly organized chain of utterances' (15).

This contrasts with the systemic view of structuralist linguistics proposed by Saussure (1966), who nevertheless prepared the way for the post-structuralism of Derrida in his disconnection between signified and signifier. For Bakhtin, language is about communication whereas for Saussure language is a system.

In the next section we can see the contrasting view of language in relation to identity between the interactional dialogism of Bakhtin and the systemic approach of structural linguistics.

The structuralism of Saussure

Saussure (1959) provides a root and branch theoretical analysis of the linguistic system including the relationship between language and the community of speakers. This is not the Cartesian rational language of mind as individual identity focusing on the grammatical system but rather an explanation of language as a social system and historical identity.

Saussure (1915; 1959: 15) defines 'language' as follows: 'It is a system of signs in which the only essential thing is the union of meanings and sound-images and in which both parts of the sign are psychological'. He goes on to say that this union is only arbitrary as there is no intrinsic bond between the word or signifier and the concept – object or signified. The association between sounds and objects which forms meaning takes place in the individual mind although the origin of both is in the social world. This is not far away from Vygotsky's position where meaning itself originates in the social world and then is internalized by the individual. The difference in Saussure's position is that the two elements that form the sign, that is, sounds and objects, are located in the social world but the meaning itself is created in the mind, rather than in the social world. Saussure (1915; 1959: 23) states that 'language is the social product deposited in the brain of each individual.'

Saussure divides language into spoken language or 'parole' and the underlying linguistic system called 'langue'. Parole is the interactional instantiation of langue where socio-historical meanings have already been formulated by 'langue'. Individual meanings are then shaped by this in their reproduction in the mind of the individual. Saussure argues that parole in terms of speaking is not the only expression of language as a system or 'langue' but rather that this could equally be sign language or gesture, for example. Therefore visual symbols could replace acoustic symbols. This is why Saussure refers to sound-image as the signifier and not simply the word. The arbitrary connection between the signifier and the signified is guaranteed by the community of speakers as, sound-images in themselves, without this guarantee, are totally meaningless and empty. The obvious exception to this are onomatopoeic words where the meaning itself is derived from sound approximation caused by nature.

Saussure (1959) regards time as having a double function in that at one and the same time its historical nature holds meaning in place and yet its continuous nature into the future causes word meanings to evolve. He refers to this as the mutability and immutability of the sign and suggests that 'the principle of change is based on the principle of unity' (74). This idea is that continuity is the basis upon which change is made. It means that change is change from something and change and continuity act as a same-difference comparison. In practice change involves a shift over time between the signified and the signifier. I consider that this is not that far from Bakhtin's view of difference and sameness in language between the individual and the supposed system aligning Bakhtin's notion of centripetal forces unifying language and centrifugal forces dispersing it. There are however differences in that, for Bakhtin, there is no real linguistic system as it is merely a notional one which is groundless. However, for Saussure, although signs are formed in the mind of individuals they are influenced by the real system of 'langue' as a social structure. Saussure is after all a linguistic 'structuralist'.

Saussure's formation of meaning through difference

In Saussure's linguistic theory meaning is produced in a process of differentiation between signs (objects linked to sounds) that stand in both association and opposition with each other. The following statement by Saussure (1915; 1959: 111) explains the basis for the construction of meaning: 'psychologically our thought – apart from its expression in words – is only a shapeless and indistinct mass'. Signs therefore allow us to differentiate phenomena into distinct categories and distinguish them from similar adjacent categories which can then be further subdivided with the use of more refined and accurate sign use. Saussure states that 'without language, thought is a vague, uncharted nebula. There are no pre-existing ideas and nothing is distinct before the appearance of language' (1959: 112).

Therefore the creation of meaning is a two-way simultaneous process. There is a vertical action of the association between sound (signifier) and object (signified) and at the same time a horizontal action between associated signs to create differentiation between them. So a word meaning or sign depends on the meanings of other word meanings, and as Saussure (1959: 114) points out, 'Language is a system of interdependent terms in which the value of each term results solely from the simultaneous presence of others'. Consequently a word-sign can totally occupy a meaning category as generic until another similar word claims some of the space by exerting a difference in meaning. An example of this would be the following proposition: vegetation in a field or on a plot of land would be seen from afar as plants especially to the untutored eye. However on closer inspection the observer might perceive flowers and he/she could do this by differentiating them from other vegetation. So we would have flowers and other plants. A subsequent refinement of perception could results in difference within flowers and the attribution of further word categories such as roses, daffodils and tulips. There may be another perception of difference for which no word is available and a new word would need to be generated, perhaps using a variation of a similar word-sign using a prefix or adding an adjective – yellow rose and so on. The result of this practically is that a rose is a rose because it is not something else and therefore a sign exists because of what it is *not* as much as what it *is* – in other words by *absence* of meaning as by its *presence* of meaning.

In recent political-media language, the term 'Brexit' was widely used in 2016 to signify the UK exit from the EU. This has meaning only in relation to Remain as its opposition and several years before the EU referendum debate, it would have been a meaningless sound, out of context. A further development was that in late 2016–early 2017, there was a division of the identity of Brexit into hard and soft and it is not inconceivable eventually, with frequent use, for a new word or word combination to be created to further designate each of these through a linguistic refinement.

Structuralist implications for identity

Word difference between similar word associations has important consequences in terms of how human identity is both constructed and constrained by language. A girl is a girl because of her resemblance to other girls but also because of her difference from boys. Saussure's theory of meaning helps us to understand how we construct meaning and how we come to define what is a boy or girl, for example, but at the same time it limits us to binary classifications. One would need to call into question such a limited view of classification in order to see that gender is not confined only to the opposites of a continuum but may lie at various points on the continuum. In educational terms simplistic binary categories could limit and constrain identity by saying all boys are inclined towards one attribute and all girls are inclined towards another. One could then end up by stating that English literature is a girls' subject and design technology is a boys' subject at school.

In the next section we will see how post-structuralism can tackle the notion of varied multiple identities as a search for emancipation from linguistically constraining stereotypes.

Before this, one other item of importance should be highlighted from Saussure's linguistic theory which is the emphasis of association of word-signs as opposed to the differentiation we have just mentioned. Saussure (1915; 1959: 126) argues that '[a] word can always evoke everything that can be associated with it in one way or another'. This means that word meanings can cohere through association and form a discourse. Saussure gives an example of this starting with the word 'education' which subsequently through usage coheres with words such as 'teaching, learning, training, apprenticeship, vocation'. Other words could then be added from use within a contemporary school setting such as 'development, assessment and progression etc.' One can easily see that this might be the start of a professional discourse around education.

The next chapter will focus on this link between language as word-sign and language as a larger discourse within the accumulated social repertoire of meanings.

Writers such as Saussure, Vygotsky and Bakhtin have demonstrated how a much wider view of human identity can be conceptualized through notions of language and meaning originating from the social world rather than from an isolated view of the individual. Language is then social communication as well as being a tool for rational thought. It is also intersubjective in its construction of meaning and Bakhtin alludes to the notion of 'I' being defined in relation to the other. This evokes the problematic as to where 'I' ends and the 'other' begins and to the idea that within one's own identity there is indeed a sense of the other and, as a consequence, a sense of interconnectedness.

Derrida (1967) picks up on this theme of fluidity of identity, not just in terms of the 'other' but also related to the future in terms of unfinished identity. Post-structuralism liberates meaning and identity from a monolithic unitary nature by looking at language in terms of interpretation as well as meaning making.

Post-structural identities

Derrida (1967; 1978) moves language and identity forward beyond Saussure's structuralism of binary meaning such that an object is identified as a particular entity because of its difference with everything else as well as its association with similarity. For Derrida difference does not mean binary opposition but a differentiation with all other possible absent meanings rather than oppositions. The post-structuralism refers to a complete decentring of meaning from what Derrida refers to as 'Logos'. Logos for Derrida comes from the false consciousness of presence which enforces finality of one meaning over another. Many writers such as Foucault (1972) refer to power in the enforcement of meaning. Power however is not a word mentioned by Derrida but is rather implied in the idea that Western secular philosophy has been dominated by the God-like status of Logos to impose meanings.

For Derrida meanings cannot be fixed and there is no transcendent signified in terms of objects. In fact this idea of our inability to grasp essences is not just the result of philosophical posturing but the result of sound argumentation by Kant in the Critique of Pure Reason. Kant (1993) argues that individuals do not really know the world as it is but only as it seems to be from sense perception. He does not deny the existence of phenomena 'out there' but maintains that we do not have direct access to it because our access and understanding are shaped by the way we perceive. Equally Derrida points out that we cannot name the world but only form ideas of it which in turn become signs. He states therefore that all meanings are signs. Therefore everything that has a meaning is a signifier which creates a meaning that in turn becomes a signifier and so on. The result is that there is no final meaning because we live in time and time itself in always unfinished; meanings therefore always move on with time and identities are always in flux.

Post-structural implications for identity

This has far-reaching consequences for areas such as education because identities, skills and knowledge should always be seen in a dynamic of development. Again Derrida stands against the enforcement of presence which is contained in the dominant voice that throughout history has been conceptualized as the closest representation of the essence of mind. Writing has then always been relegated to the external phonic representation of speech. Writing traditionally conceived as externalized speech contains hidden dominant agency and the presence of the writer enforcing meaning. However this dominant meaning is illusory and all text needs to be 'deconstructed' to locate marginalized, suppressed or absent meanings. Derrida's view is that writing and speech are not separate as in Saussure's 'langue' and 'parole', which is a sort of division between theory and practice. His view is that everything is text and a part of a linguistic system containing writing, speech and also signs, that is, in practical terms, images, designs, gestures, clothing, music and so on. His now famous statement is that there is nothing outside the text or 'il n'ya pas de hors texte' (1967: 158), a position that can be hotly debated since it situates individual identity at the mercy of language in its widest textual context. If the individual is totally constituted by the linguistic system and the language we use, then it is difficult to find objective meaning because we have to analyse language with language. Our analysis then amounts to language looking at language.

Critical discourse analysts such as Fairclough (1989; 1992) find this position of linguistic determinism unacceptable and Fairclough in particular sees individuals as only partially situated within language and therefore able to find a metalanguage to critique the influences language and sign have on the social world. We will explore critical discourse analysis in much greater detail in the next chapter. However the Derridean view is that metalanguage is nonetheless still language and we would still be using arbitrary symbols, totally ungrounded objectively, to analyse arbitrary symbols. Consequently the downside of Derrida's view is that meanings are always on the move as they go from signifier to signifier with the result that the notion of identity becomes very unstable and fragmented.

This position is the complete antithesis of Descartes's view of a stable and rational individual identity. Descartes's dominant voice of God-like status or Logos is the voice of Western philosophy that Derrida is attempting to disrupt. Consequently in texts, in order to find alternative identities and meanings which have been suppressed, the reader has to deconstruct the text. In doing this there will be semantic meaning possibilities only available through interpretation and so the outcome will not be objective truth but the subjective interpretation of meaning of word-signs. Derrida (1967: 50) underlines this as follows, 'From the moment there is meaning there are nothing but signs. We think only in signs'.

Deconstruction

Polysemia or multiple meanings occurs due to a double movement that Derrida refers to as 'Differance'. This is a Derridean neologism deriving from the merger of two words 'difference' and 'deferral'. 'Differer' in French means both to differ and to defer and Derrida has created the neologism to refer to the construction of meaning as a double action of a word's meaning occurring from both its difference from other word meanings and its journey through time within the text.

This movement through time within text is referred to by Derrida as the 'trace'. The author has a meaning intention in his/her message but there are meanings which are present that the author is unaware of, perhaps even occasioned by punctuation or grammar use. There may be omissions that the author is aware of but prefers to overlook due to ideological disposition, and this may concern official documents in, for example, areas of politics, education, public health and so on. The notion of text includes the punctuation, gaps, paragraphing, possible omissions and absences; in fact anything that might contribute to meaning and deconstruction is the project to discover all the possible meanings or in practical terms, 'to read between the lines'. Chouliaraki and Fairclough (1999: 121) point out that 'discourse is inherently open, and no hegemonic bids to achieve its closure can ultimately prevail – there is always a surplus of meaning which subverts it'. Deconstruction is not negative, its purpose is not to destroy ideas but on the contrary to find the 'surplus of meaning' which prevents the closure of meaning and keeps discourses open.

This is an emancipatory idea because it has the possibility of liberating individual identity from imposed constraints and is crucial to the notion of critical pedagogy which highlights the ideologies of institutions in shaping the lives of people. Deconstruction therefore can be conceptualized as a democratic project of foregrounding suppressed and absent meanings to include the forgotten and marginalized and in this respect it is about deconstructing hegemony to find the meanings away from the centres of power.

Conclusion

In this chapter I have argued that, far from identity being exclusively individual and isolated, which is implied in Cartesian linguistics, identities and meanings are multiple and constructed over time through difference and deferral. Identity is not unitary and should be framed as identities and consequently self is not a singular fixed object but varied, active and existential. We have seen Derrida argue against the concept of a fixed object or signified and in favour of a system of signifiers which actively make meaning. Similar ideas in terms of plural identities are argued by Bakhtin when he states that 'I' is defined in opposition to 'other' and therefore must contain something of the identity of others in the process of dialogue and dialogism. Wertsch (1991) says something similar in the concept of heteroglossia where our speech contains the voices of others. However Derrida details the process of meaning and identities through the interplay of presence and absence where presence is not final and complete but temporary invoking all the absent meanings which have been displaced to the margins. Deconstruction means unpicking the dominant hegemony and finding alternative readings in these margins. Identities therefore contain otherness in all the other possibilities and Derrida argues for open discourse and against the closures occasioned by power. Derrida (1978: 114) quotes Levinas as follows, 'If the other could be possessed, seized, and known, it would not be the other. To possess, to know, to grasp are all synonyms of power'; further on Derrida himself states, 'To see and to know, to have and to will, unfold only within the oppressive and luminous identity of the same'. Derrida provides a linguistic base for the ethics of the other or alterity although his views on language and identity amount more to a spiritual philosophy rather than an overtly political one. We have to look to sociologists of language such as Bourdieu, in the next chapter, to understand how the power of linguistic hegemony marginalizes language and culture in his concepts of language as symbolic and cultural capital. For Bourdieu (1982) language is a symbolic power that shapes cultures into hierarchies based on social class as opposed to equal differences. The power to rank language, languages and therefore cultures into hierarchies of value or capital is a political act resulting in the hegemony of same and marginalization of other. The consequence of this is the suppression of difference. However equally the act of opening up discourse and resisting linguistic and cultural hegemony is also a political act of resistance. We can see how public institutions enact discursive cultural hegemony in everyday social life such as the visual media including newspapers and advertising and education. A recent example was media's role in shaping public consciousness in the EU referendum debate of 2016 where powerful popular press highlighted problems caused by migration (sources quoted in the next chapter) and used this 'threat' to shore up feelings of nationalism. Indeed, the debate overlooked issues of pan-European importance such as intercultural understanding, knowledge and skill exchange through science and the arts. Sameness was highlighted, leaning towards Britishness, and Alterity was denigrated as the menace of the other rather than the celebration of cultural difference.

The next chapter will focus on the political nature of language and discourse in the formation of wider sociocultural identities. There will be an exploration of the nature of discourse where some, such as Derrida, argue that there is nothing outside the text and, such as Foucault, that we are entirely constituted by discourse, including our knowledge. However others argue that discourse is only one social practice among others and that we still exercise our free will through a rational critical analysis of discourse by understanding the power that lies behind it.

References

Bakhtin, M. (1981). *The Dialogic Imagination: Four Essays*. M. Holquist (ed.). Austin: University of Texas Press.

Bourdieu, P. (1982). *Langage et pouvoir symbolique*. Paris: Editions Fayard.

Chomsky, N. (2006). *Language and Mind*. Cambridge: Cambridge University Press.

Chomsky, N. (2009). *Cartesian Linguistics: A Chapter in the History of Rationalist Thought*. Cambridge: Cambridge University Press.

Chouliaraki, L., & Fairclough, N. (1999). *Discourse in Late Modernity: Rethinking Critical Discourse Analysis*. Edinburgh: Edinburgh University Press.

Cole, M. (1996). *Cultural Psychology: A Once and Future Discipline*. Cambridge, MA: Harvard University Press.

Dabrowska, E. (2015). *Handbook of Cognitive Linguistics*. Berlin/Boston: de Gruyter.

Derrida, J. (1978). *Writing and Difference*, trans. A. Bass. London: Routledge.

Derrida, J. (1967). *Of Grammatology*, trans. G. C. Spivak. Baltimore: John Hopkins University Press.

Descartes, R. (2008). *Meditations on First Philosophy*, trans. M. Moriarty. Oxford: Oxford University Press.

Fairclough, N. (1989). *Language and Power*. London/New York: Longman.

Fairclough, N. (1992). *Discourse and Social Change*. Cambridge: Polity Press.

Foucault, M. (1972). *The Archeology of Knowledge*. London: Routledge.

Hardcastle, J. (2009). 'Vygotsky's Enlightenment Precursors'. *Educational Review* 61.2: 181–95.

Kant, E. (1993). *The Critique of Pure Reason*, ed. Vasilis Politis. London: Everyman.

Lenneburg, E. (1967). *Biological Foundations of Language*. New York: Wiley.

Locke, J. (2010–15). *An Essay Concerning Human Understanding: Book 2 – Ideas*. Jonathan Bennett. www.earlymoderntexts.com (accessed August 2016).

Price, S. (2014). 'Student "Ownership" of Language: A Perspective Drawn from Bakhtin and Derrida'. *Journal of Academic Language and Learning* 8.3: A12–A22.

Roy, B. (1999). 'Reasoned Grammar, Logic and Rhetoric at Port-Royal'. *Philosophy & Rhetoric* 32.2: 131–45. Pennsylvania: Penn State University Press.

Rule, P. (2011). 'Bakhtin and Freire: Dialogue, Dialectic and Boundary Learning'. *Educational Philosophy and Theory* 43.9: 924–42.

Saussure, F. de (1915). *Course in General Linguistics*. New York: McGraw-Hill.

Saussure, F. de (1959). *Course in General Linguistics*. New York: Philosophical Library.

Saussure, F. de (1966). *Course in General Linguistics*. New York: McGraw-Hill.

Vygotsky, L. S. (1962). *Thought and Language*. Cambridge: MIT Press.

Wertsche, J. V. (1991). *Voices of the Mind: A Sociocultural Approach to Mediated Action*. Cambridge, MA: Harvard University Press.

3

Discourse Formation

David Evans

Saussure's (1966) view of language is that it is a system that operates within social structures. Meanings come from the social structure and become attached to words by conventional association. Saussure's renown comes primarily from breaking the intrinsic link between word and object or signifier and signified. Words in the Saussurean system derive their meanings from the surrounding linguistic system in a community of speakers that ascribe meaning. Alone, word-sounds are empty; there is nothing intrinsic in the letters forming the word 'house' that denotes a built structure with four walls and a roof. Evidence for this is that in different language areas and registers a different arrangement of letters designates the same object, for example, in French, 'maison' and in Spanish and Italian, 'casa'. In British slang, 'gaff' is the word for 'house' (Oxford online dictionaries, 10 January 2017). Meaning therefore is essentially social and meanings may change as long as the changes are supported by the linguistic system of the community as Saussure (1915: 77) points out, 'For the realization of language a community of speakers is necessary.'

Of course the notion of discourse goes beyond individual word, phrases and sentences. We will look at different definitions of discourse. Saussure does not use the word 'discourse' very much; however he does say that meanings do not have to be conveyed through word-sounds alone and can be carried by signs and symbols other than words such as images, sign language and gesture. This gives an indication that discourse will eventually amount to more than the linear juxtaposition of words.

In structuralism then the system contains the meaning supported by social convention, known by Saussure (1915) as 'langue' and individuals express their variations on the system in daily language known as 'parole'. Here language as a system predates individual speakers and so the meanings are already available socially and are 'the social product deposited in the brain of each individual (23).

He further points out that 'language never exists apart from the social fact' (77). So it can be seen that words by themselves are not generating meaning since meaning extends beyond the individual and into the social system. Meanings find their expression in words as they are arranged consecutively in a linear fashion. Here Saussure refers to a definition of discourse as follows: 'In discourse, on the one hand, words acquire relations based on the linear nature of language because they are chained together' (123).

Syntagmatic and associative relations in words

He describes this as a syntagmatic view of language where social meanings expressed in consecutive juxtapositions of word-sounds (graphemes and phonemes) are able to be expressed because of differences between the word functions and between the meanings. The empty materiality of the consecutive flow of graphemes and phonemes would be a continuous meaningless sound until one is able to differentiate sound-grapheme meanings from each other. Eventual meaning is therefore based on difference. Derrida (1967) also, as a post-structuralist, as we saw in the last chapter, posits difference as one of the ways in which meaning is discernible. If everything was one continuous and extended materiality, there could be no discernible meaning. Analogous to this would be a foreign language of which one has no knowledge because one is unable to make any differentiation in sound-meaning, hearing just a continuous flow of sound.

As was mentioned in the last chapter, word-object associations, in this flow of sound, are only associations in the arbitrary dividing up of sound into sense units or words. However word meanings themselves can evolve over time and place. For example, across languages such as French and English the same word, spelt the same, can have different meanings. Some common examples are everyday words such as 'duvet' which in French is a sleeping bag but has transferred meaning in English as a continental quilt now designated by the word 'duvet'. 'Spectacle' in French tends to have a positive connotation in terms of a show or a visual entertainment. In English however there is a negative connotation involving a display of inappropriate and embarrassing events. In French the word 'courrier' now refers to the mail itself whereas in English, it commonly refers to a delivery operative for parcels and so on. In all these mundane examples from everyday life, meanings have changed as the words have moved from one language and evolved separately.

In Saussurean structuralism until convention says otherwise, a word only means one thing at one time in one location because it does not mean something else and therefore has a discernible difference or binary opposition with other linguistic items in the sentence-phrase. This was discussed in the last chapter in contrast to the Derridean concept of polysemia, referred to in post-structuralism, where a word can have many meanings, in the present, according to context and also over time.

Saussure (1915) contrasts this syntagmatic view of consecutively arranged language with one of associative relations between words which resemble each other in meaning. He states that '[a] word can always evoke everything that can be associated with it in one way or another' (126). Saussure (1966: 126) uses the word 'education' to give an example, as in the last chapter, of these word associations as follows, 'teaching', 'teach', 'instruction', 'apprenticeship', 'education'. Contemporary educational discourse, as mentioned in Chapter 1, might also include 'training, pedagogy, assessment, progression, achievement, accreditation etc.' Saussure's definition of associative word relations, even back then, seems to resemble a very early conceptualization of discourse where words resembling each other in meaning gather around a subject area. This emphasizes word associations beyond individual sentence structures so that words associate to define a subject area or even constitute a hitherto unknown subject area. It should be noted however that although the words which gather around 'education' in their associative value form a nascent discourse, their individual meaning in use can only occur, in great part, due to their difference from each other. Therefore in binary terms 'teaching' has its semantic value because it is not 'instruction' or 'apprenticeship' or any of the other associated words. It is one thing because it is not something else. By way of contrast, we may recall, from the last chapter, Derrida's progression from Saussure's structuralism in which he maintains that the absent meanings displaced in Saussure's binary are still present in their absence. However they can be foregrounded by a deconstruction of all the possible meanings of associated items which have been excluded and marginalized.

Meanings then in Saussurean structuralism are from both differences and associations. Words within text can have similar meanings to form an association or a discourse but these meanings only arise, in the first place, because of their word meaning differences with each other in adjacent text.

The location of meaning

For structuralists, the location of meaning is within the system. For formal linguists, such as Chomsky, the location of meaning is within the individual mind before anything else and for post-structuralists like Derrida, as we saw in Chapter 1, meaning unfolds into the future and always remains unfinished.

However, as outlined in the last chapter social constructivists such as Bakhtin (1981) proposed that meanings emerge from dialogic interactions. Bakhtin did not acknowledge a system as in Saussure but emphasized that meanings were generated between individuals and groups of individuals. Language is therefore constantly differentiated according to the speakers. Clark and Holquist (1984: 12) state the following: 'My voice can mean, but only with others-at times in chorus but at the best of times in dialogue.'

Bakhtin's (1981) notion of heteroglossia is a diversification of meaning because one is always evoking the voices of others in one's own utterances. He takes a very spiritual view of language in terms of the relationship between self and other. This is because he views individual identity as located on the cusp of the interface between self and other where the notion of the 'I' can only be defined in relation to the 'You' and also, within dialogism, where the 'I' speaks in anticipation of the response from the interlocutor as the 'You'. There is then a sense of diglossia, or dual voice, where 'I' in its subjective definition contains elements of 'You' and therefore the boundaries between individual identities are blurred within language. Bakhtin's spiritual perspective holds that it is language which does more than just communicate; it binds people and communities together and enables us to take the perspective of the other thereby enabling us to grasp what 'I' must be in the eyes of the other. Bakhtin understood along with Derrida in a different linguistic tradition that the word cannot be exactly mapped on to the object, including the notion of the pronominal subjects of 'I' 'You', 'She', 'He' and so on, whose possible meanings and identities far exceed the words that are assigned to subjects and objects. Whereas Saussure's linguistics are restricted to binary similarity and opposition, Bakhtin and Derrida thought in terms of multiple meanings for identities or polysemia. Discourse in this view is language in social interaction and is imbued with the voices and intentions of others.

However, words inasmuch as they enable meaning can also constrain meaning. They are a 'double-edged sword' in that they embody meaning as a vehicle and yet like a vehicle contain and constrain meaning because meaning is always in surplus to words. Clark and Holquist (1984: 83) underline this notion of polysemia as follows: 'It is not only that a tree is never the same as the sign "tree" but also that I am never any of the signs that name me, least of all the pronominal signs such as "I". Non-linguists ignore the fact that the world does not correspond to the system of language.'

In terms of education, there are immense implications for Bakhtin's and indeed Derrida's views of meaning and identity in the moral and spiritual damage that labelling can do to vulnerable individuals and minorities. Derrida's particular emancipatory contribution with regard to the moral constriction of labelling is that identity is forever unfinished and also subject to modification as we go into the future. Identity is, in fact, always unfinished since it is developed in time and of course time is forever unfinished. Even after an individual's demise their post-humous identity is still subject to time and modification.

We will discuss such implications of the changing nature of multiple identities when we focus on language and power later on in the chapter. Clark and Holquist make the important point that in claiming a unitary identity through a correspondence between words and the 'self' in such pronominals as 'I', 'You', 'She', 'He', we create 'fictions of sameness'. Therefore not only is the world always more than the language used to name it but we, as humans, are also always more than the language used to describe us. Heidegger (1993) made his existential claim that '[l]anguage is the house of being' but he also needed to add that it can also be the container of being through unequal power relations. Truly, then, a 'double-edged sword' of constructing and constraining.

Dialogism, heteroglossia and ideology

Bakhtin (1981: 341) states that '[t]he ideological becoming of a human being ... is the process of selectively assimilating the words of others'. Identities then are being constructed and re-constructed within the dialogic interface between the words of self and others. Individuals appropriate words for themselves but these words are already imbued with the meanings of others. Identities therefore are constructed in the intersubjective space between self and other. The notion of 'heteroglossia' (Bakhtin 1981; Wertsch 1991) is born from our words carrying the voices of others within the content of what we say. Taking language from the common pool means not only assimilating but perhaps also processing the ideological content of language. Bakhtin (1981: 293) states the following: 'All words have the "taste" of a profession, a genre, a tendency, a party, a particular work, a particular person, a generation, an age gap, the day and the hour. Each word tastes of its socially charged life; all words and forms are populated by intentions.'

Language therefore is not neutral but saturated by the intentions and ideologies of users or social groups of language users. Discourse is therefore more than a language consisting of a neutral juxtaposition of words in a Saussurean sense. Discourse is the way people use language in a variety of ways to reflect their subject positions. It has a profound constitutive effect on identity and in particular the notion of unitary identity since one is born into preexisting language marked by ideologies and subject positions which indeed constitute different discourses. Therefore when we participate in discourse, we are using the voices of others within our own intentional speech since we are using language types already formulated in chains and threads of utterances by others who have preceded us. We find ourselves within that chain. This could be as simple as using the expressions and utterances we have heard in the media, on television or social media. We may reformulate them or appropriate them for ourselves but we have still used discursive language as our raw material and therefore we have taken part in heteroglossia. The language we use then is only partly our own, taken from a commonly used stock.

Examples of heteroglossia (Wertsch 1991; Bakhtin 1981) where identities are constituted by the voices of others can be found among stakeholders within schools in classroom interactions where we see a cross-current of interactional discourses. Teachers are in a dialogic relation with pupils in anticipating responses to classroom pedagogy and at the same time anticipating the monitoring requirements for standards expected by management discourses which in turn are shaped by external bodies such as Ofsted. Parental and local community discourses feed into this heteroglossia as do expectations for professional development and performance management. Pupils themselves interact at an intersection between the discourses of local community and family, media, peer group, classroom teacher and school managerial discourses. Interacting across these more localized voices are the wider discourses such as socio-economics and gender which derive from wider sociocultural forces but at the same time help to shape interactional discourses. If we focus on wider societal discourses such as gender and socio-economics, we can see how ideologies shape discourses within institutions and localized interactions. We can also see that Bakhtin's ideas provide a conceptualization of discourse which, unlike structuralism, is based on the agency of participants and, due to the notion of heteroglossia, contains the voices of others. However not all discourses are equal since some are more powerful than others.

Ideological discourse

Fairclough (1989; 1992) posits three levels of discourse. At the societal level the largest, most powerful he names the 'Orders of Discourse' which relate to the way society has been organized over time with regard to sociocultural history;

in the case of Western society the socio-economics of capitalism. This, he argues, is the dominant social force and through the dominant social classes, it is able to project its ideological force through government, parliament, law, education, utilities, finance and so on into its institutions as discourse types. The second level of discourse is at institutional level such as schools, universities, advertising, health care, the police, public transport and so on. An example of socio-economic discourse at institutional level is the establishment of internal markets for financial provision and profit, where public institutions serving state infrastructure are cast in the role of private companies competing against each other to improve services and attract customers, making profits for shareholders.

The third level of discourse is at interactional level such as we might see in the classroom itself at the point of contact between teachers and pupils. At this level, such discourse interacts with other discourses at more local level within a heteroglossia already mentioned.

Fairclough (1989; 1992) argues that the way economic power permeates into these more everyday levels of discourse within institutions is by means of ideology, being the ability to project a dominant way of thinking as perfectly normal. This normalization is achieved through discourse by the manufacture of the consent of the other. An institutional discourse type such as education, at the level of schools, may well express the wider socio-economic discourse, not only in its readiness to compete with other schools for funding via greater numbers of pupils, but also organize curriculum and pedagogy to prioritize knowledge and skills in the light of competitive economic forces. Consequently the important subjects on the schools' curriculum are the STEM subjects leading to employability and economic competitiveness for the nation. One should not forget that the nation is a major stakeholder in the educational system. STEM is the acronym for science, technology, engineering and mathematics. In most schools the domination of these subject areas is normalized compared with RE, music, art, dance and drama where economic outcomes are less visible.

While Bakhtin's dialogism and heteroglossia do provide an understanding of how language is dispersed and diversified into discourses, to complete this understanding, the notion is needed first of power and dominant social forces or classes. Second the means to project that power through the normalizing process of ideology by making a situation seem as though it is perfectly normal and beyond question. Hart (2016) reinforces this position with regard to ideology arguing that he views ideology as normalized systems of beliefs and values that are embedded in language so as to shape a world-view.

Consequently the concept of heteroglossia or shared voices begs the question, whose voices? This question of whose voices prevail leads to issues of power not only behind discourse but also within discourse (Fairclough 1989).

Power behind the discourse, as we have seen, is the socio-economic orders of discourse in capitalism which exist as the providers of the conditions for the discourse types in institutions and subsequent interactional discourse. Chouliaraki and Fairclough (1999) argue that discourse is but one element of social practice among others and Fairclough (1992: 66) further argues that 'social practice has various orientations – economic, political, cultural, ideological – and discourse may be implicated in all of these without any of them being reducible to discourse'. Fairclough is therefore saying that although ways of speaking and writing as discourse may be contained in socio-economic practice, he does not view socio-economic and social practices to be reducible to discourse itself. Consequently he is claiming that one can stand outside of discourse and as such opposes linguistic determinism. Whereas the post-structuralists such as Derrida argue that everything is text and Foucault (1972) that everything is discourse, Fairclough, as a sociolinguist, adopts the position of a dialectical relationship between discourse and social practice and although discourse is contained to some degree within social practice, the latter is able to have a position apart from discourse. The two interact dialectically where social practice shapes discourse and in turn discourse contributes to the construction of social practice.

Heteroglossia and discourse colonization

The different discourse types at institutional level may well interact with each other resulting in a level of hybridization of identity where discourses borrow each other's features of language. Discourse types such as advertising, counselling, education, finance companies, management discourses and bureaucratic discourses, which are all social practices, may very well borrow or even appropriate each other's ways of speaking depending upon their power relations. Chouliaraki and Fairclough (1999: 27) give an example of discourse colonization as follows, '[M]anagerial ideologies in education are discursive constructions of education which draw upon discourses which come from other practices that are closely tied in with contemporary practices in education-specifically from economic practices'. Therefore Orders of Discourse, which are primarily economic in Western societies, provide conditions for economically instrumental orientations in discourse types within institutions. The prevailing discourse type, in the example above, is then managerialism which permeates into educational institutions shaping an economically instrumental frame for schooling, hence the STEM subjects already mentioned above. Another influential discourse type in schools is that of counselling which can be framed as the manufacture of the subject's consent in getting subjects to regulate themselves in terms of dominant cultural behaviours and goals. Schools will endeavour to get pupils to 'take ownership' of academic and behavioural performance targets through counselling and guidance so that pupils engage in self-regulation rather than coercive control from an external punitive force (Foucault 1972).

Discourse types of managerialism and counselling represent voices which are traditionally outside of education, imported in from industry, commerce and mental health therapy but which in schools combine to get pupils to take ownership of target setting and managing their own performance in achieving targets. Many pupils do resist the hegemony of these dominant discourses and schools can become sites of ideological conflict rather than a totalizing consensus. Pupils may adopt resistant discourses located in their own community cultures or subcultures. However pupil unofficial discourses may interact with officially approved discourses to construct a hybridity of identities drawing upon the interaction of available discourses. Bhabba (1994) refers to this hybridity as a third space where, in this case, pupils construct their own space by creating their own voice from all the voices available. Young people in a school or other setting may well engage in subcultural discourse to express identities, using anti-establishment ways of speaking and being. Kramsch (1998) expresses this as follows, referring to language use as a way of belonging, '[Y]ou belong through language and you don't belong through language.' Therefore using an alternative anti-establishment discourse constructs two cultural markers in terms of where you belong, to a subculture, for example, and where you don't belong, for example, to the 'establishment'.

Later on in the book we will look at the interface between dominant and resistant languages and language types in various locations across the world and in United Kingdom to see how dominant and marginalized languages and cultures interact on a much larger national and regional scale.

So far we have looked at power behind the discourse where socio-economic and cultural power strives to establish a platform of domination of one discourse over another or even discourse colonization. We can now turn our attention to power within the discourse, looking at language as a symbolic capital constructing domination within language.

Symbolic capital in language and discourse

Symbolic capital accounts for power, prestige and status within language (Bourdieu 1990; 1991). Bourdieu argues that within language there is a symbolic capital which legitimizes some language types over others. There is then a linguistic capital in the type of language used within discourse. An interesting question to ask is why English dictionaries are almost always Oxford English or Cambridge English dictionaries? I have never yet seen a Liverpool, Manchester, Glasgow, Cardiff, Belfast or Birmingham English dictionary! The answer is that the interior of language, in terms of vocabulary, grammatical constructions and pronunciation, is validated by the external conditions of language in its socio-political and cultural context. Bourdieu (1991) situates this external validation of linguistic capital historically and his analysis is predicated on the historical emergence of a national standard language in France. Standard language was cultivated in the centres of economic, political and therefore cultural power in order to create national unity around the location of power. In the United Kingdom the language spoken is referred to as English even though the United Kingdom is a union of Scotland, Wales, Northern Ireland and England. Furthermore this language is very often referred to as the 'Queen's English' or in former times the 'King's English'. The locus of linguist power or linguistic capital was determined by the other forms of power-economic, political and cultural historically situated in the capital and in the medieval and oldest universities of Oxford and Cambridge. Holmes (1992) points out that the language variety spoken within the triangle bounded by London as the capital and the ancient medieval universities of Oxford and Cambridge is the variety that became standard due to its codification in the dictionaries of these universities and in the accompanying grammar books. Merchants coming into this region of the country from the provinces felt obliged to adopt the standard language to be understood and accepted by power and, of course, over the course of history standard language has become, throughout the United Kingdom, despite regional variations in accent, the language of politics, education and commerce. According to Bourdieu it is the linguistic capital of the standard which converts socio-economic capital into symbolic capital and this symbolic capital becomes the platform for legitimacy and credibility.

Bourdieu traces a parallel linguistic development in France, where the national standard centred on the capital was created for the purpose of national unity, enforced by the school system and monitored by the examination system. Against this, all other regional variations were reduced to the status of 'patois' and therefore delegitimized. Speaking a regional dialect then came to lack credibility in terms of social value or capital. Values of words also change and Bourdieu refers to the French word 'paysan' as an example which has value in rural dialects but which, when used in standard language, becomes a derogatory term. In English it should be noted that calling someone a 'peasant' is indeed now a term of abuse. Holmes (1992: 84) points out that '[a] standard dialect has no particular linguistic merits, whether in vocabulary, grammar or pronunciation. It is simply the dialect of those who are politically powerful and socially prestigious'. Consequently the value given to words as a linguistic capital is ideological. Between the two words 'peasant' and 'entrepreneur', there will be an ideological social value which is not contained intrinsically within the words themselves but is conferred by the prevailing ideological system which shapes meaning. Volosinov (1994) points out that the word is the ideological sign par excellence.

Bourdieu's notion of language as a symbolic capital and, therefore, power within discourse lies at the heart of this book. Consequently we shall see in the case study chapters how this is expressed in the areas of the world and United Kingdom where there is linguistic and cultural conflict between dominant, marginalized and ensuing resistant languages and discourses. In the United Kingdom, speaking the Queen's English with 'received pronunciation' is highly valued and seeking to undermine this by ignoring correct grammar, especially in an educational context, would be highly controversial. Although regional accent is permitted, grammatical inaccuracy would lead to lack of personal credibility in official contexts. For Bourdieu language type is crucial in access to power since linguistic capital, as Chouliaraki and Fairclough (1999) point out, converts all other forms of capital into symbolic capital. They argue that 'all forms of capital are convertible into "symbolic capital" once they are (mis) recognized as and have the effects of power' (101). There are three important and related points to make with regard to the statement above.

First for Bourdieu the concept of the state underwrites all symbolic capital and is its ultimate source. Schinkel (2015: 219) points out that for Bourdieu the state has 'the function of providing ultimate consensus regarding the symbolic order of the world' and 'has a strong symbolic and fiduciary character'. As such it provides an underlying platform for fundamental meaning. Bourdieu refers to the concept of measured time as an example of symbolic power in that the state regulates the time of day and when, in the autumn, the state decides that the clocks go back an hour, we all duly wind back our clocks. The state accredits knowledge and skill through its schools, universities and professions and so provides a platform of basic symbolic power that very few people question. Bourdieu refers to the notion of doxa which is a pre-reflective state of affairs where the symbolic power of the state guarantees all the other capitals, including social and cultural capital.

The second point is that, in Bourdieu's view, the state does not really exist but more importantly is believed to exist. Schinkel (2015: 220) points out that '[t]he state, Bourdieu argues, is a relation which exists because it is believed to exist'. The third point which comes from the quotation above concerns the notion of (mis)recognition of the effects of power. This refers to the trust accorded to symbolic power which exists only in the minds of individuals. Therefore language and culture that are accorded a superior status are misrecognized as such, given what Bourdieu regards as the transcendental and magical power of symbolic capital. In other words any hierarchy of language, power and culture as superior is a sham and only exists because it is unchallenged. Interestingly van Dijk (2008) has a slightly less deterministic view than Bourdieu of symbolic power. He also acknowledges state as underwriting symbolic power; however, this is not exclusive due to the power of private corporations which have immense financial power through advertising, marketing, investments and a worldwide internet and media reach. For van Dijk such corporations also have the power to underwrite symbolic power and produce symbolic elites. According to van Dijk, these elites have control over channels of communication and production of discourse and he cites media companies as an example of having the symbolic power to shape consciousness. He also refers to the notion of counter-power in Western democracies where as an example, novelists and some academics have the freedom to challenge the hegemonies of power.

Therefore language within discourse, or more specifically within the notion of 'field' in Bourdieu's sociology, draws upon sociocultural power externally since we have seen that there is nothing of inherent power within the structure of any given standard language variety. To think otherwise is to engage in an act of 'misrecognition' which would be to buy into a fiction. The consequences of misrecognition of dominant language and culture could be serious because the result would be that those who are dominated could end up conspiring in their own domination. The emancipatory strategy then would be to expose the dominant language and culture as a position of domination, thereby promoting a discourse of resistance. In the ensuing case study chapters we will see evidence of language struggle and resistance against language and cultural marginalization by potentially hegemonic language-culture.

We have seen that the notion of power within language and discourse in terms of linguistic capital draw upon power outside of language and discourse and how this has developed historically and, as Bourdieu suggests, is ultimately guaranteed by symbolic power.

We see with Bourdieu how important power is in securing meaning within language and in securing the prestige and status of the language itself. Foucault's (1972) perspective of language goes even further into the realms of power by suggesting that through language and discourse, power shapes the meaning of knowledge itself

Foucault's perspective on discourse

Power and meaning are two very important elements of this chapter and indeed this book. First, in Chapter 2, we discussed the construction of meaning as 'intra cranium' of Cartesian linguistics. Second, in Chapter 2 and in this chapter, we discussed systemic meaning in Saussurean structuralism; third, intersubjective meaning proposed by Bakhtin and finally alluded to in the unfinished Derridean deferred meaning was also covered in the last chapter. Eventually the notion of power has entered the debate with the sociolinguistics of Fairclough. Bourdieu also looks at the relations between power and language in his notion of linguistic capital as it converts socio-economic capital to a 'meta' capital which is symbolic capital. Bourdieu is a sociologist of language and therefore examines the relationship between linguistic capital and other capital outside of language which interacts with language, so that we see that language is indeed powered by external socio-political forces.

However for Foucault, as indeed for Derrida, there is no outside of language. We will see in this section how Foucault relates language to wider discourse in his proposal of statements and enunciations, what you can say and what you cannot say. For the moment the striking feature of Foucault is that everything lies within discourse. We will see that this is a totalizing position and indeed a deterministic one in terms of free will. The social practices proposed by sociolinguistics and sociologists of language are, for Foucault, all uniquely discursive positions and always speak from within a discursive position. This means that language and discourse always represent an ideology and never occupy a neutral position outside of discourse. So there could be no 'meta-language' of discursive analysis as an objective analytical position because this itself is a discourse, and so one ends up analysing one discourse, not with a neutral language, but instead with another discourse. We would be analysing language with language depriving us of objectivity. Therefore the non-discursive practices proposed by Fairclough (1989; 1992) such as economics, managerial practices, bureaucratic practices, counselling and so on are for Foucault all part of discourse.

Foucault (1972) looks at discourse as containing the social power within social practices to constitute knowledge itself. So ultimately the knowledge we have does not connect directly with the world but is instead constructed through discourse, meaning that the world, as we experience it, is a sociocultural construction over historical time. If discourse had followed a different path, our knowledge would have been different. Foucault (2002) argues that knowledge and language are tightly interwoven which he maintains 'share, in representation the same origin and the same functional principle; they support one another, complement one another, and criticize one another incessantly'. Further on, he remarks, 'It is in one and the same movement that the mind speaks and knows' (95) and, it is true to say, even as social constructivists claim, that one cannot have knowledge without language. Both Chomsky (2009) and Vygotsky (1962) posit that language leads to higher-order thinking and knowledge. This has enormous implications for education as we will discuss in the pedagogical section later in the book because it can be argued, within educational contexts, that ways of speaking shape ways of knowing. Ways of addressing the other and the culture of the other shape the way the other is perceived. This reinforces the notion that language is never neutral but inscribed by ideological positions that need to be critically analysed or 'deconstructed'.

Foucault (1972: 52–3) refers to the notion that knowledge is grounded in language as follows, '[T]he regular formation of objects that emerge only in discourse.' Furthermore, he states, 'To define these objects, without reference to the ground, the foundation of things, but by relating them to the body of rules that enable them to form as objects of a discourse and thus constitute the conditions of their historical appearance' (53). Here Foucault states that even objects are discursively constituted and have no transcendental basis. However this perspective is not really new. Kant (1993) claims that, apart from some a priori analytical exceptions, we do not really know the world directly. Our knowledge of the world or phenomena comes to us through perception as empirical knowledge. Therefore we can have no direct knowledge of the world, although we can say that our perceptions are based on something but we do not know exactly what it is. Foucault takes this idea much further by saying that the world itself is constituted by our way of talking about it. What perception was for Kant, discourse is for Foucault. We, as individuals, are part of the picture we constitute – we paint ourselves into the picture and cannot stand outside it as objective observers.

Consequently discourse is not about the surface language of interaction; as Foucault (1972: 52) declares,

> I would like to show that discourse is not a slender surface of contact, or confrontation, between a reality and a language, . . . the intrication of a lexicon and an experience; I would like to show with precise examples that in analyzing discourses themselves, one sees the loosening of the embrace, apparently so tight, of words and things and the emergence of a group of rules proper to discursive practice.

He further adds that 'these rules define . . . the ordering of objects'. Foucault is saying that discourse is made up of language in terms, not of words and things, but in terms of what one can say, and the conditions which govern verbal performances. These verbal performances group together into formulations of statements and propositions. Therefore to analyse a discourse, one has to analyse the conditions which have given permission for certain things to be said and for certain things to be left unsaid. Again we see that what counts here is the function of power and what power chooses to say leaves gaps and omissions regarding what cannot be said. In this regard, supporters of Derrida might be able to justify the project of 'deconstruction' in order to reveal everything that can be said of a text, exploring the gaps and omissions to bring to the surface that which power has silenced.

Foucault's (1972: 121) statements and propositions group together to form 'discursive formations' and these constitute individual discourses such as 'clinical discourse, economic discourse, the discourse of natural history, psychiatric discourse' (121). We can see that, even though both sociolinguists and post-structuralists focus on power in the construction of social realities through discourse, the post-structuralism of Foucault defines discourse in a radically different way in terms of its constitution of the conditions for the emergence of all reality.

The conditions under which certain propositions and discursive formations can be made require an analysis of who has the power to open up and shape certain discourses and in doing so what was excluded? Language, knowledge and power therefore are inextricably entwined.

Implications for identity

With regard to individual identity as an object of knowledge and self-knowledge, the 'I' or 'You' is not passively uncovered but discursively constituted in and by language and power. One's subjective identity is not therefore waiting to be patiently discovered but actively constituted and elicited not by 'who am I?' but rather 'What do my social conditions permit me to do and therefore to be?' Individual identity constituted in this way is much more existential and shaped by one's own active agency. This may also mean identities rather than identity in the singular because one may act, interact and respond differently in different situations. Post-structural accounts often refer to subjectivities rather than identities since social life and the interrelations of power are different in different situations.

Ironically, although some might view the post-structural position of a more existentially constituted identity as liberating, others view Foucault's underlying position regarding discourse as deterministic. This is because he views individuals as uniquely rooted in discourse and their a priori reality is nowhere else but in language and discourse. They can only operate within the discourses to which they have access and are therefore shaped by the power relations of their context which changes from situation to situation over time and place.

Foucault's importance is in elucidating the deep relations between knowledge, power and language and this knowledge is in itself liberating. However he does not propose any sort of critical discourse analysis to challenge and question the discursive nature of unequal power relations. A large part of the rationale of this book however is to promote critical pedagogical positions to address power imbalances in language and culture, through a revalorization of marginalized language and an awareness of resistant discourses. This position implies that the individual is not completely imprisoned by language but can use it critically in an act of free will. This recalls the Cartesian cogito where Descartes (2008) sets out to prove that he exists as a mind ergo in free will rather than as in a dream. He arrives at his conclusion of 'cogito ergo sum' or 'I think therefore I am' through doubt. The fact that he is able to question and doubt his thinking and his thoughts proves he is a thinking being rather than idly drifting away in a dream world. In terms of language, by analogy, a critical language embodies the free will to doubt the veracity of a surrounding discourse rather than uncritically reproduce it.

Aside from this Cartesian caveat, we have travelled some way from Descartes's individualism of the last chapter although perhaps we do need to return towards a more central position to acknowledge the notion of critical analysis within and by language.

Discourse analysis, text and ideology

Fairclough (1992) argues that discourse is both a social practice and also a constitutive element of non-discursive social practice. He furthermore argues that there are some social practices that are wholly constituted by discourse. Examples of the latter are advertising, marketing and counselling, which wholly depend upon language. Nevertheless all the discursive elements of social practices come to be made manifest in text. Fairclough (1992: 67) argues that discourses come to be ideologically 'invested' by the social practice in which they are situated. He further maintains that signs within discourse are 'socially motivated' (74–5). This means that the Saussurean combination of signifier and signified which make up signs becomes ideologically imbued. Therefore if the signified within social practice has a particular characteristic, this will shape the signifier or the word as its vehicle. The word or signifier will then *re*flect the underlying characteristic of the signified as both the signified and signifier or object and word come together.

A previously mentioned example in an educational setting is the choice of signifier between 'student' and 'pupil' to designate the child who learns in a school setting. The choice is an ideological one according to how one frames the learner, as either active or passive. The ideological tendency now is to view young learners as active, researching knowledge, expressing opinion and acting out individual agency in an entrepreneurial manner. Education is after all tied to the economy and society has changed where young school leavers no longer automatically follow their parents into the manual work of industry and agriculture because, in terms of industry, the UK manufacturing base has declined over the past decades in favour of service and financial sectors. Here it is vital to be able to research and manipulate information and persuasively communicate to consumers. Young learners are therefore framed as students researching knowledge, actively learning how to learn as a skill in a technologically fast changing world rather than pupils who are passive recipients of traditional knowledge. Learners are still learners but they are being shaped ideologically through word choice designating the independent, autonomous status of the 'student'.

Word usage has then a symbolic legitimacy and in Bourdieu's terms this is ultimately underwritten by state symbolic power. Another example of this would be in the ideology of military terminology where a member of the British armed forces is a 'soldier' and not a 'fighter'. The word 'fighter' may be designated by the news media as those combatants who are in irregular armies or terrorist groups. Fairclough (1992) quotes the age-old example of the ideological difference between 'freedom fighters' and 'terrorists'. In Second World War–occupied France, the French resistance were viewed as 'freedom fighters' by the French and British and 'terrorists' by the occupying German forces.

Word-signs are therefore ideologically saturated by the social practice and conditions in which they are situated and some words are contested. For example, in industrial disputes a word such as 'modernization' carries ideological baggage connoting, on one side of the dispute, efficiencies and, on the other side, job cuts where technologies are seen as cost cutting. A concept such as 'modernization' is therefore a double-edged sword of being both a benefit and a deficit relative to where one is situated in society.

Often the ideological nature of a word is much more powerful where its contested nature is concealed resulting in its matter of fact routine normalization. An example of this is in gender ideology where the verb 'to man' is frequently used rather than to staff and 'man power' used instead of 'work force'. 'Mankind' is often used rather than 'human kind' in the media. Critical analysis or deconstruction is able to foreground the suppressed alternative meanings revealing the power, in this case, to appropriate male gendered 'man' to represent all genders and humanity, thereby suppressing 'woman'. 'Woman' becomes a hidden subsidiary in favour of 'man' as universalized concept for humans.

A focus on ideological meaning in language does not just concern vocabulary but also the way in which language is structured. Some texts may be impersonal and bureaucratic making language seem scientifically objective and official, thereby hiding agency. Therefore a bureaucratic notice from an employer could read thus: 'It is expected that all employees arrive at meetings on time' rather than '"I" or "We" expect all employees to arrive at meetings on time.' The message is thereby rendered more objective and less the result of the power of an individual who has made a decision affecting the lives of many.

Hart (2016) points out that metaphor as imaged language is another means of constructing normalized ideology. He states, 'Ideologically, however, metaphor may be exploited in discourse to promote one particular reality over another' (137). Examples of this can be seen in the recent debates on immigration surrounding the 2016 UK referendum on remaining in the EU or leaving where immigration into the United Kingdom was one of the arguments against remaining, citing taking back control of UK borders. The notion of 'taking back control of our borders' was depicted metaphorically in the imaged language of long queues of migrants try to gain entry into the United Kingdom. The following popular UK newspaper headlines illustrate the language used to normalize a sense of invasion.

Text 1

One million migrants heading this way
(And we took 558,000 last year)
BY LYNN DAVIDSON
22nd September 2015, 11:01 pm *The Sun* newspaper

Text 2

A vote for Remain is a vote for mass immigration from Turkey
• PETER BONE – *THE DAILY TELEGRAPH* 17-05-2016

Text 3

MILLIONS of EU migrants grab our jobs: Time for Brexit to FINALLY take
    control of borders
DAVID Cameron's plan for cutting the migration surge suffered a shattering
    blow last night when new figures showed that the number of EU
    nationals working in Britain soared by nearly 200,000 last year.
Daily Express 18-02-2016

Text 4

Why we MUST speed up EU exit: New migrant surge on the way ahead of
    Brexit curbs
BRITAIN risks falling victim to an immigration 'surge' as people seek to
    beat post-Brexit curbs
Daily Express 27-07-2016

These headlines are from newspapers with mass readership in the United Kingdom both in print and online and have an intention of constructing a sense of invasion. Text 1 talks of 'a million migrants heading this way' giving a sense of a mass invasion and Text 2 is directed at Turkey, leading people to believe that, as a future likely EU member, the United Kingdom would be invaded by large numbers of Turks. Finally Text 3 refers to migrants who already 'grab our jobs' creating an illusion of theft given that the jobs are referred to as 'our jobs'. Finally Text 4 uses the metaphor of a 'surge' to create the sense of a tidal wave and consequent fear.

We can see therefore that metaphors in language can create, due to mass circulation, popular images and a hegemonic vision of the refugee from economic misery and war as a threat, constructing a social reality of a country under siege.

The critical discourse analysis model of sociolinguistics and the deconstruction project of post-structuralism can be brought to bear on hegemonies of ideology by foregrounding the hidden and alternative meanings in texts and highlighting the motives behind such ideologies.

We see in this chapter that language and discourse are not neutral but politicized by ideologies and invoke such questions as to who is authoring the spoken or written text, what are the motives and what effects are the author(s) trying to produce? The fact of being able to conduct textual analysis throws again into question the extent to which individuals are determined by discourse. A meta-language of analysis is still language, and it is true to say that such analysis amounts to language investigating language. However critical analysis through awareness of the effects of language rather than using any separate specialist language nevertheless serves a purpose of highlighting social injustice and inequality. This, again, recalls the Cartesian cogito, where Descartes's ability to use his mind to doubt and question his thinking actually proves the reality of a reasoning mind. Descartes, in this way, shows that he is not locked into a dream and, in the same way, an analytical language, by casting doubt on hegemonic discourse demonstrates that individuals are not locked into discourse and can at least step outside of the prevailing ideology, even though they can never step out of language itself. This reinforces the real existence of not necessarily a separate analytical meta-language, but rather using existing language, as a critical device of challenge to analyse and doubt by questioning prevailing discourse.

Conclusion

The direction of travel of this chapter shows how notions of discourse have developed from structuralist words, phrases and sentences to the way in which discourses shape identities. Of course discourse is more than words, phrases and sentences although it does contain them. In its wider sense, discourse is about both language and sign in their external social use. The latter includes gesture, dress, music and images, all of which can be found in multimodal media discourse which will follow in a later chapter. The extent to which the individual and his/her social group are shaped by discourse depends on one's definition of discourse. We have shown in this chapter that there is not just one definition of discourse but many and some of the discourse types compete with one another within power relations. We have looked at discourse colonization and heteroglossia where linguistic items infiltrate less powerful discourses and the most powerful may achieve a status of hegemony where, within the discourse, ideological meanings have become normalized. It is true in the Foucauldian sense that such powerful discourses can determine what counts as knowledge, which cultures and languages are framed as superior and which are marginalized. Discourse in this sense deprives individuals of agency. Fairclough's (1992) version of discourse is much less totalizing, in that through critical discourse analysis, it is possible to see the relationship of language and linguistic items to the discourse in which they are situated. Foucault, by contrast, says very little about linguistic items and grammatical structures but concentrates always on the notion of statements, discursive formations and the conditions of power which make them possible.

Fairclough's position is much more hopeful, where, through critical discourse analysis, we have seen that discourses are supported by ideologically saturated words, metaphors and grammatical structures concealing agency. Combined with Bourdieu's notions of linguistic and symbolic capitals, discourse analysis promotes social justice through the realization that individuals are positioned by ideologically saturated language and become more and more positioned the more they use such language. Discourse analysis enables, through critical pedagogy within education, individuals to step outside of totalizing discourse in order to question the agency of statements, what they are trying to achieve and the linguistic devices they use in order to achieve the desired effects.

In the following chapters, narratives and analysis will bear witness to the various linguistic and cultural struggles in several continents of the world: Asia (China), the Indian subcontinent and Africa as well as in UK urban life.

The linguistic situations are indeed varied and diverse but the core issues are the same. Language and identity as a site of opportunity for some, but marginalization and then resistance for others. However underlying these opportunities and conflicts exists a defining rationale which is the construction of discursive identities within power and power relations.

References

Bakhtin, M. (1981). *The Dialogic Imagination: Four Essays*. M. Holquist (ed.). Austin: University of Texas Press.

Bhabba, H. (1994). *The Location of Culture*. London: Routledge.

Bourdieu, P. (1990). *Outline of a Theory of Practice*. Cambridge: Cambridge University Press.

Bourdieu, P. (1991). *Language and Symbolic Power*. J. P. Thompson (ed.). Cambridge: Harvard University Press.

Chomsky, N. (2009). *Cartesian Linguistics: A Chapter in the History of Rationalist Thought*. Cambridge: Cambridge University Press.

Chouliaraki, L., & Fairclough, N. (1999). *Discourse in Late Modernity: Rethinking Critical Discourse Analysis*. Edinburgh: Edinburgh University Press.

Clark, K., & Holquist, M. (1984). *Mikhail Bakhtin*. Cambridge: Harvard University Press.

Derrida, J. (1967). *Of Grammatology*. Baltimore: John Hopkins University Press.

Derrida, J. (1978). *Writing and Difference*, trans. A. Bass. London: Routledge.

Descartes, R. (2008). *Meditations on First Philosophy*, trans. M. Moriarty. Oxford: Oxford University Press.

Fairclough, N. (1989). *Language and Power*. London/New York: Longman.

Fairclough, N. (1992). *Discourse and Social Change*. Cambridge: Polity Press.

Foucault, M. (1972). *The Archeology of Knowledge*. London; Routledge.

Foucault, M. (2002). *The Order of Things*. Abingdon: Routledge.

Hart, C. (2016). *Discourse, Grammar and Ideology: Functional and Cognitive Perspectives*. London: Bloomsbury.

Heidegger, M. (1993). *Basic Writings*. New York: Routledge.

Holmes, J. (1992). *An Introduction to Sociolinguistics*. London: Longman.

Kant, E. (1993). *The Critique of Pure Reason*. Vasilis Politis (ed.). London: Everyman.

Kramsch, C. (1998). *Language and Culture*. Oxford: OUP Oxford online dictionaries (accessed 10 January 2017).

Saussure, F, de (1915). *Course in General Linguistics*. New York: McGraw-Hill.

Saussure, F. de (1966). *Course in General Linguistics*. New York: McGraw-Hill.

Schinkel, W. (2015). 'The Sociologist and the State: An Assessment of Pierre Bourdieu's Sociology'. *British Journal of Sociology* 66.2.

Van Dijk, T. A. (2008). *Discourse and Power*. London: Palgrave Macmillan.

Volosinov, V. N. (1994). 'Language and Ideology'. In J. Maybin (ed.), *Language and Literacy in Social Practice*. Clevedon: Multilingual Matters.

Vygotsky, L. S. (1962). *Thought and Language*. Cambridge: MIT Press.

Wertsch, J. V. (1991). *Voices of the Mind: A Sociocultural Approach to Mediated Action*. Cambridge, MA: Harvard University Press.

Newspaper Extracts

The Daily Express Headline (18 February 2016).

The Daily Express Headline (27 July 2016).

The Daily Telegraph (17 May 2016). Headline by Peter Bone.

The Sun (22 September 2015). Headline by Lynn Davidson.

Part Two

Urban Discourses

Editor's introduction

This section examines discourses in the urban world in two UK sociocultural contexts and how they are able to construct subject positions.

Chapter 4 focuses on the ideological power of metropolitan 'hipster' discourse in the sociocultural category of 'DFL' (Down from London) and how this discourse attempts to marginalize local discourse in an English seaside town.

Chapter 5 explores the empowerment of a youth discourse to creatively construct identity in the face of more powerful media voices.

Both chapters see discourse as a possible site of conflict, expressing marginalization, resistance and empowerment.

'DFLs' versus 'Locals': Discursive Conflict on Social Media and the Battle for Regional Identity

Christopher Anderson

Introduction

This chapter concerns the discourses of 'gentrification' seen in a social media conflict between a 'gentrifier' and those who resist her 'gentrifying' discourse. 'Gentrification' (Glass 1964) is the process whereby impoverished working-class urban areas are initially found as an attractive place to locate to by artists, students and bohemians for its cheap but architecturally attractive accommodation and central locality. With the exponential rise of rents and house prices in London as a whole, there has been a recent new form of 'gentrification' whereby artists and people working in the creative industries more generally are relocating to socially deprived seaside towns in Kent and Sussex which, with improving transport links, offer cheap, architecturally attractive accommodation combined with a closeness to the capital.

This chapter then explores a micro-level incident of online discursive resistance to a dominant discourse of gentrification applying Holliday's (1999) notion of small cultures to provide a framework for understanding how interpersonal communication conflict can be conceptualized within a critical paradigm of intercultural communication (Humphrey 2007: 5).

On Wednesday, 7 November 2012, an article was published in an online lifestyle magazine (Richards 2012a). On Thursday, 8 November 2012, the writer of the article published an apology for her article on the Facebook page of her pizza restaurant (Richards 2012b). The apology was a reaction to controversy and complaints that her article created. Both the article and the apology were subsequently deleted from their respective sites. On Friday, 9 November 2012, BBC South East Today television news covered the controversy with a written version published on the BBC News website (BBC 2012) in what was to be known as 'Pizzagate' on social media (Thanet Life 2012). I was made aware of the original article on the day of its publication and followed the controversy it caused with great interest as the subject was my own home town, Margate.

In following this controversy on social and mass media and in also examining a whole range of related media texts subsequent to this on my region, it became clear that this was worthy of an academic analysis. Beyond the fact that this is an interesting case of how social media enables an incredibly quick turnover of publication, reaction and then wider media coverage, it demonstrates how social and mass media can be used by those with cultural and social capital as a means to discursively support the process of gentrification, while at the same time being used by the readers of the text to create feedback extremely quickly – what I call *reactive discourses*. This chapter then concerns how the underlying gentrification discourse in the original text (referred to as the *article*) caused the initial controversy as well as looking at how the reactive discourses were also created from the perspective of certain residents in Margate. An important consideration in this work is my own place in this research. In dealing with analysis that divides people into groups, one of which I am a member of, I have to tread a careful line of reflexivity (Usher & Edwards 1994: 148). To that extent this is a piece of insider research and I had to be conscious of my own subjectivity and biases throughout the process (Hammersley & Atkinson 1995: 103–12).

Geographical and historical context

In order to make sense of the chapter, it is necessary to understand the geographical and historical context in which it occurred. The article concerns the town of Margate on the Isle of Thanet in Kent in the southeast of England. Margate developed in the nineteenth century as a seaside resort primarily servicing London (Jackson et al. 2016; Ward 2016). It serviced in particular the working classes from northeast, east and southeast London. This link to London was maintained with many Londoners relocating in the 1950s, 1960s and 1970s to the coast either to retire or work in the tourism industry. As with more recent migrant patterns of the British either moving or having second homes in southern Europe, the internal migrant patterns to southeastern coastal towns was a result of their holiday experiences, that is, positive holiday experiences led to holidaymakers moving to the holiday destination. In demographic terms, therefore, often the people moving to the coastal towns reflected the social classes of the holidaymakers they attracted. In addition to attracting Anglo-Londoners, a notable Jewish community was established in the more middle-class Cliftonville district of Margate and later in the early 1970s a Greek-Cypriot community developed.

Like many other UK seaside resorts, Margate suffered a decline from the 1970s onwards in its tourism industry as holidaymakers chose the cheaper and warmer destinations in the Mediterranean. During the 1980s a majority of the hotels, guest houses and B'n'Bs were closed down. Many of them were converted into multiple-occupancy dwellings and rented out to the unemployed who moved to the area. Other buildings were converted into children's homes, homes for the mentally ill, nursing homes and retirement homes. These phenomena were particularly noticeable in the wards of Cliftonville West and Margate Central where many of the larger guest houses and hotels were, and which were not easy to convert into single-occupancy dwellings. The 1990s saw waves of immigration into these wards initially as a product of the Yugoslavian civil war but then followed by others seeking asylum including Roma Gypsies and finally a wave of eastern Europeans. The Isle of Thanet was ranked 65th out of 354 of most socially deprived local authorities in England (Thanet District Council 2010). Cliftonville West and Margate Central were ranked as the most socially deprived in Thanet (ibid.).

From the beginning of the 2000s onwards there was a concerted effort to have an arts-led regeneration of Margate built around the final opening of the Turner Contemporary art gallery in 2011, which was originally conceived of in 1998. A model following precedents set with former industrial towns such as Liverpool and Gateshead (Ward 2016). Prior to the opening of the Turner, there began a redevelopment of the 'Old Town', an area close to the then proposed Turner site which had many empty buildings and vacant shops. The redevelopment could be seen with the opening of both art galleries and artists' studios as well as the opening of cafes, bars and niche shops (vintage clothing, antiques and so forth). Following the opening of the Turner, this regeneration slowly expanded beyond the 'Old Town' towards the main high street and into the Cliftonville area.

This regeneration saw a concomitant new internal migration of Londoners to Margate, typically hailing (but not originating) from the east-end of London often from the borough of Hackney. Unlike their predecessors they were middle class, typically working in the creative industries or actually artists. One of the principal attractions of Margate was the cheapness of Regency, Victorian and

Edwardian property in Cliftonville West and Margate Central; areas that were avoided by many working-class and middle-class people from Thanet due to the reputation of the area being socially deprived and therefore associated with criminality. With the incessant rise in property prices in London in the 2000s; it was quite feasible for Londoners to sell a small flat in London and get a large house for less in Margate. The second attraction was the closeness of Margate to London made more accessible by the opening of the high speed rail link in 2009. Third, the perceived attractiveness of the area was its seaside location. The final attraction was the perception of the town having a creative community shown explicitly through the opening of galleries and studios.

This new migration was coupled with mass media coverage particularly within broadsheet national newspapers (e.g. Turner 2011), lifestyle magazines (e.g. Smith 2015) and property television programmes (e.g. *Inside Out: London* 2016) as well as coverage on social media typically in blogs presenting from those who had either visited or relocated to Margate (e.g. the article). Common to all of these forms of media was Margate being recommended for either a visit or as a place for relocation.

Analysis of 'Every Day Is Like Sunday'

The article, entitled 'Every Day Is Like Sunday', appeared in the London-based 'digital magazine' *Civilian* (2017a). The magazine is subtitled 'global intelligence, style and culture', whose aims are 'to inspire, inform and entertain you' (*Civilian* 2017b). To 'inspire' suggests that beyond the functions of providing information and entertainment, it wishes to institute change in its readers' behaviour, that is, to perhaps imitate the experiences their writers have had. In the 'About' page, a great deal of effort is given to create an identity for the magazine itself given in the first person (ibid.). It recognizes itself as a form of travel magazine but at the same time it constructs an identity of 'difference' from what it defines as a conventional 'luxury travel' magazine. This is done through a comparison to the 'conventional' stating how it is 'not like' the others in a way it is not easy to pigeonhole; in its attitude; in how it treats its subject matter; and in what it does not do.

> Civilian is contemporary, intelligent, inspiring, luxe, provocative, witty, offbeat, literary, human . . . and largely in the first person.
>
>   If you insisted on the utmost brevity, we'd identify ourselves as a luxury travel magazine. But, while many magazines execute 'luxury publishing' superbly and

intelligently, and many of our writers – and readers – are very much a part of that world, we feel that there's room for something that embraces individuality and irreverence. (*Civilian* 2017b)

The list of adjectives in the first sentence proposes a complex identity that cannot be easily pigeonholed. This avoidance strategy can be seen in the way it reluctantly identifies itself as a 'luxury travel magazine'. The only other place this is mentioned is on the title page to the left of the title 'Civilian' where there is a vertical Japanese script that translates as 'posh travelling'. In the 'About' page it gives its own definition of 'luxury' as being not about the consumption of expensive goods and services, but rather an abstracted interpretation of an experience. Avoidance can also be seen in how it states that it 'embraces individuality and irreverence'. The avoidance strategies help to create an identity of being alternative and individual which is emphasized in a '0' conditional sentence addressed to the reader. 'If you're looking for "best beach" lists, celebrities or a bunch of picture galleries, then this isn't the place' (*Civilian* 2017b). This rhetorical identification device is not actually directly addressed to the perceived reader that the editor conceives but to a reader not suited to the magazine. I would suggest that the person looking for that type of content in a magazine would not be reading this text in the first place, and so in essence it means *we don't write for that normal type of reader and we know really that you are like us and not like them.*

The way in which this magazine constructs its identity as not mainstream, as alternative and as not easily pigeonholed, I would argue, makes it part of the 'hipster' culture that emerged in the early 2000s. 'Hipster' is a highly contested term but what it appears to signify is a set of people who live in urban areas often previously impoverished (e.g. Williamsburg in Brooklyn, New York; Shoreditch in Hackney, London) and construct an alternative consumer lifestyle in opposition to the mainstream in, for example, dress, food, transport, work and leisure (Maly and Varis 2016; Schiermer 2014; Scott 2017), a nomenclature that those described as 'hipster' often reject. Civilian is very much in contrast to the mainstream and purports alternative consumption patterns. Such consumption patterns are always threatened by the fact that particular style choices made by 'hipsters' can become mainstream (Michael 2015). The article is then located in this challenging dynamic of what Saul (1994: 130) calls the self-destructing paradox of fashion: 'In order to be fashionable you must avoid everything in fashion'. As will become apparent in the following analysis, the article fits into the magazine's identity and perceived readership.

Aims and structure

In this section I will look at the text as a whole in terms of purpose and structure. A close reading of the text reveals that there is one primary and three secondary purposes of the article, and therefore, one assumes, of the writer:

- Primary:
  - To persuade the reader to visit or to move to Margate permanently or to have a second home there.
  - The underlying argument is that although Margate has social problems it is in the process of regeneration due to Londoners moving there.
    - This is done through a 'parallel' narrative, that is, this was my experience and it could be your experience which fits into the magazine's aim to inspire.

- Secondary:
  - To demonstrate to the reader how a successful business was set up and established in Margate (the writer's own business).
  - To promote the writer's business.
  - To promote the writer herself as a successful businesswoman who has set up a 'hipster' restaurant.
    - Perhaps to engender in the reader an admiration for what the writer has done, that is, moved to a risky place and achieved success.

The text, although not demarcated as such through organization features such as subheadings, can be easily identified as having four distinct sections.

- Section 1 (Paragraphs 1–3): Description of Margate as a location with potential
- Section 2 (Paragraphs 4–5): An imagined itinerary for a day trip to Margate
- Section 3 (Paragraphs 6–14): Narrative of the writer's relocation to Margate
- Section 4 (Paragraphs 15–16): Persuasive conclusion

Section 1 argues the potential of Margate in terms of its cheap property and physical beauty, but at the same time notes the people of Margate and their poverty as being problematic. This is counterbalanced with the identification of the town being in a process of regeneration due to 'DFLs' (down from London). This term is used in the article and has become a common term for describing these new internal migrants from London by residents of Kent and Sussex (*Wiktionary* 2017). This section has the primary purpose of persuading the reader to visit or to move to Margate.

Section 2 creates an imagined itinerary for a middle-class London visitor on a day trip starting from St Pancras Station in London to catch the high-speed rail connection to Margate. The narrative both identifies the negatives in Margate and the positives beginning with more negatives on arrival at Margate station but leading to more positives as the imagined visitor gets to the Old Town. As with Section 1, this also shares the primary aim.

Section 3 is the writer's own narrative of her relocation with her partner to Margate. It begins with her initial visits from London leading to her conversion to the place; then continues with her efforts to get accommodation and start her catering business there eventually leading to her business success with her restaurant. This section covers all the purposes while Section 4, the conclusion, focuses on the primary aim. The main argument (reflecting the introduction) is that it is a good place with a bright future despite its problems.

Paratext features: title, quotations, photographs

I adapt the term 'paratext' from literary theory (Genette & Maclean 1991) to describe all the features additional to the actual text written whether verbal or visual. These features are either the choice of the editor and subeditor or the actual writer. What they do in this article is orient the reader to the subject matter of the article while positioning the reader verbally and visually as a London-based 'hipster'.

The title of the article 'Every Day Is Like Sunday' is a reference to a song by Morrissey with the same title released in 1988 as a single and as a track on the album 'Viva Hate'. The song recounts the misery of visiting a seaside town in the United Kingdom reflecting the writer's discussion of the negative features of Margate and therefore is an apt title. However, there is another distinct signifier in choosing this song. Morrissey and his former band, The Smiths, as the leading purveyors of UK indie music in the 1980s is very much a 'hip' choice that one could assume would fall in the musical lexicon of the target reader.

The subheading of the title is 'The Art and Pizza-Based Regeneration of a Forgotten Seaside Town'. On one level this describes the content of the article in terms of the regeneration of a town. However, there are two elements of note. First of all, 'pizza-based regeneration'. While it could be acknowledged that the regeneration of Margate is arts-led with the opening of the Turner Contemporary central to this, the author's opening of a pizza restaurant is a by-product of the regeneration rather than an engine of it. A reading of this phrase then could be that the writer or subeditor is attempting irony; the use of irony being a key 'hipster' trope (Schiermer 2014). Second the use of the adjective 'forgotten' is of interest. A town that is forgotten suggests that people have lost all memory of it rather like a lost city discovered in an archaeological dig. Yet Margate was evidently not forgotten by its residents. This suggests then that it is forgotten by the assumed readers of *Civilian*. In that sense it is off the 'hip' radar but through regeneration may gain recognition.

There are three large quotations from the text embedded in the right hand side of the main article paragraphs to illustrate the subject matter of the text. The first quotation, which comes from the Section 2 imagined itinerary, is a description of the 'locals' using wordplay for assumed humorous effect based around the root 'waste' to counterpoint the literary traditions of Margate with the intoxicated state of the inhabitants. 'Carry on along the seafront, past the shelter where T.S. Eliot wrote lines of The Wasteland, whose latter-day inhabitants create their own take on wasted' (Richards 2012a). The second quotation from the Section 4 conclusion contrasts the 'excitement' about the regeneration of the town using the metaphor of scent, 'There's the whiff of excitement and possibility in the air in Margate' (Richards 2012a) which is contrasted to the smells associated with the traditional seaside and the smell of social deprivation: 'It mixes headily with the potent seaweed, sickly sweet candyfloss and the stench of a polarised populace facing crippling levels of unemployment' (Richards 2012a). While there appears to be sympathy for the unemployed plight of the 'locals', the use of the noun 'stench' with its negative connotations draws on an history of the middle and upper classes describing the poor in terms of their uncleanliness and resultant body odour (Classen et al. 1994).

The final quotation comes from the writer's narrative of relocation to Margate in Section 3. This is from a description of the writer setting up her pizza restaurant with her partner which is part of an explanation of the kind of restaurant they have established. 'There's no theme or back story here – no witty press release or cloying food trend. Small plates are banned' (Richards 2012a). This is an interesting example of the dynamic flow of always trying to be fashionable. The denial of having a press release describing the theme or back story and not being part of a food trend (cf. 'small plates') marks out the establishment as being different; an alternative to how other restaurants are promoted. Yet Section 3 acts as a back story establishing a clear theme for the restaurant that actually does follow a food trend for 'gourmet' pizza restaurants which she discusses as an influence in paragraph 9. The three quotations highlight the different sections of the text and more importantly function to pick out the themes of how the old

Margate is contrasted with the new regenerated Margate while also promoting the writer's business.

The photographs used in the article also have a similar function of illustrating the different aspects of the article while being oriented to the assumed tastes of the readers. There are five photographs, four of which were taken by the author. In order, they are of:

1. A young man jumping off the end of Margate pier into the sea
2. The Turner Contemporary art gallery
3. A pizza – presumably from the author's restaurant
4. Margate harbour, the Turner Contemporary and the Old Town
5. Stencilled graffiti image of the artist Tracey Emin on a wall

In the examination of the style of the images, what these photographs share in common is an abstracted quality in terms of framing, composition and use of colour effects. In the 'About' section of the magazine, the importance of visual imaginary for the magazine is made clear: 'We are as driven by text as we are by images' (*Civilian* 2012b). In the example of the jumping man, it is not immediately clear what he is jumping from and what he is jumping into with a colourized sky dominating the frame. This abstracted theme is, I would argue, part of the magazine's aforementioned remit to be 'different' and therefore a further signifier of 'hipness' oriented to the reader. A more standard composition and lighting would be less attractive to the target reader.

The man is actually jumping off the end of Margate pier (renamed in the regeneration process of Margate as the 'Margate Harbour Arm'). At the time this photograph was taken, this activity was associated with local male working-class youth and the man's Union Jack shorts acts as a class signifier (Jefferies 2014). To that extent he represents an example of the 'locals' discussed in the article. The second photograph, of the Turner Contemporary gallery, is again abstracted with two angular exterior walls and a blue sky. This photograph centres on the architectural modernism of the gallery and could be seen as a signifier of the new to the town. The photograph of the pizza is itself slightly abstracted in being a close up of the item on what appears to be a wooden base typifying an 'artisanal', slightly rough-hewn food product. Thus the writer is not only promoting her product but is positioning what is a common type of fast food as something alternative to the mainstream. The fourth photograph while not abstracted appears to be heavily colourized. It is moodily lit at sunset emphasizing the beauty of the location of the 'harbour' area, the gallery and the Old Town – in essence the original focus of the regeneration of Margate.

The final photograph is abstracted in the sense it is not clear where the wall is or indeed if it is a wall. The photograph works on two levels. First of all, it is an example of stencil art which has become fashionable particularly due to the work of Banksy (Lewisohn & Chalfant 2009). Thus the choice of this type of art work is another 'hip' signifier. Second, the picture is of the artist Tracey Emin. The London-based artist originally from Margate acts as a transitional signifier of both the old Margate which she refers to her in own art (Brown 2006) and the new Margate of artists and creatives.

These paratext features are designed to be aesthetically appealing to the target reader and give a set of recognizable signifiers that form part of the presumed verbal and visual lexicon of this reader. At the same time it orients the reader to the subject matter of the changing town, its people, the writer and her achievements.

Constructions within the text

The writer through discursive strategies such as arguments, descriptions and narratives constructs the key elements of the text. At the centre of this is her construction of Margate that is dichotomous being both 'down at heel' (Richards 2012a) but also in the process of change, that is, improving through regeneration. More subtly, as already discussed, the writer constructs the reader as a London 'hipster'. The writer indicates in her language a shared knowledge with the reader of what is 'hip' by reference to signifiers that demonstrate a cultural knowledge and therefore a cultural capital (Bourdieu 1992; Robbins 2000). In other words, *you know about this stuff, they don't*. Furthermore, with its primary aim to persuade the reader to visit or move to Margate, the writer positions the reader as a potential 'DFL'. The writer then by addressing the reader as someone with a shared cultural capital (as well, it would be assumed, financial capital to be able to relocate) is constructing herself to be similar to the reader. However, at the same time she constructs herself as a 'DFL' – she privileges her relocation in terms of being an early example of this, that is, a 'pioneer' (Richards 2012a). Thus she is in the privileged position to explain to the uninitiated about Margate.

The construction of writer and reader contrasts with the construction of the preexisting residents of Margate which primarily led to the negative reaction to the article. The residents, referred to as the 'locals', are constructed as an ill-educated impoverished underclass of either the unemployed or in low-status occupations with many social problems: a construction that posits these people as a negative, problematic 'other' (Edgar and Sedgwick 1999; Said 1978). This construction is not erroneous as Margate has suffered from poverty and unemployment (Thanet District Council 2010; Margate Coastal Community Team 2016), but what is absent from this construction are other types of residents in the area such as the skilled working class, the middle classes and the migrant communities in Margate, many of whom similarly suffer from poor social conditions. The writer choses one particular subsection of the local population and from that creates a stereotype of all 'locals'.

The two major narratives in the text

Using the above constructions, there are two distinct but related narratives that occur in the text. The first is a narrative of relocating to Margate. While most explicitly realized in section 3 of the text with the narrative of the writer's own relocation, elements of this narrative occur in all sections. The narrative is as follows:

1. **Londoners visit Margate** (Through increasing media coverage they become aware that this is good place to visit for a day trip or weekend. Margate beginning to regenerate.)
2. **Londoners fall in love with Margate** (They love its beauty – architectural, historic and scenic – and see that there are more and more features of 'hipster' London life there, but they also recognize its social problems with a white underclass.)
3. **Londoners move to or buy a second home in Margate** (Its social problems mean that it is a lot cheaper to live in than London in terms of property and general living costs. London is getting more and more expensive to live in. Yet Margate is not far from London with improved transportation. Due to the fact that they live in Hackney, they are used to having social problems around them so are more willing to move to the poorer wards than those from east Kent.)

The second narrative concerns the regeneration of Margate. Underpinning the narrative of the 'DFL' is a narrative that in relocating to Margate (and possibly setting up business), the 'DFL' will contribute to the regeneration of Margate which in of itself will attract further Londoners which will increase the value of their properties.

1. Margate has negative qualities
2. It is, however, going through a process of change
3. Which leads to positive qualities (there are still negatives but in the process the positives are outweighing the negatives)

This regeneration involves bringing from London aspects of 'hipster' culture in terms of leisure and consumption. The local 'unemployable' (Richards 2012a) culture is of no attraction to 'DFLs' so the 'hipster' culture and 'unemployable' culture is in conflict with the new culture taking over the old. Implicit in this is the notion of gentrification although it is not recognized as such in the article only being mentioned as a reason for people relocating from London. 'This time they've moved because the gentrification of London's wildest boroughs has forced out those that don't earn six-figure sums' (Richards 2012a). The locals are unable to bring about change themselves while 'DFLs' can bring about change for them and improve the locals' world. The writer uses negative language to describe Margate (e.g. 'grimy, down-at-heel') but contrasts this with a process of change that is positive: for example, 'dragged itself up', so the town has agency.

Binary of the two cultures

The writer establishes in her constructions of 'DFLs' and 'locals' two distinct and separate cultures. I used the term 'culture' following Holliday's (1999: 247) notion of small cultures as 'the composite of cohesive behaviour within any social grouping'. These cultures can be identified in how she describes people, their behaviour and the artefacts they use, consume or venerate.

In her construction of a people binary, the writer, in her choice of adjectives and adjectival phrases, nouns and noun phrases, creates a clear distinction in her description of the two groups (see Table 4.1). 'Locals' are unattractive ('grubby kids'; 'thick-necked'; 'paunched'), 'unloved' and in a state of intoxication ('uncontrollable'; 'drunks'; 'wasted'). 'DFLs', however, are 'well-heeled' and fashionable ('perfectly topiaried facial hair'; 'bespoke heeled'; 'avant-garde fashions'). As already stated, 'locals' are either unemployed or in low-status occupations, while 'DFLs' are in a range of professions in the creative industries and in other white-collar occupations. In terms of tastes and values, locals are racist and anti-immigrant while 'DFLs' are 'cultured and knowing' and 'clued up'. In other words, they are knowledgeable about what is fashionable and hip. Locals then lack cultural and financial capital; the 'DFLs' do not.

Table 4.1 People (descriptions and roles) in the article

Nouns; adjectives + nouns	
Locals	**DFLs**

Locals	DFLs

• Naming
  ○ lowlifes
  ○ locals
• Description
  ○ grubby kids
  ○ thick-necked driver
  ○ younger, slightly less paunched version of him
• Occupation
  ○ unemployable
  ○ polarized populace facing crippling levels of unemployment
  ○ cab driver
• Taste/values
  ○ racist
  ○ anti-Eastern-European bile
  ○ prime specimens of the master race – tattooed thugs with short foreheads
• Condition and behaviour
  ○ unloved
  ○ uncontrollable
  ○ drunks
  ○ wasted
• Tracey Emin problem
  ○ she is both
	• Naming
	  ○ hipsters
	  ○ day-trippers
	  ○ Pioneers
	  ○ discoverers
	  ○ visitors
	  ○ gallery-goers
	• Description
	  ○ bespoke heeled
	  ○ well-heeled Thanet dwellers
	  ○ hipsters visiting with their Leicas and perfectly topiaried facial hair
	  ○ the avant-garde fashions of visiting Londoners
	• Occupation
	  ○ architects, gallery owners and designers
	  ○ running a theatre
	  ○ artists, designers
	  ○ creatives
	  ○ artists, designers, furniture makers, printmakers, chefs, photographers, civil servants, stylists, shopkeepers, hoteliers, restaurateurs, PR folk and journalists
	  ○ business owners and their businesses in the Old Town
	• Taste/values
	  ○ cultured and discerning
	  ○ clued-up people
	• Tracey Emin problem
	  ○ she is both

Through verb phrases and clauses, the writer makes a strong distinction between how the two cultures behave (see Table 4.2). For the writer, the behaviour of 'locals' is violent and disruptive ('girl fights in Morrisons'; 'marauding the streets') to the point of nihilism ('launching themselves into the shallow water'). As mentioned earlier there is much emphasis in her construction on far-right politics; this is combined with a sedentary lifestyle associated with unemployment. This contrasts

Table 4.2 Behaviour in the article

Clauses; S+V+O, verb phrases etc.	
Locals	**DFLs**

• Violent/disruptive
  ○ girl fights in Morrisons
  ○ marauding the streets
  ○ launching themselves into the shallow water
 	
• Alcohol and drug use
  ○ in-your-face drug use
  ○ wielding tins of Tennents Extra
  ○ sinking cans of Stella
 	
• Far-right politics
  ○ planning their manifesto for white supremacy
 	
• Sedentary/unemployed lifestyle
  ○ waiting for their benefit cheques to clear
  ○ sat at home sinking cans of Stella while playing his Xbox bought on the never-never from Brighthouse
	• Consumer behaviour
	  ○ property
	    ▪ scouring . . . the streets for property
	    ▪ sensed an opportunity
	    ▪ artists . . . sniff out cheap studios and gallery spaces
	    ▪ searched for property
	    ▪ found a one-bed flat
	  ○ furnishing and decoration
	    ▪ bought furniture
	    ▪ discovered dusty emporiums filled to the rafters with sticks of mismatched furniture, vintage finds and upcycled lighting
	    ▪ stripping floorboards, plastering, painting and sourcing furniture
	    ▪ vintage furniture was found
	  ○ food and drink
	    ▪ put together a picnic
	    ▪ sipping pots of tea surrounded by their shopping bags and pedigree pooches
	    ▪ finished up with pints of Kentish cider at The Lifeboat and perfectly formed burgers at Fort's Café
	  ○ art
	    ▪ wandered around brilliantly curated exhibitions at the Turner
	• Alcohol and drug use
	  ○ sip a glass of bubbly
	  ○ pints of Kentish cider at The Lifeboat
	
	• Establishing businesses
	  ○ set up shop, scrubbed their doorsteps and filled their stores with cleverly chosen pieces and work by local artists
	  ○ tweeting
	  ○ built up a knowledgeable, passionate support network

Clauses; S+V+O, verb phrases etc.	
Locals	**DFLs**
	○ branding was created with the help of a close friend who happens to be one of the United Kingdom's best art directors
	• Process of regeneration and gentrification
	○ cleared the way for new inhabitants
	○ talked of the promise of this town
	○ gentrification

with 'DFLs' establishing businesses, buying properties and renovating them. There is also a distinct difference in consumer behaviour. Alcohol consumption for the locals is cheap, mass-produced beer ('Tennents Extra'; 'Stella') while 'DFLs' consume more expensive drinks such as Champagne and craft cider. Underlying this is a social-class based legitimization of consumer behaviour. While the consumption of mass-produced beer in either public or in 'rough pubs' is framed in derogatory terms, the consumption of more expensive alcoholic drinks in the context of 'a picnic' or in a micropub (i.e. 'The Lifeboat') is acceptable.

Linked to behaviour are the actual artefacts associated with each culture. By artefacts, I mean the anthropological notion of objects either made for or made by a culture that are used by members of a culture in everyday life and ritual (Hodder 1994). Thus artefacts can stretch from simple everyday tools to objects that hold important symbolic meaning. Artefacts identified in nouns and noun phrases generally involve what people buy and consume (see Table 4.3). There is a distinction between the kinds of shops frequented by the locals, that is, mass-market supermarkets and shops aimed at those on a low income ('Morrisons'; 'Brighthouse') and the 'DFLs' in the Old Town with a range of niche shopping in small independent shops. Property in terms of homes that 'DFLs' have bought are distinctly period: 'Georgian, Edwardian and Victorian', which forms part of a narrative of buying a property to renovate and furnish with objects that can be found in shops in the Old Town.

Places to eat also show a class distinction between mass-market fast-food restaurants ('Wimpy'; 'Pizza Hut') and independent, more expensive eateries from those in London that inspired the writer's restaurant ('Pizza East, Franco Manca, Santa Maria and Pizza Pilgrims') to new Margate eateries ('Cup Cake Café'; 'Fort's Café'). As already stated, alcohol is strongly separated between mass-market and more expensive products. Leisure beyond food and alcohol

Table 4.3 Artefacts in the article

Nouns; noun phrases	
Locals	**DFLs**

Locals	DFLs

• Shops
  o Morrisons
  o Brighthouse (shop for poor where consumer products can be bought on hire purchase)
 	
• Food and restaurants
  o Formica-clad Wimpy 'restaurant'
  o Pizza Hut
 	
• Alcohol
  o cans of Stella
  o Tennents Extra
  o Sambuca and Jägerbomb deals
  o rough pubs
 	
• Other forms of leisure
  o Xbox
	• Shops
	  o Old Town
	  o Qing interiors
	
	• Property
	  o Georgian, Edwardian and Victorian properties
	  o oldest Georgian square
	  o bare plaster and brick wall
	  o vintage furniture
	
	• Arts
	  o theatre
	  o studios and gallery spaces
	  o Cinema
	  o T.S. Eliot's The Wasteland
	  o Margate Gallery
	
	• Food and restaurants
	  o types of food
	    ▪ a picnic
	    ▪ street food
	    ▪ wood-fired pizza,
	    ▪ olives
	    ▪ ices by Gelupo Gelato
	    ▪ chocolate brownies
	    ▪ flat whites
	    ▪ locally roasted beans
	    ▪ good, simple food
	  o restaurants
	    ▪ pop-up
	    ▪ Sourced (Sourced market trendy food shop and café at St Pancras station copying on farmers' markets)
	    ▪ Pizza East, Franco Manca, Santa Maria and Pizza Pilgrims in London
	    ▪ Cupcake Café
	    ▪ Fort's Cafe
	  o equipment
	    ▪ pizza oven/Roman-style oven
	    ▪ La Marzocco coffee machine
	    ▪ GB Pizza Company
	
	• Alcohol
	  o a glass of bubbly
	  o pints of Kentish cider
	  o The Lifeboat (micro pub)
	  o Bloody Mary
	  o barrels from Borough Wines

Nouns; noun phrases	
Locals	DFLs

	• Transport
	  ◦ VW Campervan
	  ◦ fixed-wheel bicycle
	
	• Internet and social media
	  ◦ Twitter
	  ◦ website
	  ◦ Tripadvisor
	  ◦ Facebook

for the 'DFLs' involves art, theatre, cinema and poetry while for the 'locals' it involves computer games.

In behaviour and the artefacts that people utilize in their behaviour, a strong binary is evident between a rather limited world for 'locals' and a more elaborate, sophisticated one favoured by 'DfL's. In literal terms, note that the 'DFL' list in both categories is far longer. In terms of consumption patterns, 'locals' are limited explicitly by poverty and more implicitly by a lack of sophistication in taste and lifestyle choices. The text is replete with verbal signifiers of social class in terms of consumer consumption. Among the many examples of this, two are particularly illustrative in paragraphs 2 and 14 respectively.

> My first sighting of a fixed-gear bicycle pedalling (sic.) along the seafront gave me joyous palpitations. (Richards 2012a)
>
> Margate might not have seen anything like it, but we're pretty sure visiting Londoners will spot the La Marzocco coffee machine and barrels from Borough Wines immediately. (Richards 2012a)

The fixed-gear bicycle is for the writer a sign that as an early indicator others are moving to Margate as this object is a key signifier of 'hipster' culture and would be assumedly ridden by a 'DFL'. The second quotation concerning the objects in her restaurant makes this even more explicit – signifiers of a London culture that locals would not recognize.

Another binary is of the description of Margate itself contrasting the old Margate which is associated with the locals and a new regenerated Margate instigated by the 'DFLs' (see Table 4.4). What has to be noted is that it is the same town being described but the writer identifies it as having two, at times contradictory, sets of qualities. Thus in the description of the state of the town it is 'exciting' and 'vibrant' but also having evidence of a lack of investment ('grimy, down-at-heel'; 'rough around the environs'). In the description of buildings, you

Table 4.4 Margate (buildings, locations etc.) in the article

Nouns; noun phrases	
Old – locals	**New – DFLs**

• Description of state of town
  ○ this grimy, down-at-heel town
  ○ no-go area
  ○ rough-around-the-environs
  ○ bags of rubbish ripped open by ASBO gulls
 	
• Buildings: condition and current use
  ○ boarded-up pubs
  ○ looming brutalist building
  ○ arcades with their ringing slot machines and glass cases filled with China-made toys
  ○ Currently home to privately run children's homes and hostels housing those on probation, Cliftonville's slipped into a less than salubrious state.
 	
• Echoes of the past as seaside resort
  ○ sickly sweet candy floss
  ○ potent seaweed
  ○ donkeys
  ○ sea
	• Description of state of town
	  ○ exciting, vibrant little town
	
	• Old buildings/property
	  ○ Georgian, Edwardian and Victorian properties
	  ○ Cliftonville, once the holiday spot for wealthy Victorians and which currently makes the 'burbs of West London look cheap with its incredible housing stock, was where we found a three-bedroom flat with enormous proportions on the frontline of Walpole Bay for less than £90,000
	  ○ Victorian train station
	
	• Arts
	  ○ theatre
	  ○ studios and gallery spaces
	  ○ glimmering piece of modern architecture by Chipperfield (Turner Contemporary)
	
	• Scenery
	  ○ a sweep of fine, golden sand, an enormous sky that wouldn't look out of place in the Caribbean
	
	• Old town
	  ○ vintage furniture stores, cute cafés and alehouse

have a sense of buildings in a bad condition ('boarded-up') or being converted to homes for children or ex-prisoners which is contrasted with these older Victorian buildings being aesthetically attractive yet cheap. What is not made explicit is that the very reason that these buildings are cheap is because of the poverty. To that extent the text does not critically engage with the social conditions that create this situation, but celebrates the possibility for internal migrants to buy old, cheap properties ripe for renovation. Combined with this is the fact that despite the run-down elements of the town, there is a broader attractiveness due to its coastal location: 'a sweep of fine, golden sand, an enormous sky that wouldn't look out of place in the Caribbean'.

The binaries have so far been identified through the selection of lexis and clauses. I will now examine how they operate by examining an extract of the text in detail, that is, paragraph 4 in the section 2 imagined reader itinerary starting at St Pancras station.

> Sip a glass of bubbly at St Pancras, put together a train picnic from Sourced and jump on the high-speed train to Margate as we did before making the move here. As you're emptied out onto the concourse of Margate's Victorian train station and are invariably met by lowlifes wielding tins of Tennent's Extra, you may well wonder whether the hype is really true or even possible. But try to look past the boarded-up pubs and the looming brutalist building that has seen better days. Carry on along the seafront, past the shelter where T.S. Eliot wrote lines of *The Wasteland*, whose latter-day inhabitants create their own take on wasted; past the rough pubs, with their Sambuca and Jägerbomb deals, and which are filled on some nights with prime specimens of the master race – tattooed thugs with short foreheads planning their manifesto for white supremacy. (Richards 2012a)

Using the imperative mood the writer makes a series of suggestion of what to do and what the reader will experience on their trip. The first sentence tells the reader to have a drink and buy food for a train picnic at the café-food shop 'Sourced' in St Pancras station which identifies itself as a market built on its selling of locally sourced food thus mentioning a 'hip' signifier. 'Sip a glass of bubbly at St Pancras, put together a train picnic from Sourced.' Compare this clause to the description of what the visitor will meet at Margate station – 'lowlifes wielding tins of Tennent's Extra'. Here there is a contrast between legitimized consumption of alcohol in a train station to that which is non-legitimized, that is, it is perfectly acceptable to drink Champagne in a fashionable food market/café in a train station but it is not acceptable to drink a strong lager on a train concourse. This is further emphasized by the verbs used. Compare 'sip', which suggests taking small amounts of the beverage to appreciate the taste, to 'wield', a verb that typically collocates with nouns such as knife and sword. Therefore the local holds the beer as if it were a weapon. This violence of the 'local' is emphasized later in the paragraph where local unattractive 'thugs' drink to get 'wasted' in 'rough pubs' with far-right politics which is contrasted later with drinking craft cider in a micro-pub.

Thus the following contrasts:

- Sourced – concourse (places to drink in a train station)
- sip – wield (verbs to describe the drinking process)
- bubbly – Tennents Extra (expensive wine versus cheap mass-produced lager)

What these binaries create is a social class distinction between an affluent middle class and a poor underclass who look different, do different things and consume different things. Like all binaries this concerns one binary privileging another (Foucault 1991: 199; McQuillan 2000: 8). It is quite clear in the author's writing that she privileges the 'DFL' in every way over the 'local' in these areas. Everything about the 'local' is problematic and negative. Everything about the 'DFL' is positive. Furthermore, 'DFLs' have the agency to change their environment in terms of work, starting businesses, buying and renovating properties, while 'locals' appear to have no agency stuck in a spiral of poverty and ignorance.

An unwitting gentrification discourse

I would argue that the constructions, narratives and binaries discussed above are part of a discourse of gentrification, central to which is the otherizing representation of residents of areas being gentrified. This representation was central to the offence and subsequent controversy the article caused. Such offensiveness is implicit to such a discourse in that the discourse operates by justifying the actions of the gentrifying by identifying the need for change to an area that has declined due in part to its indigenous population. This discourse was unwitting on two counts. First, the author states in her Facebook apology a complete surprise in the offence she caused and that she had no awareness that her article could cause offence (Richards 2012b). Second, there is no direct recognition that she is promoting gentrification and indeed as stated above, only sees gentrification in London as the cause for the internal migration to Margate.

The two major narratives in the text are then integral to the discourse of gentrification. Gentrification is a term coined by Ruth Glass (1964), which is now well-established in urban geography and sociology (e.g. Butler & Robson 2003; Lees et al. 2007; Brown-Saracino 2010; Lees 2010; Smith 2010) to explain the phenomenon of bohemians (artists, students etc.) moving to impoverished areas of cities attracted by their central locality and the cheap but architecturally attractive accommodation. The impact of the new residents is the bringing about of a material 'improvement' to the area in terms of renovated properties, new shops and leisure facilities. This in turn makes the area slowly become attractive to the more conventional middle class who move there leading to rising house prices, the selling of rented properties and the rise in rents of any rented properties still in existence. This process leads to the displacement of the original working-class inhabits who can no longer afford to live there (Slater 2006); Notting Hill in London is a good example of this process starting in the 1960s. I would argue further that this article is not unique in producing this discourse. There is a large body of texts, whether personal blogs, print newspaper and magazine articles, and television programmes, that form a complex discourse of gentrification for Margate and similar coastal towns in Kent and Sussex. What marks out this text as particular is the reaction it caused.

The explicit otherization of the residents that caused the reaction related to what Wacquant et al. (2014) call 'territorial stigmatization'. 'Locals' consist of only an impoverished, uneducated underclass lacking any agency to change their neighbourhood for the better. Thus it is the role of the gentrifier to come and improve an area. Yet in this discourse, other types of 'locals' are missing: skilled working classes, the middle classes and recent immigrants. I would argue that the first two groups were ignored because they do not fit the narrative as they indeed do have more agency to improve the area than the 'underclass'. Indeed, regeneration activity has not been exclusively in the hands of 'DFLs', for example, The Turner Contemporary gallery was a local initiative (Jackson et al. 2016) and several of the shops in the Old Town were locally owned. The immigrant group, who populated the 'down-at-heel' area of Cliftonville where the author bought her property, are ignored even though some of them are as socially deprived as the 'locals'. An argument for this omission is that if they were portrayed in a similarly negative light, the author would be open to accusations of racism. A key point to note is that 'hipster' culture is one associated with the progressive liberal left (Schiermer 2014: 170).

Underlying the discourse is that gentrifiers have the financial capital to buy property and set up (or relocate) businesses while they also have the cultural capital to be able to organize activities to engender gentrification (e.g. community associations, neighbourhood groups and campaigns). Furthermore, financial and cultural capital give gentrifiers a confidence and independence that easily allows for internal migration, resettlement and change of work. This cultural and financial capital combined with the otherization of locals legitimize gentrification. The central negative consequence of gentrification, the displacement of the indigenous residents as rented properties are bought up and rents increase (Slater 2006), is not considered in this discourse as problematic and in fact advantageous in the article. The otherization of 'locals' means that they are not consulted within the text; their opinions are not sought apart from cited examples of their backwardness and ignorance. For example, the author cites a generic conversation with a taxi driver:

> Not a cab journey goes by without having to firmly tell a thick-necked driver to keep his anti-Eastern-European bile to himself – 'Coming here, stealing our jobs. My son can't get no work . . .' I imagine a younger, slightly-less paunched version of him sat at home sinking cans of Stella whilst playing his Xbox bought on the never-never from Brighthouse. (Richards 2012a)

In considering how the discourse is unremittingly positive about the processes of gentrification and unremittingly negative about the 'locals', it is possible to identify a level of regional and class prejudice that suggests an important element of gentrification discourse is a colonialist discourse.

A colonialist discourse

Following the work of Said (1978) and Pennycook (1998), I would state that a colonialist discourse is a construction that makes exotic stereotypes and simplifies the colonized. This otherization process with the 'locals' lacking agency is then a justification for colonialism. Somewhat akin to the Anglo-colonial spread of Christianity to save the natives' souls, there is a subtext that the 'DFLs' can regenerate an area for the 'locals' that have not been displaced. While the internal migration of middle-class Londoners to seaside towns is not colonialism in its truest sense, that is, taking over a country or region with physical force, there is a remarkable similarity to actual colonialism. There is a justification for moving to an area and changing it not only in terms of economic regeneration but also in terms of bringing the cultural artefacts and behaviours of the colonizers' culture.

In addition to this otherizing in the article, there is language that more directly pertains to the 'DFLs' being like colonialists in the process of taking over the area and removing the indigenous population. Paragraph 6 in the section 3 narrative of the writer's relocation to Margate illustrates this element of the colonialist discourse in the most clear and direct manner. This begins with the narrative of the writer's relocation.

> We'd been coming to Margate for two years. Firstly as day-trippers, stumbling across the Old Town with its vintage furniture stores, cute cafés and alehouse, feeling like we were its first discoverers. These shop and gallery owners were the pioneers – when the Old Town was just another no-go area, full of drunks waiting for their

benefit cheques to clear, they set up shop, scrubbed their doorsteps and filled their stores with cleverly chosen pieces and work by local artists. Janet Williams at the Margate Gallery, Anne-Marie Nixy and her Qing interiors store and Lisa Hemingway's Cupcake Café cleared the way for new inhabitants. These days the Old Town is packed with visitors and well-heeled Thanet dwellers, sipping pots of tea surrounded by their shopping bags and pedigree pooches. (Richards 2012a)

The paragraph describes the Old Town with its shops, cafes and pubs. The writer describes how she and her partner felt like Margate's first 'discoverers'. The verb 'discoverer' is a quintessential colonialist lexical item discounting the fact that people have actually already lived there for some time. Furthermore, the shop and gallery owners are described as 'pioneers' – again a familiar term in colonial language – the Europeans setting up communities in the newly discovered lands. However, the language also emphasizes the displacement of the 'native' locals. It is apparent that the owners of the new businesses have helped to remove the previous unemployed drunk residents in the choice of the verb phrase 'scrubbed their doorsteps'. This suggests a cleansing of an area; removing the dirt left by the predecessors (cf. the discussion above of the smell metaphor to describe the 'locals'). These businesses thus 'cleared the way for new inhabitants' further emphasizing the displacement of the locals. These are unfortunate metaphors as they appear to be unwitting intertextual references to ethnic cleansing and the Highland clearances.

Reactive discourses

As can be seen in Table 4.4, the internet and social media are key artefacts of the 'hipster' culture. In the article, the author stresses how she used social media to promote her restaurant while the actual article appeared in an online magazine. As already argued, the magazine and the article were aimed at a particular London-based reader. However, with the openness of the internet, the article was easily accessible to a far wider readership as can be seen in how quickly there was a reaction to it. In a very fast process, the article was accessed by a large audience it was not aimed at, that is, 'locals'.

Table 4.5 illustrates the timeline from Wednesday, 7 November to Saturday, 10 November 2012 of the article's publication and the various reactions to it on social and mass media. It should be noted that these dates are for the publication of the texts; the comments that followed the texts extended over a longer period. For the social media posts on 7 and 8 November, there are three examples: Margate & Local Family History (2012) and We Make

Table 4.5 Discourse timeline

Date	Discourse Event	Media	Reaction
7 Nov	Publication of 'Every Day Is Like Sunday' on *Civilian*	Mass (online magazine	
7–8 Nov	Posts on individual and group Facebook pages and Twitter conversation	Social media	Majority negative; some positive
8 Nov	Boycott GB Pizza Facebook page started (earliest reference 12.40)	Social media	Negative
8 Nov	Apology by the writer on the Facebook page of her restaurant (at 18.17)	Social media	Negative and positive
9 Nov	Item on BBC South East Today news at 6.30 pm and on BBC news website	Mass media (broadcast and internet)	Neutral reporting negative & positive
9–10 Nov	Item on local blogs concerning local politics and issues (Thanet Online; Thanet Life; Thanet Waves)	Social media	Positive

Margate (2012) both on Facebook; and a Twitter conversation with the author (Glimbrick 2012). From the references made in the subsequent social media posts and comments, it is evident there existed a far greater range of posts but they are difficult to access for the following reasons. First, many of the people whom I identified as the original instigators of the protest had private Facebook settings so their past posts were not accessible. Second, those with public settings such as Ian Driver (a local independent district councillor who was a main instigator of the boycott campaign) had deleted their posts from their Facebook accounts.

The discourse timeline shows the linear pattern of text production but also reveals the range of responses in what I call the 'reactive discourses'. Using Foucault's notion of discourse (McHoul & Grace 1993: 31; Foucault 1998: 100), I would argue that the article is an example of a dominant gentrification discourse. Dominant in the sense that gentrification is integral to capitalist societies and in the sense that the gentrifiers are perceived to have a greater financial and cultural capital than the indigenous residents. Yet, the indigenous peoples were capable of reacting to the discourse through social media. The complexity and range of the responses means there was not a singular resistant discourse in the Foucauldian sense (Foucault 1998: 100–101); rather, there was a complex range of reactions some of which formed a resistant discourse. This resistant discourse had its own power in that it led to an apology and mass media coverage, which itself led to further blog reactions.

The social media response on 7 and 8 November formed the resistant discourse being highly negative in response and linked to the instigation of the boycott campaign with a Facebook page which was subsequently deleted (Boycott the GB Pizza Company Margate 2012). There were, however, some positive comments posted. The apology on 8 November was followed by 230 comments that were both negative and positive, with the latter including comments from friends of the author and people not located in the Margate area. The mass media response on the BBC on 9 November examined both perspectives interviewing Ian Driver and the editor of *Civilian*. The Friday and Saturday blog responses took a more measured overview of what had happened from publication, boycott campaign to TV coverage. The blogs (and their comments) tended to be more sympathetic to the writer with a great deal of criticism towards Ian Driver for his role that drew on past criticisms of his behaviour as a councillor. Furthermore, the writers of the blogs took a wry, ironic stance rather reminiscent of *Private Eye* magazine which is reflected in some of their comments.

On analysing all the reaction texts, a clear division can be found between those positive towards the article and those who were negative. Emerging from this data was a consistent set of themes in the comments which are described in Table 4.6 above. It should be noted though that a few comments were more balanced, particularly following the apology seeking a compromise that recognized both perspectives. The following example from the apology illustrates this.

I don't think you deserve a total backlash, you are doing great things here, and it's true that a lot of people in Thanet are exactly as you describe. But by no means all – they are the minority, honest! The problem comes, sometimes, when people who have moved here from other areas (often but not always London) come across as if they have somehow come to save the day, and that without them, we would all be jumping around like monkeys, unable to articulate proper sentences. So you may have touched a few nerves is all, but not deliberately . . . I think maybe the article doesn't give enough credit to the fact that Thanet is also home to many, many intelligent people with no criminal records or dependency issues, some incredibly good schools and some amazing home grown businesses . . . and most have either stayed or returned because it's home, we love it and it's

Table 4.6 Reactions to the article

Negative	Positive
• Overall assessment of article ○ 'Nasty little review of Margate' (Margate Local & Family History)	• Overall assessment of article ○ thought provoking, well written, amazing, love it
• Construction of 'locals' and Margate ○ personal criticism (e.g. taxi driver) ○ insulting, rude and offensive to locals ○ stereotyping, negative, patronising ○ colonialist ○ don't insult the family metaphor	• Construction of 'locals' and Margate ○ balanced, accurate – shows negatives and positives of town ○ these people exist ○ honest, truthful
• Tone ○ snobbish, condescending	• About Margate and regeneration ○ optimistic, positivity ○ more positive than negative about the future of the town ○ DFLs/London improving town – needed
• Comparison ○ reaction if about Brixton or Newcastle?	
• Perceived attitudes and beliefs of writer and DFLs/Londoners ○ arrogant, smug ○ DFL/London snobbery ○ DFLs/writer 'saviours' of Margate and its peoples	• Writer's role in Margate and DFLs ○ supportive of local community ○ commitment to Margate ○ invested in Margate
	• Positive about the restaurant
• Imbalanced/factually incorrect ○ critical without dealing with issues ○ positives only about DFLs/hipsters ○ similar social problems in London/ UK	• Non-local comments ○ positive towards writer as friend ○ positive as fellow DFL
• Problem people came from London, UK, abroad	• Reaction to the negative reactions ○ in general 'you should be ashamed' addressing other locals; 'jealous of success' ○ Richards victim of cyber bullying ○ critiquing Ian Driver's behaviour (boycott, seeking publicity on TV etc.)
• Writer – naïve/error/backfire ○ alienate locals as customer base	
• Boycott restaurant • Personal criticisms of writer ○ don't like it here, leave ○ the restaurant ○ cashing in on the area	• Acceptance of apology ○ assumption that previously critical

ace! . . . Some would say it takes a while to qualify to slag off Thanet – my dad's been here since 1962 and still gets told he's not a proper local! My tip – never underestimate the pride of Thanet. The seafront may have a few drunks and crappy arcades, but they are OUR drunks and crappy arcades, and we'll defend them till we die. (Comment on Richards Facebook Apology 2012)

This comment recognizes why offence has been caused citing some of the aforementioned themes. In terms of the positives, the writer acknowledges the construction of 'locals' and Margate but notes that they are a 'minority'. What is particularly interesting, and something that comes up in many comments, is how the 'minority' forms part of the group identity of writers. Therefore denigrating them is a broader face-threatening act – they *don't insult the family metaphor*. This is then a strong sense of a Margate identity including its negative elements which locals will defend even if they do not recognize themselves to be part of the problematic group. In both negative and positives comments, the construction of the 'locals' was accepted but the majority of locals writing did not seem themselves as part of that grouping. The writer also picks out the negative perceived attitudes of 'DFLs' of a patronising snobbery and being 'saviours'.

There is then in the negative texts a concern with how Margate and 'locals' are constructed in terms of the stereotyping which does not pertain to them. Therefore, there was a clear anger that all locals were tarnished with the same brush. 'Whoever is behind writing this article is clearly well educated, and yes you have hit the nail on the head that with time, effort and regeneration projects Margate will flourish. However, the constant stereotyping and pompous belittling of us "Margate people" who live here is awful' (Comment on Margate Family & Local History 2012). The concerns with how the writer and 'DFLs' more generally stereotype locals was linked in the negative comments with the attitude towards the area and its peoples in terms of how 'DFL' actions (e.g. setting up businesses) are the engine of regeneration helping to improve the lives of the 'locals', that is, being 'saviours'. One commentator made the link, as I have, with colonialism.

> When I read the article my gut reaction was 'Shit! this sounds like the justification of Colonialists'. 'Colonialism is a relationship between an indigenous (or forcibly imported) majority and a minority of foreign invaders. The fundamental decisions affecting the lives of the colonized people are made and implemented by the colonial rulers in pursuit of interests that are often defined in a distant metropolis. Rejecting cultural compromises with the colonized population, the colonizers are convinced of their own superiority and their ordained mandate to rule'. Jürgen Osterhammel's book; Colonialism: A Theoretical Overview. (Comment on Richards Facebook Apology 2012)

It is interesting here that the writer used her cultural capital with an academic quotation to rebuke the article. In essence, the negative commentators often recognized the negative elements pointed out in the article but it was the tone of the article, the stereotyping and the perceived attitude of the writer that caused the negative response. Like the positive commentators, many of the negative commentators recognized the improvements to the town brought about by 'DFLs' (if not exclusively by them).

Another very important element was the use of humour by both groups. This was often ironic and sarcastic referencing elements of the article, or critics of the article particularly Ian Driver who was at the centre of much criticism. The humour used the themes noted in Table 4.6 but it was not always clear whether the authors were being positive or negative. 'Taxi for pizza Gb. . . oh hang on . . . taxi! Taxi!' (Comment on Margate Family & Local History 2012). The following clearly negative comment particularly plays on the fact that a key part of the restaurant's online publicity was photographs of the owner's dog in situ. 'This woman must be out of her mind writing this. Rule number 1. Don't insult the locals. Rule number 2. Don't insult the Taxi Drivers. Rule number 3. The environmental health officer doesn't like large slobbering dogs in catering establishments no matter how POSH your pizza's are' (Comment on Margate Family & Local History 2012). The 'Don't insult the locals' element was a very common among the negative comments as a whole, that is, the author has made a naïve error in insulting locals, her key customer base, particularly during the off season. The following positive comment on one of the blogs plays on the local perception of local government (n.b. TDC = Thanet District Council). 'I can certainly agree with the comment regarding bigoted cab drivers! Why don't they become TDC Tory councillors instead?;)' (Comment on Thanet Waves 2012).

Of all the posts and comments, I found only one where the writer recognized themselves as part of the people being represented and, in the case, vehemently disapproved of the perceived stereotype.

> I have been driving a Cab in Margate for 22 yrs . . . And didn't just live in Hackney. For your yuppie NAZI effect I was born there . . . How dare you insult my children by suggesting they drink Stella Artois . . . And play on games consoles that are on HP . . . Damage Done. And I will refuse to take anyone or pick up anyone from your establishment!!!! And I will spread the word believe me You are a NAZI.(Comment on Richards Facebook Apology 2012)

This comment emphases a personal hurt that the article caused. In the actual apology, there is no recognition of why she caused offence beyond being arrogant. She claims that her article was an expression of her experiences which were positive and negative; she was not aware that how she framed and described these experiences could be offensive. There is a focus on how the town is improving which was emphasized in the article and was for her the focus of article – she is surprised that readers did not get this element. Much of the apology is concerned with the business and how it supports Margate and then how the business communicates to customers outside of Margate the positives of Margate. What is interesting here and perhaps unsurprising is that she is doing this from the perspective of the business rather than as individual writer – it therefore reads as a public relations exercise in protecting her business.

A final consideration is that the writer in both her portrayal of the 'locals' and 'DFLs' may have been using stereotypes for humorous purposes. This could well have been the case and indeed this would fit into the irreverent identity of Civilian. The author may have intended to give an irreverent and arch tone using stereotypes that the reader recognizes and finds funny. Indeed some of the humorous comments also played with these stereotypes. Furthermore, it could be assumed that she had met 'locals' who did not fit that stereotype. Whether she was being humorous or serious, the article offended many 'locals' through their representation. Furthermore, whether humorous or serious, this is still an example of gentrification discourse.

These clashing discourses can be understood in terms of intercultural communication conflict (Ting-Toomey and Oetzel 2001: 17). While in more traditional understandings of communication, this would be classified more in terms of interpersonal and (social) media communication conflict as all the participants theoretically share national culture and identity, taking the more recent critical paradigm of intercultural communication (Humphrey 2007: 5), one can see that this is an intercultural conflict based around culture and cultural identity in terms of region and class (cf. Collier 2003). The article contains within it a set of face-threatening acts threatening the positive face of the 'locals' (Brown & Levinson 1987). In other words, it threatens their own self-identity in the way that she denigrates the 'locals' and their regional identity in the way she denigrates the old Margate. Finally, I would argue that her position of her culture and cultural identity being superior to the indigenous one is also face threatening. The resistant texts are evidence of this. This cultural superiority with a presumed cultural and financial capital was particularly irritating to those residents who felt they were being patronised and felt that they indeed had cultural capital and possibly financial capital. I would include myself in this category.

Conclusion

This chapter has considered a social and mass media discourse event consisting of the publication of an article and the reaction to it including the writer's own apology. This event is an example of how computer-mediated communication allows for a far quicker response time to a publication when compared to traditional print media in the pre-internet age. It would have been inconceivable then for an magazine article to be published one day followed by an apology the day after, and mass media coverage the day after that. For discourse researchers, this new online operation of social and mass media is a rich vein of textual data not only in illuminating on how readers respond to texts but examining the complex patterns of discourse production and reproduction.

This particular example of discourse production and reproduction provides textual evidence of a new type of gentrification where movement is to beyond the city rather than within it. Necessitated here by London accommodation prices but also made easier through new remote working patterns enabled by new media technologies and high-speed public transport, whereby the provincial gentrified town is conceptualized as a satellite of London rather than geographically remote from the metropolis. As evidence of this, Margate has gained in the media the new nomenclatures of 'Shoreditch-on-Sea' and 'Dalston-sur-Mer' (Smith 2015; *Inside Out: London* 2016). What is interesting about looking at gentrification from a discourse perspective is that it gives an insight into how gentrifiers construct themselves and their actions, and how preexisting residents construct the gentrification in terms of themselves and the gentrifiers.

The examination of discourse in providing evidence of intercultural relations (in this case intercultural conflict) is what I call an ethnographic approach to discourse analysis where language is examined as a rhetorical device for constructing self and other as well as cultural behaviour, identities and norms. As with much recent qualitative work (Merrill & West 2009), this is partly a research of the self in that I am a native of Margate and I was offended like many other 'locals' by the article. Beyond using reflexivity to monitor how I dealt with these texts, an examination of my own reaction provided another complex example of seeing this as a face-threatening act to my own cultural identity by an *outsider* but at the same recognizing that the people described in the article existed.

References

BBC News (2012). *Margate Article by Restaurateur Lisa Richards Leads to Row*
    Available at: http://www.bbc.co.uk/news/uk-england-kent-20276948 (accessed 11
    November 2012).
Bourdieu, P. (1992). *Language and Symbolic Power*. Polity Press: Cambridge.
Brown, N. (2006). *Tracey Emin (Modern Artists Series)*. London: Tate Publishing.

Brown, P., & Levinson, S. (1987). *Politeness: Some Universals in Language Usage.* 2nd ed. Cambridge: Cambridge University Press.

Brown-Saracino, J. (ed.) (2010). *The Gentrification Debates* (The Metropolis and Modern Life). Abingdon: Routledge.

Butler, T., & Robson, G. (2003). *London Calling: The Middle Classes and the Remaking of Inner London.* Oxford: Berg.

Civilian (2017a). Available at: http://civilianglobal.com/ (accessed 20 July 2017).

Civilian (2017b). 'About'. Available at: http://civilianglobal.com/about/ (accessed 20 July 2017).

Classen, C., Howes, D., & Synnott, A. (1994). *The Cultural History of Smell.* London: Routledge.

Collier, M. (2003). 'Understanding Cultural Identities in Intercultural communication: A Ten-Step Inventory'. In L. Samovar & R. Porter (eds), *Intercultural Communication: A Reader.* London: Thomson Wadsworth. 412–30.

Edgar, A., & Sedgwick, P. (1999). *Key Concepts in Cultural Theory.* London: Routledge.

Foucault, M. (1991). *Discipline and Punish: The Birth of the Prison*, trans. A. Sheridan. London: Penguin.

Foucault, M. (1998). *The Will to Knowledge: The History of Sexuality: 1*, trans. Robert Hurley. London: Penguin.

Genette, G., & Maclean, M. (1991). 'Introduction to the Paratext'. *New Literary History* 22.2: 261–72.

Glass, R. (1964). *London: Aspects of Change.* London: MacGibbon & Klee.

Glimbrick (2012). An Argument: After a Pretty Offensive Article Was Written I Confronted the Author on Twitter. Available at 'Storify' (accessed 23 November 2017).

Hammersley, M., & Atkinson, P. (1995). *Ethnography: Principles in Practice.* London: Tavistock.

Hodder, I. (1994). 'The Interpretation of Documents and Material Culture'. In N. K. Denzin & Y. S. Lincoln (eds), *Handbook of Qualitative Research.* Thousand Oaks: California. 393–402.

Holliday, A. (1999). 'Small Cultures'. *Applied Linguistics* 20.2: 237–64.

Humphrey, D. (2007). *Intercultural Communication Competence: The State of Knowledge.* Report prepared for CILT The National Centre for Languages. 3–17.

Inside Out: London (2016). BBC 1 Television. 31 October.

Jackson, A., Nettley, A., Muzyka, J., & Dee, T. (2016). *Turner Contemporary: Art Inspiring Change Social Value Report (15/16).* Canterbury: Canterbury Christ Church University.

Jefferies, S. (2014). 'Patriot Games: How Toxic Is the England Flag Today?' *The Guardian.* 26 November. Available at: https://www.theguardian.com/uk-news/2014/nov/26/patriot-games-battle-for-flag-of-st-george-english-identity (accessed 20 July 2017).

Lees, L. (ed.) (2010). *The Gentrification Reader.* Abingdon: Routledge.

Lees, L., Slater, T., & Wyly, E. (2007). *Gentrification.* Abingdon: Routledge.

Lewisohn, C., & Chalfant, H. (2009). *Street Art: The Graffiti Revolution.* London: Tate Publishing.

Maly, I., & Varis, P. (2016). 'The 21st-Century Hipster: On Micro-populations in Times of Superdiversity'. *European Journal of Cultural Studies* 19.6: 637–53.

Margate Coastal Community Team (2016). *Economic Plan 2016 and Beyond; A Living Document*. Available at: http://www.coastalcommunities.co.uk/wp-content/uploads/2016/05/Margate-CCT-Economic-plan-2016.pdf (accessed 20 July 2017).

McHoul A., & Grace, W. (1993). *A Foucault Primer: Discourse, Power and the Subject*. London: Routledge.

McQuillan, M. (2000). 'Introduction: Five Strategies for Deconstruction'. In M. McQuillan (ed.), *Deconstruction: A Reader*. Edinburgh: Edinburgh University Press. 1–43.

Merrill, B., & West, L. (2009). *Using Biographical Methods in Social Research*. London: Sage.

Michael, J. (2015). 'It's Really Not Hip to Be a Hipster: Negotiating Trends and Authenticity in the Cultural Field'. *Journal of Consumer Culture* 15.2: 163–82.

Morrissey (1988). *Viva Hate* [vinyl]. London: His Master's Voice.

Pennycook, A. (1998). *English and the Discourses of Colonialism*. London: Routledge.

Richards, L. (2012a). 'Every Day Is Like Sunday: The Art and Pizza-Based Regeneration of a Forgotten Seaside Town'. *Civilian* (7 November 2012). Available at: http://civilianglobal.com/ (accessed 9 November 2012).

Richards, L. (2012b). [Facebook] 8 November. Available at: http://www.facebook.com/GreatBritishPizza/posts/277343362386885?comment_id=1173500&notif_t=like (accessed 12 November 2012).

Robbins, D. (2000). *Bourdieu and Culture*. London: Sage.

Said, E. (1978). *Orientalism*. New York: Pantheon.

Saul, J. (1994). *The Doubter's Companion: A Dictionary of Aggressive Common Sense*. New York: The Free Press.

Schiermer, B. (2014). 'Late-Modern Hipsters: New Tendencies in Popular Culture'. *Acta Sociologica* 57.2: 187–1.

Scott, M. (2017). ''Hipster Capitalism' in the Age of Austerity? Polanyi Meets Bourdieu's New Petite Bourgeoisie'. *Cultural Sociology* 11.1: 60–76.

Slater, T. (2006). 'The Eviction of Critical Perspectives from Gentrification Research'. *International Journal of Urban and Regional Research* 30.4: 737–57.

Smith, M. (2015). 'How Margate Became the New Hipster's Paradise'. *Esquire* (4 April). Available at: http://www.esquire.co.uk/food-drink/travel/8101/how-margate-became-the-new-hipsters-paradise/ (accessed 8 April 2015).

Smith, N. (ed.) (2010). *Gentrification of the City (Routledge Library Editions: the City)*. Abingdon: Routledge.

Thanet District Council (2010). *Cliftonville Development Plan*. Margate: Thanet District Council. Available at: https://www.thanet.gov.uk/media/437121/Cliftonville_Development_Plan_Document.pdf (accessed 19 July 2017).

Thanet Life (2012). 'BBC – A Great British Pizza Crisis'. *Thanet Life* (12 November). Available at: http://www.thanetlife.co.uk/2012/11/bbc-great-british-pizza-crisis.html (accessed 21 November 2014).

Ting-Toomey, S., & Oetzel, J. (2001). *Managing Intercultural Conflict Effectively*. Thousand Oaks: Sage.

Turner, S. (2011). 'Top 10 Art Attractions in Margate'. *The Guardian* (14 April). Available at: https://www.theguardian.com/travel/2011/apr/14/margate-art-kent-turner-contemporary (accessed 20 July 2017).

Usher, R., & Edwards, R. (1994). *Postmodernism and Education*. London: Routledge.

Wacquant, L., Slater, T., & Pereira, V. (2014). 'Territorial Stigmatization in Action'. *Environment and Planning* 46: 1270–80.

Ward, J. (2016). 'Down by the Sea: Visual Arts, artists and Coastal Regeneration'. *International Journal of Cultural Policy*. doi: 10.1080/10286632.2016.1153080.

Wiktionary (2017). 'DFL'. Available at: https://en.wiktionary.org/wiki/DFL (accessed 20 July 2017).

Youth Identities: Media Discourse in the Formation of Youth Identity

Patricia Giardiello

Introduction

In today's postmodern society the media has become as important as food and clothing. It plays a significant role in 'informing' a society and notably our current generation of children and young people spend more time with media than engaged in any other activity (Zemmels 2012).

Using data from a recent qualitative study of teenagers attending Millgate Community School's Extended Day and Residential facility this chapter seeks to uncover some of the ways in which the media, in its multimodality, shapes youth's personal and social identity and sense of belonging. In carrying out the research I was particularly concerned with how the media influences the identities and aspirations of youth and also how youth use the media to define self. Individual decisions about *who they are* and their lifestyle choices, while often appearing to be unbounded and, therefore, solely a consequence of agency, are, in reality, made within cultural and social constraints, what Bourdieu (1977) terms 'habitus'. In my small-scale study of youth's everyday encounters with the media, Bourdieu's theory of habitus provides the theoretical framework from which to examine how the media impacts on youth perspectives within the cultural and social contexts of their community.

This chapter begins with unravelling what is meant by identity and how the sense of self emerges from our earliest experiences and what others do to us and for us. It then moves on to explore the way in which media has potentially profound effects on the social identity formation of young people. The chapter will present ideas concerning new technologies such as digital media, internet and social networking sites and the way they have transformed youth culture in the home, school and community. Discussion will include the way in which youth culture draws from the media to collectively construct what is valuable and worthwhile including how adolescents develop identities by adapting to these peer cultures through social processes (Manago et al. 2012; Larson 1995). Finally, by allowing a more nuanced understanding of the relationship between youth identity and the media I intend to reverse the traditional research stance which focuses on what the media does to children and youth (Heim et al. 2007) by discussing instead what children and youth do with the media in developing their own intersectional identities within a postmodern society.

Unravelling what is meant by identity

> I wonder if I've been changed in the night? let me think, was I the
> same when I got up in the morning? I almost think I can remember
> feeling different. But if I am not the same, the next question is
> 'who in the world I am? As that's the great puzzle.
>
> – *Alice in Wonderland* by Lewis Carroll

Alice's words are both nonsensical and comprehensible yet serve to illustrate the struggle many young people experience in developing a clear sense of self or identity. As Buckingham (2008: 1) points outs, '[I]dentity is an ambiguous and slippery term.'

In unravelling what is meant by 'identity' it can be useful to distinguish between two main types. There is the personal identity, which Alice is grappling with, and there is something often referred to as the 'social identity'. Social identity theory posits that a portion of one's self-concept is dependent on the importance and relevance placed on the group membership(s) to which an individual belongs (Turner & Oakes 1986).

By contrast dictionary definitions of 'identity' tend to reflect a more simplistic notion of 'identity' made popular during the 1950s by the developmental psychologist Erik Erikson (1959; 1968) through his work on psychosocial stages of development and his coining of the term 'identity crisis'. For example: 'The characteristics determining who or what a person or thing is' (OED, Online).

Erikson's concept of 'ego identity', a term extending from Freud's (1938) psychoanalytic personality theory, suggested that identity is shaped by the interaction of three elements: a person's biological characteristics, their psychology and the cultural context. Erikson focused on the concept of identity as it emerged and changed in developmental stages across the life course but that in childhood it was only a provisional type of identity, for example, in role playing or when girls want to be princesses and boys want to be superheroes. In Erikson's view such identifications do not have the same depth and directing functions as those of adult identity, believing that the essential development of proper identity takes place during the period of youth. According to him the development of a coherent and organized sense of identity is a key task in adolescence (Erikson 1950; 1968; Illeris 2014). Erikson proposes that, in order to move on, adolescents must undergo a 'crisis' in which they address key questions about their values and ideals, their future occupation or career and their sexual identity. Through this process of self-reflection and self-definition, adolescents arrive at an integrated, coherent sense of their identity as something that persists over time (Buckingham 2008). Erikson's use of the term 'crisis' reflects the tradition of treating adolescence as a period of *Sturm und Drang* (storm and stress) imported into psychology from German literature in the late 1880s by the American psychologist Granville Stanley Hall who is usually accredited with the 'discovery' of adolescence (Rattansi and Phoenix 1997). Ching and Foley (2012) point out that Erikson's description of what he believed to be a universal picture of human development based on the experiences of Western middle-class individuals has come under criticism. Erikson, like many of his contemporaries in early developmental psychology such as Piaget (1969), sought to articulate a universal hierarchical framework of development that could account for human change over time. It is particularly the aspiration for a universal, stage based model of development that lacks resonance in the context of a new discourse on human development that privileges the long-neglected role of culture (Hammock 2008). Rogoff (2003) reinforces the view that human development must be understood as a cultural process, not simply a biological or psychological one.

A number of individuals have attempted to extract operational definitions and to derive testable models and hypotheses from Erikson's writings. The most commonly used conceptualization of Erikson's identity theory is Marcia's (1966) identity status paradigm. Building on Erikson's account, Marcia focused on the notion of adolescence as a period of 'identity crisis'. Through this period, the young person has to consider potential life choices and eventually make a commitment or psychological investment in particular decisions. Marcia suggested, based on the amount of exploration and commitment,[1] that an adolescent's identity can be classified into either one of four distinguishable identity statuses: *diffusion*, which is low in exploration and low on commitment; *foreclosure*, which is little exploration but strong commitments; *moratorium*, which is high on exploration but no stable commitments as yet; and *achievement*, which is high on commitment after a period of extensive exploration (cited in Klimstra et al. 2010). Much of the research in identity formation has traditionally used Marcia's identity status paradigm to examine the ways in which adolescents move through a period of identity exploration to a state of commitment, that is, dedication to an autonomously negotiated set of stable self-structures that is adaptive to one's social world (Manago 2015). From this perspective, adolescence is seen primarily as a state of transition, a matter of 'becoming' rather than 'being'. A further perspective is that adolescents' key dilemmas are to do with what they will become, particularly in terms of their future occupation and their relationships; their current experiences are only significant insofar as they help them resolve their crisis and hence move on (Buckingham 2008). However, Marcia's identity status paradigm is criticized for its narrow focus and its failure to take into account the sociocultural aspects of identity formation (Bennett and Robards 2014). For example, Adam and Marshall's (1996) developmental contextual approach to identity formation draws on Bronfenbrenner's (1977) ecological model of development which takes the view that development is influenced by embedded and connected environmental systems.

During adolescence youth are increasingly identifying themselves within social peer groups as they distinguish themselves from their parents or primary carers (Erikson 1959; 1968; Harter 1999). This involvement in the task of identity building leads to concern with marking one's identity for others. According to Deutsch and Theodorou (2010: 231), '[T]his dual exercise, of individuation of self and connection to a social group, results in a relationship with material culture wherein consumption is used to both mark and mask difference.' The omnipresent physical displays of identity through clothing, hairstyles and accessories not only reinforce individual identity but also establishes one's place in the larger peer group (ibid.). Here, identity is about identification with others, presumed as being similar, if not exactly the same, in some significant ways, which brings us back to social identity as mentioned earlier. According to Hammock (2008: 227): '[T]o understand the full embellishment of an identity, beyond what Erikson would term its "ego" functions but what we might prefer to dub its purely "cognitive" features, we must theorize the formation of social identity – that part of identity that, as Erikson argued, contains an awareness of an individual's location within the solidarity of a particular group.' Using data from my recent small-scale qualitative study of teenagers attending Millgate City School, the chapter moves on to report on some of the ways in which the media, in its multimodality, shapes youth's identity both personal and social.

In order to place the teenagers' narratives into context the next section of the chapter discusses the influence of media in youth identity formation.

Media and the construction of identity

The sociocultural context in which young people live is characterized by competing, complementary and divergent values and beliefs provided by parents, school, the consumer society, peer relations and of course the media. However it is this last element that has gained significant importance as it has come to play a more central role in the way children and young people interpret the world, particularly since the inception of the internet (Marôpo 2014). Part of young people's lived experiences growing up in the United Kingdom and other industrialized countries around the world is the frequent exposure and often daily use of a variety of media. Media has potentially profound effects on the social identity formation of young people. The various media including local radio, film, television, music and print media such a magazines, newspapers and comic books privilege either sight or sound, or both as well as playing on a broad range of emotions influencing how young people think and behave and how they construct their identities. According to Kellner (2003: 1): 'Media culture provides the material to create identities whereby individuals insert themselves into contemporary techno-capital societies and which is producing a new form of global culture.' Emerging from his concerns about the dominance of television Gerbner et al. (1994) pointed out as far back as 1994 that children heard more stories and facts through different media than through parents, schools or community. Livingstone (2002) identified this phenomenon as a mediated childhood which emphasizes the role of media and its importance for children and young people in everyday life. In contrast to over twenty years ago television is viewed in different ways depending on the audience. Many young people in current times use devices to 'zap' from one programme to another, channel 'hopping' or 'grazing' to merely see what is happening and to go with the disconnected flow of images (Kellner 2003). A more recent notable development in the tie between television and youth media culture is the shift to video sharing internet websites such as YouTube, together with the advanced capabilities of video recording and educating equipment, that has fostered the creation of content for and by youth (Bronner and Clark 2016). Hamley (2001) adds that as we live in a media-saturated environment it is an inevitable consequence that young people make use of imagery derived from the use of popular media to construct their identity. Similarly Coiro et al. (2008: 526) argue that today's youth experiment with different identities in 'dynamic and shifting constructions and presentations of self'. Furthermore in an era that is often referred to as the 'digital age' children and young people do their learning and entertain themselves through technologies that were unimagined just twenty years ago. Hague and Williamson (2009) concur that many young people are now spending significant amounts of their own social and leisure time using digital media such as video games, social networking sites, video sharing, music editing, animation and different forms of online communication, as well as carrying out a host of more prosaic activities. Media and the tools of modern technology play an important role in the developmental processes of childhood, including adolescence, as they learn 'to find their [*sic*] way around in the world' to discover who they are in relation to the wider human family and their social and physical environment (Edgar and Edgar 2008). For many young people, especially in the industrialized parts of the world, digital media are significant modalities through which they are seeking, consciously or unconsciously, the answers to identity questions, looking for what Buckingham (2008: 28) describes as 'the me that is me'. This also has implications for schools; Buckingham points out that young people need to be equipped with a new form of digital literacy that is both critical and creative. In today's society new technologies and new social practices rapidly and repeatedly redefine what it once meant, in traditional literacy terms, to be able to read, write and communicate effectively in the shared language of a culture. Just as school subjects provide young people with the knowledge and skills to make sense of their world, including its history, geography, religions, arts, languages and sciences, education should also supply the skills and knowledge to make sense of this digital media world. It is worth noting however that the success or otherwise of school-based innovation is often related to local circumstances and to the characteristics of particular schools, teachers and children.

Stemming from Bloom's (1956) original taxonomy of learning domains in 2008 a digital taxonomy was produced which supplied a number of verbs related to technology and media under each of Bloom's headings. This taxonomy suggested that 'creating' in a digital context might involve 'designing, constructing, planning, producing, inventing, devising, making, programming, filming, animating, blogging, video blogging, mixing, re-mixing, wiki-ing, publishing, videocasting, podcasting, directing or broadcasting' (Hague and Williamson 2009: 18). The children and young people who attend the school used in my small-scale study are fortunate as they are given the opportunity to develop these skills as a direct result of attending the extended day and residential facility. For example, some young people have been involved in film-making. To showcase their work, recent films made by these young people are shown annually at 'The Millgate Oscars' ceremony (Ofsted report, 2016). Research has shown that what young people learn from their participation in film-making indicates that these are learning environments for multimodal production that involve identity construction. Willett et al. (2005:2), for example, argue that 'identity' features prominently in multimodal composition: 'New media production is as much about producing identities and social spaces as it is about creating media . . . Through different media forms young people are described as performing, defining, and exploring their identities.' This can be seen in the productions available on the school's YouTube website,[2] most notably 'Mighty Mighty Millgate' which was part of a whole school project nurturing the pupils' clear sense of self and identity.

The small-scale study

Identities are more like spots of crust hardening time and again on the top of volcano lava which melt and dissolve again before they have time to cool down and set.

– Bauman (2000: 71)

The study set out to explore a group of young people's quest for identity and the influence the media has on the formation of both their personal and social identity. The influences that shape teenager's choices and the wider challenge that they face to conform to the notion of being media 'savvy' were also explored. I chose to carry out my study in a community school's residential facility, currently operating for five nights a week, term time only, and accommodating up to ten students, as it gave me an opportunity to chat with the young people in a relaxed homely atmosphere. These are young people with emotional, behavioural and social challenges who benefit from the school's ethos and values of 'respect', which is also used as an acronym for responsibility, education, safety, perseverance, excellence, caring and tolerance. This positive approach within the school emphasizes the manifest potentialities rather than the incapacities of these young people, often from the most disadvantaged backgrounds and those with the most troubled histories. Furthermore, experiences that promote a sense of personal identification with one's school and local community provide a young person with a positive set of aspirations that point the way to a socially and personally productive future (Damon 2004).

Who I Am –	Name	Age

Thanks for taking part in this study about your use of media. There are not many questions to answer

1. What type of music do you like best?
   Please circle one: Indie / Guitar – Rock / Heavy Metal – Emo – Soul – Hip / Hop / Rap -
   R&B -   Dance / House -   Pop -   Drum & Bass -   Garage -   Other (please state)

2. What group do you think your friends and classmates would describe you as being part of? Please circle one
   Trendy - Goth - Emo - Chav - Skater - Greb - Punk – Other

3. Why do you think this is? Please circle if it is your . . .
   Personality - Clothes - Music preference - All three – Other

4. Please circle the different kinds of electronic devices you use
   PC/Laptop, Radio - mobile /smartphone - tablet pc / I pad - TV - music player Xbox/Nintendo - other (if other please state)

5. Please state how strongly you agree/disagree with the following three statements.
   - My friends are really important to me; they understand me more than my family
   1 = Strongly Agree   2 = Agree   3 = Disagree,   4 = Strongly Disagree
   - I feel very much a part of my city, local town/community
   1 = Strongly Agree   2 = Agree   3 = Disagree   4 = Strongly Disagree
   - I feel very much a part of my school community
   1= Strongly Agree   2 = Agree   3 = Disagree   4 = Strongly Disagree

6. How do you talk or meet with friends outside school? – circle the two most important ways:
   in person / Face to face - text message - email - facetime/ skype - social media (e.g. facebook, Instagram, Snapchat, twitter)

7 I feel very much a part of web community such as Facebook, Instagram and Snapchat
   1 = Strongly Agree   2 = Agree   3 = Disagree   4 = Strongly Disagree

8. Social network is an important part of my life
   1 = Strongly Agree   2 = Agree   3 = Disagree   4 = Strongly Disagree

9. Why do you use an online social network? (you can circle more than one choice)
   To find information - To play games - To keep in touch with friends - To get opinions - To share videos, pictures, music - To share experiences

10. The use of social networks helps me to find out who I am (my identity)
    1 = Strongly Agree   2 = Agree   3 = Disagree   4 = Strongly Disagree

Many thanks for answering these questions

Figure 5.1 The questionnaire (adapted from Cassidy and Van Schijndel 2011)

Bourdieu's (1990) concept of habitus is used to discuss how the social context in the varying 'fields' shapes young people as they are in the process of shaping themselves. Young people internalize 'rules of the game' and 'ways of being' from the institutional rules and interactions in their social context (68). Hence, the social discourse and values of the school are integrated into the students' attitudes and identity formation, as can be seen in the research findings discussed below. Marcia's (1966) identity status paradigm will also be used in the discussion of the young people's identity formation.

With the ethical considerations and logistics completed I chose as my methodology a focus group approach. This approach provided the ability to capture deeper information more economically than individual interviews. The focus group also provided authentic insights into how the young people thought about identity and their use of media. In order to set the tone and for the participants to not feel too intimidated they were given beforehand a short questionnaire (see Figure 5.1) using a Likert scale and funnelling technique, with the first question being very general enquiring into the young person's musical taste and thereafter probing further and deeper. The length of the questionnaire was deliberately short using appropriate adolescent language and terminology. The results of the questionnaire were used to facilitate the later focus group discussion and were effective in keeping the young people focused on the topic area.

A discussion of the findings

Popular media was represented through the music preference of the participants. The majority of the group preferred rock/heavy metal but rap and hip hop also proved to be popular among the group. However heavy metal and rap/hip-hop, have a particularly negative image, especially in the media. Media reports often invoke moral panics surrounding the negative effects on 'vulnerable minds' of the aggressive composition and dark lyrical content of heavy metal. Dan Silver, assistant editor of the music magazine *New Musical Express* (NME), in defence of heavy metal is reported as saying that 'many themes of heavy metal are about alienation. If you have these kinds of feelings there is a lot you can get out of the music and the community of fans who are into it' (cited in Fleming 2007). This is supported by research carried out by Miranda and Claes (2004) who found that music taste plays a unique role in explaining adolescent transgressive behaviours. Their research suggests that the unique explanatory value of music taste lies in the strength of the sociocultural identity some types of music can offer. For example, in response to question 2 on the questionnaire Xander, aged 15, indicated that his group identity is dependent on his music preferences. He enjoys listening to rock music through his headphones and expressed an interest in becoming a Radio DJ although conversely he does not listen to the radio which would place him in Marcia's (1966) category *identity foreclosure* which in this case is little exploration of radio but a strong commitment to listening to rock music. On average, adolescents listen to music for up to three hours daily and accumulate more than ten thousand hours of active music listening throughout adolescence (Roberts et al. 2009). Moreover, time spent listening to music keeps increasing due to ever more media-socializing and multitasking smartphones and tablets. Xander's knowledge of music has resulted in numerous school prizes for the category of *Best Sound and Visual Effects* in film production as part of performing arts.

Other participants used question 2 to reflect on how others saw them. Brendon, aged 13, and Syrus, aged 11, who are both heavy metal fans have a developing sense of self with Brendon using a self-abusing language term 'dick head' to describe how others in the community regard him. When asked why he thinks this he replied because of the way other young people talk to him. During adolescence, when belonging to a peer group can become vital, language and naming is a primary resource to establish the self, social categories and social relations. It is the continual vocal branding of 'other' in order to identify 'self' and the combination of exclusion and bonding which make slang and swearwords especially attractive to teenagers (de Klerk 2005).

Syrus revealed that his peers often find him annoying and a 'funny little monster'; however he does not set out to be annoying but he does like to make people giggle. Although Syrus falls into the category of *identity foreclosure* he is also closely aligned to Marcia's category of *Identity Moratorium* as he is lively, engaging but conflicted, and sometimes tiring to be around as can be seen from the comment about being annoying. With adolescence come heightened interest, concern, commitment and conflict associated with interpersonal relationships, especially with peers. As yet these two young people are finding it hard to connect to a specific group identity but both felt a sense of belonging to the school community.

As discussed in the first part of this chapter, adolescence is known to be a period of exploratory self-analysis and self-evaluation ideally culminating in the establishment of a cohesive and integrative sense of self or identity (Erikson 1968). Based on Marcia's (1966) categories, Brendon and Syrus display *identity foreclosure* as they tend to correspond to the expectations of others. In contrast

Pratham, aged 15, sees his identity as being strongly tied to the words or label used to describe him in his Education and Health Care Plan (ECHP). When challenged by others in the focus group that this label, a standard social and emotional problem child (Pratham's interpretation), is not his real identity he argued that without this label he 'wouldn't be me'. This suggests something about how strong and influential labels can be. Certainly labels are harmful when, as a result of that label individuals are degraded, discriminated against, excluded from society or placed in classrooms without regard for their individuality but this is clearly not the case with regards to Pratham. Describing his identity as someone who is a sensible, trusted young man and, good looking, Patham clearly displays Marcia's category of *identity achievement* as using (Kroger and Marcia 2011) the description he impresses one as being solid with an important focus in his life and while retaining some flexibility he is not easily swayed by external influences in his chosen life direction.

In response to question 4, all research participants indicated that they use electronic devices such as Xbox and PlayStation on a daily basis. These are known as Massively Multiplayer Online Role-Playing Games (MMORPGs) which are fully developed multiplayer universes with an advanced and detailed visual and auditory world wherein players create an individualistic character (Griffiths et al. 2004). Brendon and Xander play online with each other, in their own room at home, thus maintaining their media related identity while away from school. They told me they also play with other friends online. Yee (2001, 2006, 2007) has carried out research into MMORPGs and notes that they allow new forms of social identity and social interaction. Yee's research has shown that MMORPGs appeal to adults and teenagers from a wide range of backgrounds, and they spend on average more than half a working week in these environments. Gaming devices such as Xbox and PlayStation encourage users to join an online global community of online players; in these virtual realms new social relationships are developed within youth culture when playing role- games. Forms of successful play and being able to cope with the technical challenges often lead young people to a feeling of success and personal self-stabilization. Furthermore in a virtual realm 'adolescents are able to express themselves as competent and powerful . . . and [*sic*] as a coping strategy . . . transfer forms of rationality recognised within the virtual realms to their real lives' (Dinter 2006: 239). Internet based role play was featured in a short film that Xander made as part of his performing arts coursework where he acted out different roles and characters from an online 'shooter' game which opened up powerful new perspectives around the difference between fantasy and reality.

Pratham identified using just three electronic devices: laptop, smartphone and TV. He told the focus group that he hasn't got time for playing games on the internet, or PlayStation saying that he is a busy person preferring to do more constructive activities such as baking. A recent media phenomenon that has had an impact on Pratham's identity as a baker is the television show *The Great British Bake Off* (GBBO, BBC). Joining Millgate's vocational catering course, Pratham learnt the skills and techniques of baking so proficiently that his teacher entered him into a local GBBO competition which he won much to his obvious satisfaction. Credit must also be given to the teacher whose understanding of how to blend the teaching and learning of baking skills with the ideas from the show enabled Pratham to discover both his talent and identity as a baker. With regards to GBBO, here is a perfect example of a factual entertainment mix that appeals across a double demographic; the traditional older audience and also the younger audiences such as Pratham with an interest in how to get on in the world of employment and/or business (Hill 2015). Here we see how secondary involvement of the media has impacted on Pratham's transformative learning and identity formation. According to Illeris (2014) when reasonable stable structures are gradually developed in more and more areas the young person has reached a situation or habitus in which identifiable patterns take form and a fairly comprehensive identity has been reached. However this does not always happen so easily as for many young people in today's neoliberal and globalized society identity development is considerably more uneven and problematic. This is because on the one hand there is an enormous variety of what could be seen as identity offers or suggestions, for example, in the form of celebrities as role models appearing in commercial adverts and mass media. There are also a range of activities, forms of behaviour and language use as differing form of expression that can contribute to identity formation. One example is the use of street slang and ungrammatical codes mainly made up from exotic terms. On the other hand there are more normative or conventional identity offers from society, policymakers, parents, teachers and the many categories of supporters who give advice, guidance and supervision, when at the same time they are trying to assist, to help, to push and to press young people through to a result that is acceptable and desirable to both the young people themselves and to society (ibid.). This serves to illustrate the long and often complex processes that young people today must cope with and overcome to fulfil the development of their identities.

The role of friends was evaluated through the findings of question 5 which showed that all the participants either strongly agree or agree that friends understood them more than family. This is an expected result as in the course of adolescence, relations with peers assume increasing importance. Friends gradually come to occupy just as central a position in the relational network as the parents. However, only some of the focus group feel part of their local community. This is not surprising taking into account the multilayered and complex sense of identities and how young people relate to and engage within the wider world. According to Bourn (2008) young people are in one sense citizens of a mediated global culture but at the same time struggle for a sense of acceptance in the local societies in which they live. Where the young people in the focus group have a sense of acceptance is in the school community. It was clear from their comments that the young people in my study feel that there is a bond and friendship between staff and themselves. For instance, Xander feels that he has become a lot more caring about people and that the staff here are a lot more encouraging and that 'if you take time to get to know them they are not much different to being with the students'. Given the role of the school community in the young people's personal, social, emotional and moral development, including attachment to the teachers and the residential childcare officers, there is good reason to believe that important links exist between the school climate and their moral and social identity.

The majority of the group meet with friends outside school through social media and face to face contact. Syrus, who is the youngest in the group, does not feel part of an online community but did circle all the choices with regards to the way he uses online social networks. He admitted to being too lazy to read a book and prefers to get his information from online news channels such as YouTube FTD News which is a new kind of visual targeting the younger audience with the strap line: *Stay up to date with the latest and craziest news Monday to Friday.* Whereas, earlier generations turned to conventional media such as newspapers and television to feed their curiosity and explore others' and their own identities, today's young people have an unprecedented array of powerful new digital tools to help them with these processes.

Conclusion

Drawing on Bourdieu's concept of 'habitus' I have endeavoured in my small-scale study to capture a sense of the mediated environment of the participants' lived experiences. Habitus describes the individuals' way of seeing, interpreting and acting in the world, in accordance with their social position and it is internalized and consolidated in childhood and youth through family, educational structures and circumstances. What emerged from my investigation into the young people's use of the media was their strong sense of belonging to the school community. It was clear the residential provision was very well organized and run for the benefit of these young people who clearly had ownership of their own school habitus. This made my role easier as investigator, as the participants were forthcoming in their views about their own identity formation and the role media played in this process. This reinforces Bourdieu's (1992) notion that when 'habitus encounters a social world of which it is the product, it is like a fish in water, it does not feel the weight of water and it takes the world about it for granted'.

I turned to Marcia's identity status paradigm to understand further the young people's identity formation. However, I discovered that there can be a great variation in determining a young person's personal and social identity and I question whether or not the identity statuses are sensitive enough to measure the identity formation process. A broader longitudinal study is needed in order to provide more compelling results.

The study set out to explore a group of young people's quest for identity and the influence the media has on the formation of both their personal and social identity ownership. In this regard my aims were met, however due to the small sample in one location larger-scale surveys using many locations are now necessary in order to make strong generalizations about young people's use of media. This brings to conclusion the discussion of the findings from my small-scale study.

This chapter began by unravelling what is meant by identity using a range of theoretical lenses. This was followed by an exploration of the media and its role in constructing identities. The final section was a discussion around my recent empirical small-scale study which set out to explore a group of young people's quest for identity and the influence the media has on the formation of both their personal and social identity.

Notes

1 'Exploration' refers to the adolescent's active questioning and weighing up of various identity alternatives. 'Commitment' refers to the presence of strong convictions or choices.

2 Millgate School YouTube website: https://www.youtube.com/channel/UCpxXqwQokAR75mXFF1B7Teg

References

Adams, G. R., & Marshall, S. K. (1996). 'A Developmental Social Psychology of Identity: Understanding the Person-in-Context'. *Journal of Adolescence* 19.5: 429–42.

Bauman, Z. (2000). *Liquid Modernity*. Cambridge: Polity Press.

Bennett, A., & Robards, B. (eds) (2014). *Mediated Youth Cultures: The Internet, Belonging and New Cultural Configurations*. London: Palgrave Macmillan.

Bloom, R. S. (1956). *Taxonomy of Educational Objectives, Handbook I: The Cognitive Domain*. New York: David McKay Company.

Bourdieu, P. (1977). *Outline of a Theory of Practice*. Cambridge: Cambridge University Press.

Bourdieu, P. (1990). 'Structures, Habitus, Practices'. In *The Logic of Practice*. Cambridge: Polity. 52–65.

Bourdieu, P. and Wacquant, L. (1992). *Invitation to Reflexive Sociology*. Bristol, England: Policy Press.

Bourn, D. (2008). 'Young People, Identity and Living in a Global Society'. *Policy & Practice: A Development Education Review* 7.1: 48–61.

British Broadcasting Corporation. *Great British Bake Off* (last accessed online at http://www.bbc.co.uk/programmes/b013pqnm/clips on 1 July 2017).

Bronfenbrenner, U. (1977). 'Toward an Experimental Ecology of Human Development'. *American Psychologist* V 32.7: 513–31.

Bronner, S. J., & Clark, C. D. (2016). *Youth Cultures in America*. Santa Barbara, CA: ABC-CLIO,LLC.

Buckingham, D. (2008). *Youth, Identity, and Digital Media*. Cambridge: MIT Press.

Cassidy, T., & van Schijndel, H. (2011). 'Youth Identity Ownership from a Fashion Marketing Perspective'. *Journal of Fashion Marketing and Management: An International Journal* 15.2: 163–77.

Ching, C., & Foley, B. (2012). *Constructing the Self in a Digital World*. Cambridge: Cambridge University Press.

Coiro, J., Knobel, M., Lankshear, C., & Leu, D. J. (2008). *The Handbook of Research on New Literacies*. Mahwah, NJ: Erlbaum.

Damon, W. (2004). 'What Is Positive Youth Development?' *Annals of the American Academy of Political and Social Science* 591.1: 13–24.

De Klerk, V. (2005). 'Slang and Swearing as Markers of Inclusion and Exclusion in Adolescence'. In C. Thurlow and A. Williams (eds), *Talking Adolescence: Perspectives on Communication in the Teenage Years*. New York: Peter Lang. 109–26.

Deutsch, N., & Theodorou, E. (2010). 'Aspiring, Consuming, Becoming: Youth Identity in a Culture of Consumption'. *Youth and Society* 42.2: 229–54.

Dinter, A. (2006). 'Adolescence and Computers. Dimensions of Media-Related Identity Formation, Self-Formation and Religious Value as Challenges for Religious Education'. *British Journal of Religious Education* 28.3: 235–48.

Edgar, P., & Edgar, D. (2008). *The New Child: In Search of Smarter Grown-Ups.* Melbourne: Wilkinson Publishing.

Erikson, E. H. (1950). *Childhood and Society.* New York: Norton.

Erikson, E. H. (1959). *Identity and the Life Cycle.* New York: International University Press.

Erikson, E. H. (1968). *Identity: Youth and Crisis.* New York: Norton.

Fleming, N. (2007). 'Heavy Metal "a Comfort for the Bright Child"'. *The Telegraph* website: http://www.telegraph.co.uk.

Freud, S. (1938). *An Outline of Psychoanalysis*, trans. J. Strachey. London: Hogarth Press.

Gerbner, G., Gross, L., Morgan, M., & Signorielli, N. (1994). 'Growing Up with Television: The Cultivation Perspective'. In J. Bryant and D. Zillman (eds), *Perspectives on Media Effects*. Hillsdale, NJ: Lawrence Erlbaum Associates. 17–40.

Griffiths, M. D., Davies, M., & Chappell, D. (2004). 'Online Computer Gaming: A Comparison of Adolescent and Adult Gamers'. *Journal of Adolescence* 27.1: 87–96.

Hague, C., & Williamson, B. (2009). *Digital Participation, Digital Literacy, and School Subjects.* Bristol: Futurelab.

Hamley, K. (2001). 'Media Use in Identity Construction'. Available at: www.aber.ac.uk/media/students/kl9802.

Hammock, P. (2008). 'Narrative and the Cultural Psychology of Identity'. *Personality and Social Psychology Review* 12.3: 222–47.

Harter, S. (1999). *The Construction of Self: A Developmental Perspective.* New York: Guildford Press.

Heim, J., Brandtzeg, P. B., Kaare, B. H., Endestad, T., & Torgersen, L. (2007). 'Children's Usage of Media Technologies and Psychosocial Factors'. *New Media & Society* 9.3: 425–54.

Hill, A. (2015). *Reality TV.* Abingdon: Routledge.

Illeris, K. (2014). *Transformative Learning and Identity.* Abingdon: Routledge. Kellner, D. (2003). *Cultural Studies, Identity and Politics between the Modern and the Postmodern.* London: Taylor & Francis e-Library.

Klimstra, T. A., Hale III, W., Raaijmakers, Q., Branje, S., & Meeus, W. (2010). 'Identity Formation in Adolescence: Change or Stability?' *Journal of Youth and Adolescence* 39.2: 150–62.

Kroger, J., & Marcia, J. (2011). 'The Identity Statuses: Origins, Meanings and Interpretations'. In S. J. Schwartz, K. Luyckx, and V. L. Vignoles (eds), *Handbook of Identity Theory and Research.* New York: Springer Science+Business Media. 31–53.

Larson, R. J. (1995). 'Secrets in the Bedroom: Adolescents' Private Use of Media'. *Journal of Youth and Identity* 24.5: 535–50.

Livingstone, S. (2002). *Young People and New Media.* London: Sage.

Manago, A. M. (2015). 'Values for Gender Roles and Relations among High School and Non-High School Adolescents in a Maya Community in Chiapas, Mexico'. *International Journal of Psychology* 50, 20–8. doi:10.1002/ijop.12126.

Manago, A. M., Taylor, T., & Greenfield, P. M. (2012). 'Me and My 400 Friends: The Anatomy of College Students' Facebook Networks, Their Communication Patterns, and Well-Being'. *Developmental Psychology* 48.2: 369–80.

Marcia, J. (1966). 'Development and Validation of Ego-Identity Status'. *Journal of Personality and Social Psychology* 3.5: 551–8.

Marôpo, L. (2014). 'Youth, Identity, and Stigma in the Media: From Representation to the Young Audience's Perception'. *Journal of Audience and Reception Studies* 11.1: 199–212.

Miranda, D., & Claes, M. (2004). 'Rap Music Genres and Deviant Behaviors in French-Canadian Adolescents'. *Journal of Youth and Adolescence* 33.2: 113–22.

Office for Standards in Education (2016). Millgate School Residential Report. London: OfSTED.

Oxford English Dictionary website, OED Online, 25 June 2017.

Piaget, J. (1969). *The Psychology of the Child*. New York: Basic Books Inc.

Rattansi, A., & Phoenix, A. (1997). 'Rethinking Youth Identities: Modernist and Postmodernist Frameworks'. *Identity: An International Journal of Theory and Research* 5.2: 97–123.

Roberts, D. F., Henriksen, L., & Foehr, U. G. (2009). 'Adolescence, Adolescents, and Media'. In R. M. Lerner and L. Steinberg (eds), *Handbook of Adolescent Psychology, Volume 2: Contextual Influences on Adolescent Development*, 3rd ed. Hoboken, NJ: Wiley. 314–44.

Rogoff, B. (2003). *The Cultural Nature of Human Development*. Oxford: Oxford University Press.

Turner, J. C., & Oakes, P. J. (1986). 'The Significance of the Social Identity Concept for Social Psychology with Reference to Individualism, Interactionism and Social Influence'. *Social Psychology* 25.3: 237–52.

Willett, R., Burn, A., & Buckingham, D. (2005). 'New Media, Production Practices, Learning Spaces'. *Education, Communication, and Information* 5.1: 1–3.

Yee, N. (2007). 'The Psychology of Massively Multiuser Online Role Playing Games; Motivations, Emotional Investments, Relationships and Problematic Usage'. In R. Schroder and A. Axelsson (eds), *Avatars at Work and Play: Collaborations and Interactions in Shared Virtual Environments*. London: Springer. 187–201.

Yee, N. (2001). 'The Norrathian Scrolls: A Study of EverQuest' (version 2.5). Available at: http://www.nickyee.com/eqt/report.html (retrieved 22 November 2017).

Yee, N. (2006). 'The Labor of Fun: How Video Games Blur the Boundaries of Work and Play'. *Games and Culture* 1.1: 68–71.

Zemmels, D. R. (2012). 'Youth and New Media: Studying Identity and Meaning in an Evolving Media Environment'. *Communication Research Trends* 31.4: 4–22.

Part Three

Marginalized Discourse

Editor's introduction

This section focuses on the socio-political nature of language itself across countries and regions in Africa, India and China. In each case languages and cultures are locked into conflict with each other where dominant languages-cultures attempt to colonize or marginalize minority languages and cultures. The nature of language as symbolic and cultural capitals are examined, and in their sociocultural interaction we see how languages become ranked within hierarchies of varying degrees of sociocultural capital and power. The consequence of such linguistic hierarchies are marginalization for some, often with acts of resistance, and opportunities for others.

6

Language-Culture: Marginalization or Opportunity in Cameroon's Official 'State Bilingualism'

Henry Kum

Introduction

Hoffmann (1991: 13) believes that 'over half the population of the world is bilingual'. This view cannot be more credible considering the cosmopolitanization of citizenship and the move towards globalization rather than towards nationalistic and border-protected politics. Appel et al. (1987) highlights the fact that language contact is a persistent and irreversible trend happening every second of human life, and it becomes even more evident that the passing of each day witnesses, at least, one language user becoming bilingual to some degree, whether at home or abroad. Being bilingual would be an opportunity to increase access to people who are different from the speaker; however it also poses practical managerial implications for individual and societal language usage, but, most importantly, for the short-term and long-term implications for language legislation at the national or macro levels. It becomes even more complex when the perceived bilingualism in a country embraces two or more foreign languages at the expense of the national languages of that country. This often leads to a disconnect between local realities and official political discourses with local communities valuing their cultures through their indigenous languages while the politicians look outward on how to gain access to the international community using a medium of expression that opens more economic, social and political 'doors'. Cameroon is one such country where a foreign biculturalism based on colonial identities has enshrined English and French as the two officially recognized languages of a country made up of over 300 tribes, each with its own local language. There is an inherent conflict between state language policy and reality not just between indigenous languages and the two official languages but also between English and French as the only official languages of the country.

Jikong (2001) problematizes the inherent bilingual cultures of French and English speaking Cameroon as marginalization and opportunities and he further argues that the linguistic and cultural complexity of Cameroon is a source of both wealth and misfortune. As the political class of the country is of the dominant Francophone ethnicity, French has become the language of power and leadership (Fonlon 1969; Kouega 1999; Anchimbe 2005). In this chapter, I adopt a historico-sociological approach (Rosemary 2001) to elaborate on the identity conflict that is a product of the colonial languages of English and French in a postcolonial Cameroon. This chapter examines the internal cultural and linguistic issues in Cameroon in order to determine how Cameroon's postcolonial language identity is a source of marginalization and of opportunities. These internal cultural issues are explored through the theoretical lenses of Bourdieu's language and symbolic power and Skutnabb-Kangas's theory of linguicism or languagism. This is discussed within a climate of colonial and postcolonial discourses.

Cameroon: history and politics

Cameroon's population is estimated to stand at 23,924,407 million inhabitants as of January 2017 (Countrymeters.info 2017). It is located in the Central West of Africa bordered by French speaking countries of Chad, Central African Republic, Gabon and Congo; a Spanish speaking country of Equatorial Guinea and an English speaking country of Nigeria. Of the estimated population above, over 70 per cent is made up of French speaking Cameroonians (Francophones) who make up eight of the ten governing regions of the country. The English speaking Cameroonians make up less than 30 per cent of the total population and occupy two of the ten administrative regions of the country.

Founded in 1472 by a Portuguese navigator called Fernando Po, Cameroon has passed through the colonial rule of Germany, Britain and France (Fanso, 1989). The Germans were defeated in 1918 during the First World War and that paved the way for Cameroon to be divided between Britain and France, and administered first under the League of Nations mandate and later under the United Nations trusteeship. Britain got one-third of the country in which the north was called 'Northern British Cameroons' and the south was called 'Southern British Cameroons' (Echu 2004). The French got two-thirds of Cameroon and administered it as an independent territory, whereas the British administered theirs from Lagos in Nigeria. French Cameroon became independent on 1 January 1960. On 11 February 1960, British Southern Cameroons voted to start unification negotiations with the Republic of Cameroon, which already had independence from France. This commencement of the desire for unification between the two entities was decided in a UN plebiscite on 1 October 1961 in which a federation made up of two states called West Cameroon and East Cameroon was created. The federation survived till 20 May 1972 when a unitary state made up of provinces was created. Later in 1984, the number of provinces was increased to ten through a presidential decree which also changed the name of the country from 'The United Republic of Cameroon' to 'The Republic of Cameroon'. Therefore, although Cameroon has been the product of two equal states of two different colonial cultures of English and French, the realities in the country render a verdict of opportunities to one culture and marginalization of another.

The language situation in postcolonial Cameroon is often described as official state bilingualism where French and English are the two official languages. While opening the Bilingual Grammar School in Buea in 1962, the first secondary education institution in the country located in the English speaking region, Ahmadou Ahidjo, Cameroon's first president, stated that '[b]y bilingualism we mean the practical usage of our two official languages, English and French, throughout the national territory' (Ayafor 2005: 127). That statement defined the official language policy of Cameroon which was enshrined in its constitution. Thus, state bilingualism functions within a complex framework of over 270 indigenous languages, several regional lingua francas and a quasi-national Pidgin English (Koenig et al. 1983). It is what Mbassi-Manga (1973) describes as the presence of French and English in a multilingual setting. This complex postcolonial setup has led to, among other individual discontentment, several complaints of sociolinguistic disadvantages by various groups which affect the people's interaction with others, their choice of identity and their socio-economic opportunities (Anchimbe 2005; Fonlon 1969; Kouega 1999; Bobda 2003). Nationally, the most visibly marginalized identities are the minority English speaking Cameroonians (Anglophones) who make up less than one-third of Cameroon against the more privileged majority French speaking Francophone ethnicity that has also been in political power since the birth of independent Cameroon in 1960 (Kouega 1999; Bobda 2003). The marginalization of Anglophones and the abounding opportunities of Francophones posit competing tensions where one group closes its social borders to the other;

identity construction and preservation of in-group qualities become the norm and continue to affect the internal stability of Cameroon as a country.

The broad stratification of Cameroonians into two major linguistic subgroups of Francophone and Anglophone has built identity boundaries around them which have become predominantly exclusionary in a country whose political catch phrase is 'national integration'. It has led to tensions where the minority Anglophones view their majority Francophone counterparts as a privileged neocolonial clan that is determined to assimilate and stifle the Anglophone culture. However the majority Francophones view the minority Anglophones with suspicion as an emerging force that seeks the reterritorialization of itself into social, political and economic spaces that were earlier dominated by the Francophones. In most social, economic and political spheres, English speaking Cameroonians are disadvantaged and therefore feel compelled to speak French in order to be recognized as Cameroonians within Cameroon. In high profile professional schools like the National School for Administration and Magistracy (ENAM), the National School for Police, the Military Academy (EMIA), Advanced School for Mass Communication (ASMAC) and the International Relations Institute (IRIC) at least 80 per cent of the courses are taught in French (Mforteh 2006). Where similar schools exist in English speaking territory, they are often devalued to first cycles and annexed to the main schools in French speaking Cameroon where power is centralized. This phenomenon resonates well with Bourdieu's (1977) theory of language, power and politics, for he concludes that language is not only a means of communication but also a medium through which power is enacted. The ruling elite of Francophone Cameroon has protected the status of French above English in order to assert their authority and influence over Anglophones. French doubles up as a medium of communication and as an oppressive weapon to marginalize Anglophones.

Cameroon's indigenous languages

Cameroon has over 300 tribes with over 270 languages (Breton & Fohtung 1991; Wolf 2001). The Cameroon government refers to these languages as local or indigenous languages (also known as local, tribal, vernacular and sometimes national languages) thereby acknowledging that Cameroon functions within a biculturalism of foreign languages of English and French in a multilingual context. These languages comprise of 55 Afro-Asiatic languages, 2 Nilo-Saharan languages, 4 Ubangian languages and 169 Niger-Congo languages (Bitja'a Kody

1999). The Niger-Congo languages are further divided into Fulfulde which is a Senegambian language; 28 Adamawa languages and 142 Benue-Congo languages. These local languages are limited to oral usage mostly in rural and family circles and for the conduct of petty trading. For example, Bitja'a Kody (1999) carried out a survey to determine the spread of the three most popular local languages of the tribes in Yaoundé (the nation's capital) and found that 32 per cent of young people between the ages of 10 and 17 did not speak any local language. The conclusions of these findings reveal that the population would have increased alarmingly because the younger generation would not have been able to transmit the language to the future generation due do their incompetence in the local languages. French has become the language of prestige, public service, education, law and all aspects of meaningful communication. It has become the currency to access the linguistic market. Bourdieu (1977) maintains that linguistic utterances or expressions can be understood as the product of the relationship between a 'linguistic market' and a 'linguistic habitus'. Many young people, as shown by Bitja'a Kody's (2001) research, deploy their accumulated linguistic resources in the French language in relationship with the social, economic and political markets which French as a currency can grant them access. It is a similar trend in most cities including Anglophone Cameroon where the younger generation will invest in English as well as French as a currency to access the country's resources.

After the defeat of the Germans in Cameroon in 1918, indigenous languages were and are still restricted to ethnic or tribal settings and for the transmission of the cultural heritage of their respective communities (Chumbow 1980). The French and the British continued with the erosion of indigenous languages. Although the British colonial policy was that of indirect rule where indigenous cultures were encouraged, this was partially applied as far as the use of indigenous languages was concerned. While encouraging the colonized Cameroonians to develop their cultures, English became the language of business, politics and education. It was pronounced as a language that should be taught and employed as a medium of instruction and by 1954, Britain declared that it was no longer possible to use any vernacular (indigenous language) as a medium of instruction in English speaking Cameroon (Ndille 2016). As English was protected as the preferred language of English speaking Cameroon, it was a much more assimilatory policy in French speaking Cameroon because French colonial policy was that of direct rule and complete assimilation. France passed an Order in 1917 emphasizing that French was to be the only language of instruction in schools and later in all state affairs. All schools in which indigenous languages were taught or served as the medium of instruction were closed down. By 1938, there were 1,061 unrecognized schools with over 30,914 pupils that had been required to shut down because of their use of indigenous languages (Ndille 2016). Earlier in 1936, the French colonial administration prohibited the production, sale, collection or distribution of publications written in indigenous languages and a tax of 12.8 per cent was imposed on books written in other foreign languages while books written in French only paid a tax of 4 per cent (Stumpf 1979). All indigenous languages were classed as foreign languages and paradoxically, French was the nationally recognized language. Therefore, in terms of citizenship and functioning in the social, political and economic institutions of Cameroon and in terms of relating to the international community, English and French became the only officially recognized languages at work 'nationally' in Cameroon. In line with Skutnabb-Kangas and Philipson's (1995) theory of linguicism, the focus of the state on a bicultural policy based on two foreign languages has been interpreted as fostering linguistic discrimination against local languages whose speakers continue to be placed in a dilemma as they struggle to address the convergence between home language, identity and access to economic opportunities (see also Bourdieu's theory of language and symbolic power).

Indigenous languages have suffered a reclassification and a redefinition and have become under-resourced (Breton & Fohtung 1991). Fourteen of the local languages are extinct and four others (Duli, Gey, Nagumi and Yeni) are on the verge of extinction (Ethnologue 2006). Some of the local languages that have survived and continue to spread regionally include Fulfulde, Ewondo, Basaa, Duala, Hausa, Wandala, Kanuri, Arab Choa and Bamun; these are languages used by highly populated tribes or include opportunities for local trade and have surviving folklores and music. Some of the languages, such as Bali Mungaka and Bafut in the northwest, were used by missionaries to spread Christianity but such preference quickly reduced as soon as most local people started to understand English or French and also as more interpreters became available (Bitja'a Kody 1999). Some of the tribal leaders of these languages fought hard to standardize their languages in the precolonial and colonial eras but received minimal or no support from the colonial masters and subsequent Cameroonian politicians. For example, some two main indigenous languages – the Bamun language, used in education long before the arrival of the German missionaries; and also Fulfulde, which had been used for the dissemination of Islam in the three northern provinces – became undervalued and extinct in education. Schools that taught in these languages were closed down. For example, the 47 schools opened by

King Njoya of Bamun in his tribe were all closed down and 1,800 schools run by the American Presbyterian missionaries in which Bulu was taught for the spread of Christianity were also closed down (Bitja'a Kody 2001).

With the closure of schools that had indigenous languages as the medium of expression, a huge and significant amount of the Bamun and Fulfulde culture disappeared. This move could be interpreted as a systematic process of increasing the social and economic dominance of French and English in public services, education, law, the military, commerce, health and all national life. And with this was the rise of French and British history, literature and foreign ways of life in Cameroonian public life as opposed to indigenous Cameroonian cultures. Cities and towns like Victoria were renamed along colonial lines, street names changed, for example, Avenue Charles de Gaulle, and people changed their accents and names to adapt to their new colonial languages (Alobwede 1998; Mbangwana 1983, 2002.). This shows the marginalization of indigenous Cameroonian identities. Although in 1998, parliament passed a bill on the general orientation of education in Cameroon with special emphasis on the teaching of national languages, very little has been done to promote the survival of indigenous languages (Mba and Chiatoh 2000; Echu 2004). None of the indigenous languages is studied at university or teacher training institutions. Therefore, there is no expertise in this area and that explains why the policy is not implemented.

The denigration of Cameroon indigenous languages has become at best exclusionary, whereby many of the indigenous populations of the country remain largely ignorant of the emblems and general policy direction of the country. They are deprived of understandings and debates about the constitution, awareness of the penal code and legal systems, presidential briefings and mainstream political discourses that affect their daily lives because these are rendered in French and English which are not their indigenous languages (Makoni & Ulrike 2003). According to Echu (2004) the ignorance of most indigenous populations on public affairs has made the state function as an elitist society of a selected few who are able to operate more importantly in the traditions of the French and less importantly as Anglophones rather than native Cameroonians. Chumbow et al. (2000) do not see any future for indigenous languages in Cameroon partly because these languages are not tolerated or encouraged in schools and also because the present language policy excludes indigenous languages from the curriculum thereby encouraging parents to clamour for their children to be introduced to French and English at the earliest opportunity in their schooling and education.

Evidence from the French colonial reports (1921, 1924 and 1952) show that the French provided financial incentives to schools that embraced French as the language of instruction and also rewarded Cameroonians who could demonstrate a mastery of the French language. Such individuals were fast tracked into administrative roles and they further helped the French to stamp out the traces of indigenous languages in official circles. The support given to French and English over indigenous languages is linguistic discrimination leading to prejudice in public life. Ngugi (1986: 3) blames colonialism for the erosion of indigenous languages and concludes that '[t]he biggest weapon wielded and actually daily unleashed by imperialism is the cultural bomb. The effect of a cultural bomb is to annihilate a people's belief in their names, in their languages, in their environment, in their heritage of struggle, in their unity, in their capacities and ultimately in themselves'.

Ngugi adds credence to the Skutnabb-Kangas's (1985) theory of linguicism whereby language is used to promote discrimination and prejudice and to denigrate a particular ethnicity while protecting another. Drawing from this stance of linguistic discrimination, Ashcroft et al. (1995: 325) quote Fanon's summation of the colonial impact on indigenous languages as a situation in which speakers of vernaculars are forced to be seen as 'hating the negro-vernacular' and 'reaching out for the universal' (in this case being English and French) as a result of linguicism. In the words of Fanon (1967: 190), '[C]olonialism brought about a strong sense of inferiority; a divided sense of self . . . a veritable emaciation of the stock of national culture . . . banished the native customs . . . created a sense of alienation in the self-identity of the colonized peoples'. It is what Ndille (2016: 17) refers to as 'the intentionality and colonial representation and the failure of a Cameroon-centric identity'. The French and British have continued with their colonial policy of cultural deracination started by the Germans. The Germans had earlier banned the public use of indigenous languages in schools and other state-run affairs (Ndille 2016). The Duala language which had been far advanced in its vocabulary and dictionary was banned in 1904 and 1910 by the Germans and only German was authorized. The French and British simply continued with this systematic and persistent trend of linguistic marginalization which excluded the indigenous Cameroonians from national public life and forced them to give up or renegotiate their devalued identity in order to share in the country's territorial rights. The Cameroonian was subjugated by the colonial masters to deny them their original identity through an oppressive language policy first by the adoption of German and later through a policy of biculturalism in a multilingual country in which French and English are now promoted as superior languages.

Official state bilingualism: French and English

As stated above, Cameroon is estimated to be made up of over 270 indigenous language and 2 colonial languages of English and French (Breton & Fohtung 1991). As a result, most Cameroonians are considered to be bilingual or multilingual – speaking either more than one indigenous language or one or the two official languages with one or more indigenous languages. Mackey (1970) describes this linguistic competence in more than one language as individual bilingualism. However, speaking more than one indigenous language even with one of the two official languages is without merit in Cameroon as the state does not recognize or accord national status to indigenous languages. Therefore, the state in Cameroon will not consider somebody bilingual if he or she speaks many indigenous languages and even if in addition to competence in indigenous languages, he or she is competent in one official language of English and French. Therefore, the official state definition of 'bilingualism' in Cameroon is the ability to speak English and French.

Thus, Cameroon is ethnically heterogeneous comprising of more than 300 tribes and 2 main political Anglophone and Francophone national identities, which already posit a fundamental challenge to a national policy of integration and language policy. Ayafor (2005: 124) indicates that 'although multiculturalism in terms of ethnic diversity is unexpectedly not yet a problem for national unity, ethnicity along the Francophone-Anglophone dichotomy is, and has whisked away attention such that it threatens national unity in terms of territorial integrity more than anything else in the country'. Ayafor maintains that these ethnic differences have led to a preference of a foreign 'biculturalism' that has been adopted to dominate an existential national multiculturalism based on the historico-cultural strengths of Cameroon as a country. And this has impacted on the choice of state languages when language policies are enacted. According to the Cameroon government, the bicultural acquisition of English and French as national languages helps to solidify the link between 'state bilingualism' and the recognized national identities of Cameroon. The Cameroon government also argues that because of the multi-ethnic tribal groupings of the country into regional local languages, a national language from one of the ethnic groups will be a source of conflict as other groups will feel excluded. It therefore argues for a foreign colonial language in line with Cameroon's history to serve as a policy instrument for national integration. In addition, these foreign languages offered common grounds between the many tribes of English speaking Cameroon and French speaking Cameroon to form a unity state in 1961. However, this unity through foreign biculturalism also paved the conflicting direction of official state bilingualism as an opportunity as well as marginalization for some parts of Cameroon.

The state has been able to make more political capital of its bicultural policy by aligning Cameroon to two political and economic blocs: La Francophonie and the Commonwealth of Nations, giving its citizens wider international choices in gains made as a result of its membership to these two blocs. La Francophonie is made up of former French colonies under the leadership of France while the Commonwealth of Nations is made up of former British colonies under the leadership of the United Kingdom. Arguments to join these two blocs were made for economic, political, social advantages offered. It also offered employment opportunities in the translation and interpretation sectors, education and trade. The government, for instance, created a pool of pedagogic animators and inspectors for each of these languages in the ten provinces and the central administration in Yaoundé, the nation's capital. Central services at the Presidency, the Prime Ministry, the Ministries and most parastatal companies have permanent translators and interpreters who make texts available to the population in both official languages. The use of foreign languages as national medium of expression exposed Cameroonians to funding opportunities in Francophonie and Commonwealth countries as fluency in French and or English as well as an awareness of educational systems common to these countries led to Cameroonians gaining scholarships to study abroad in fields that were not offered in Cameroonian universities. Some scholars may challenge this and accuse it of brain drain where the brightest Cameroonians left on scholarship and ended up being employed on better wages where they studied (see Tebeje 2010; Nguyen et al. 2008). But it is important to point out that most managers, governors and ministers, including the president and high profile private and state employees in Cameroon, studied abroad. Thus, Cameroon's political elite saw its bilingual culture as a window of opportunity internally and externally.

The adoption of one dominant cultural policy of French traditions in Cameroon where the French-styled administrative system and territorial integration indicates patterns of gross political centralization has exposed the weaknesses of official state bilingualism. The geographic and demographic division of the country makes the English speaking region a minority. The territorial representation of English and French automatically follows this division, hence giving French a numeric ascendancy over English. This ascendancy is the factor which also makes the English speaking region a linguistic minority in the view of Francophones. Besides, due to the fact that Anglophones have to make both a linguistic adjustment from English to French, and a geographic movement from the English to the French speaking region to perform most of their civic duties, it has become one negative impact of the lack of language planning. Thus, it pushes them to feel assimilated; hence, language policy has become one major factor among the socio-political grievances of Anglophones which has led to social and political unrests threatening the existence of a united Cameroon. The Anglophones view bilingualism as an obligatory one-sided push for Anglophones to move towards French while Francophones do not have the need, political will or choice to embrace the English language. By implication, Anglophones are conscious of bilingualism as a tool to assimilate Anglophones into a dominant French culture and erode any traces of their Anglo-Saxon traditions.

The policy of bilingualism has been more in text than in practice (see Tchoungui 1983; Kouega 1999; Anchimbe 2005) leading most critics to conclude that Cameroonians as individuals are monolingual and it is the state of Cameroon that is bilingual (Bobda 2003; Anchimbe 2005). This conclusion is drawn from what Anchimbe refers to as 'anglophonism and francophonism'. Echu (2004) challenges the stance on official state bilingualism by emphasizing that the language policy in the country lacks an implementation strategy and does not sufficiently promote or guarantee the opportunities for Cameroonians to function as bilingual citizens but rather promotes Cameroonians to identify under an Anglophone identity (anglophonism) or a Francophone identity (francophonism). According to Echu, the policy of official state bilingualism, originally aimed at guaranteeing political integration and unity in Cameroon, now seems to constitute a source of conflict and political disintegration. The constitution of Cameroon (1996) states that '[t]he official languages of the Republic of Cameroon shall be English and French, both languages having the same status. The State shall guarantee the promotion of bilingualism throughout the country. It shall endeavour to protect and promote national languages'. The interest in the clause above is in the emphasis on 'English and French, both languages having the same statuses'. Official state bilingualism was intended to foster a unified national identity but this has existed only in theory because of the Francophone-Anglophone divide. Therefore, French, which is the language in over 70 per cent of the territory of Cameroon, dominates national service, the media, public works, the military, administration and education among others

French speaking Cameroon: francophonism

As earlier stated, Francophones are the French speaking Cameroonians who make up over 70 per cent of the population of Cameroon and occupy eight of the ten administrative regions of the country. Their sociocultural identity in postcolonial bilingual Cameroon is described by Anchimbe (2005) as 'francophonism', a term coined from the subscription of Francophones to the French way of life that distinguishes them from Frenchmen from France and English speaking Cameroonians from Cameroon. Francophones, until recently, never had the motivation to learn and speak English, not only because of failure in government policy to enforce state bilingualism but also due to the fact that discourse in Cameroon public life including government, education, professional life, politics was a preserve of the French language. For example, Bobda (2003) states that the total number of Francophones learning English in the various language centres is far below 10,000, which is insignificant compared with the total population of 12 million Francophone Cameroonians (Bobda 1986; 1993; 2002; 2003). This was in the 1980s and the number would be higher now with the increase in the population of Cameroon. English remained the less favoured and generally marginalized of the two official languages. Administrative, political and diplomatic transactions were and are still conducted in French. For example, the president of Cameroon, who took power in 1982, is French speaking; he addressed Cameroonians during his inauguration speech in English in 1982 and for over thirty-four years now, he has never again addressed the country in English. This means that all state policies are presented in French and are sometimes poorly translated into English.

On 13 November 1995, Cameroon, which had been a member of the Economic and Customs Union (CEMAC) of neighbouring French speaking countries and of La Francophonie of former French speaking colonies, joined the Commonwealth of Nations, thus ushering in a new wave of cultural and economic opportunities of relating to English speaking communities in the world. This exposure enabled Francophones to realize the influence of English as a major world language and to ascertain that educational and business opportunities could be available for them in countries like the United Kingdom, the United States, Australia and Canada among others. Francophone Cameroonians did not perceive embracing English as a shift in cultural identity; rather it was perceived as a negotiation of opportunities for political and economic benefits within the international community. English is not considered as one of the identity markers of Francophone Cameroonians but it is seen as that bridge to international success that everyone, irrespective of official language background, wants to cross. Francophone families now send their children to the most high profile English speaking schools in the two regions of English speaking Cameroon and also to schools that the government of Cameroon has classified as 'bilingual schools'. There is a proliferation of privately owned English speaking nursery, primary and secondary schools in French speaking cities owned by Francophones but staffed by English speaking teachers.

Many former French-medium schools have gained bilingual statuses to include education along the Anglo-Saxon educational culture. Eighty per cent of these schools introduced the teaching of the English language to pupils as young as 4 years (Bobda 2003). In the 2004/2005 academic year, for example, Francophone children constituted up to 28 per cent of the total number of students admitted to the first year of studies in some schools in English speaking Cameroon (Mforteh 2006). This new breed of Francophone children who are drilled in the English speaking curriculum add this opportunity to their acquired French competencies as an advantage to dominate their English counterparts in Cameroon and compete with them in English speaking countries outside Cameroon. Their 'francophonism' is challenged outside Cameroon but remains a currency as they access national services and the political landscape both in Cameroon and in countries of La Francophonie. Francophone Cameroonians have become interested in English language as an opening to embracing globalization in which English has reinforced its position as the main international language.

English speaking Cameroon: anglophonism

Anglophone Cameroonians are the English speaking Cameroonians who make up less than 30 per cent of the population of Cameroon and occupy two of the ten administrative regions of the country. These two regions are former colonies administered by the British after the Second World War and in a UN organized plebiscite of 1961, they joined the Republic of Cameroon to become the United Republic of Cameroon as two equal states. Their sociocultural identity in postcolonial bilingual Cameroon is described by Anchimbe (2005) as 'anglophonism', a term coined from their subscription to the British way of life that distinguishes them from Francophones and British citizens from the United Kingdom. The union with the French speaking Republic of Cameroon has become highly contested with the English speaking Cameroon losing its political, cultural and economic institutions to the French speaking political class. Anglophone Cameroonians consider themselves to have been stripped of the political and cultural autonomy that they exercised under British rule, and they look back with nostalgia, discomfort and frustration at the 'second class' citizenship they enjoy as a minority population in Cameroon. Appointments of senior administrators in the country do no longer subscribe to legible rationality with no Anglophone heading any important ministry out of fifty-one ministers and fifteen secretaries of state (*Cameroon Post* 2015). Of the two presidents that the country has had since unification in 1961 till 2017, both are from the French political class (Amado Ahidjo: 1960–82; and Paul Biya: 1982–till date). All ministries, the presidency, national inspectors, important government branches covering law, the military, education, finance as well as most professional colleges and universities/branches are located in French speaking Cameroon. Up till 1990, there was only one university, the University of Yaoundé, which was located in French speaking Cameroon where English speaking students who had been educated in English in nursery, primary and secondary school were registered to be taught in French.

Faced with what they see as accumulated injustice perpetrated against their language, themselves and their culture, Anglophones have, after a quarter of a century of coexistence with their Francophone countrymen, started to react in all kinds of ways. Reactions to the alleged marginalization of the Anglophones have grown to include pressure groups and civil disobedience, which crystallized in the 1990s into a force that seriously threatened the unity of the country with the creation of the first opposition party, the Social Democratic Front (SDF), by an Anglophone Cameroonian (Ni John Fru Ndi). After a huge militarization and police brutality of the two Anglophone provinces, the party was recognized and is considered by many to have won the presidential elections of 1992 which were rigged to favour the incumbent French speaking president. Anglophone nationalism rose and led to civil disobedience and they were branded as 'les enemis dans la maison' (meaning, enemies in the house). By implication, Anglophones were not considered as Cameroonians and they were often branded as 'Biafrans', a tribe in Eastern Nigeria.

Anglophones have united through various pressure groups like the Cameroon Anglophone Movement (CAM), Southern Cameroons National Council (SCNC), Cameroon Anglophone Students Association (CANSA) and Confederation of Anglophone Parent-Teacher Associations of Cameroon (CAPTAC) which continue advocating for the restoration of the linguistic, cultural, political and infrastructural cultures of Anglophone Cameroonians either through federalism or the complete separation of the English speaking Cameroon from the Republic of Cameroon. In 2016/2017, these accounts of the alleged marginalization of Anglophones in Cameroon led to violence in which many Anglophone Cameroonian lawyers, teachers, students and other professionals took to the streets demanding a restoration of the Anglophone system of education, law and the federal state that was the product of unification in 1961. Students were tortured with some deaths reported and massive arrests made. The stalemate continues with teachers and lawyers on an indefinite strike in Anglophone Cameroon where there are no court hearings and schools are closed indefinitely.

The bridging language: Cameroon Pidgin English

The arrival of the colonial masters and the struggle for territories meant that colonial and postcolonial countries emerged along geographical lines rather than on cultural or tribal identities. Boundaries were drawn and redrawn according to the treaties that colonial masters concluded with other colonial masters. That gave rise to Francophone Cameroon and Anglophone Cameroon which emerged as colonial territories awarded to the French and English after the Germans were pushed out of Cameroon. The inhabitants of Cameroon were now faced with new colonial masters whose language and way of life was new. However, there was the need to interact with these newcomers who had become the new masters of Cameroon. As Cameroonians in the territory accorded to the British tried to learn the language, a new form of language emerged that was neither English nor any of the indigenous languages. It was a mixture of the English words that the native Cameroonians could master and their indigenous languages. As many tribes had merged into one country now known as British Southern Cameroon (Anglophone Cameroon), this medium of expression did not only serve the local population to interact with the colonial masters but also became a bridging language among tribes whose languages were not mutually intelligible. This became known as Cameroon Pidgin English (CPE; Alobwede 1998), which is a mixture of formal English expressions and local languages, in which the speaker is fluent. Cameroonians who served the British colonial masters needed a medium of expression for official interaction but their competence in English was minimal. They resorted to code switching in their local languages with a blend of the few English sentences or words that they could afford.

When the two Cameroons united in 1961, Pidgin English widened to include words from local languages, English and French and linked many tribes across the united Cameroon. CPE has become a widely used lingua franca in most communities in Cameroon and even the political elite that condemns this lingua franca in official circles use it during election campaign to get across their messages to a varied and linguistically diverse population. CPE has become a bridging language. It is used in business milieus, in churches, and many informal situations. It is a 'no man's language' that is structurally closer to the indigenous languages and English language. It has no rules of grammar, no exclusive vocabulary thereby enabling every Cameroonian to use it, blend existing components with French and new indigenous words in order to pass across their message. It is the only lingua franca in Cameroon which is not associated with a tribe, religion or any foreign power. The absence of ownership of this language enables it to be a unifying language. As earlier stated, although its lexicons have a high proportion of words of English origin, it has a neutral identity as the interlocutors can add to it drawing from their own repertoires. Most Cameroonians would advocate for this language to be developed, standardized and promoted to become the official language of Cameroon replacing French and English. It is Cameroon Pidgin English that Cameroon can claim ownership of due to the fact that it draws significantly from the Cameroon local setting, cultures and geography, and offers a much more unique identity to Cameroonians than the foreign bicultural languages of French and English. Despite this, the ruling political elite of Cameroon discourages its use and does not allow it in schools, publics service, mass media and state institutions.

CPE is considered as a non-standard form of English by the state and this allows the state to allocate it an inferior status. Speakers of CPE are often the target of linguicism as they are often perceived to be of low intelligence, illiterate and limited education who resort to CPE because they cannot construct a meaningful sentence in French or English. In most schools, there are billboard signs written in bold prohibiting the use of CPE in and out of the classrooms and prescribing strict punishment to anybody caught speaking in CPE. Users of this lingua franca cannot use it to get employment, or admission into schools and universities especially as any reference to it during official state business is judged as a mark of intellectual limitation. Sometimes Francophone Cameroonians who cannot speak English will retort to Anglophone Cameroonians that they are 'Biafran Nigerians' (Nigerian immigrants) or that they are speaking in 'Pidgin English' which is not allowed. In official state circles, CPE has no currency; it has no power and no pride. Take, for example, the caption at the entrance of the University of Buea, the first English speaking university in Cameroon, shown in Figure 6.1.

Bourdieu (1977) states that every linguistic interaction, however personal or insignificant it may seem, bears the traces of the social structure that it both expresses and helps to reproduce. This explains why linguistic usage varies according to considerations such as class and gender. Bourdieu therefore expands on the process through which the state (infused with the authority and values of the dominant group) helps in the preservation of that group's linguistic and social power. The political class in Cameroon seeks to protect the colonial languages and inherent values, identities, power and values of French and English against a widely spoken and understood lingua franca like the CPE. The Cameroon state is not prepared to give up the prestige of French and English as foreign colonial languages for a unifying CPE that is original, inclusive and draws more from the Cameroonian cultural settings. The official languages are bound up with the state of Cameroon, both in its creation as a state from colonial ruins and now in

Figure 6.1 A pro-English sign from the University of Buea. This caption shows the extent to which Cameroon Pidgin English is devalued and discouraged in institutions of the state.
Source: Signboard obtained at entrance of University of Buea.

its determination of the social values of the state. As a result, CPE is devalued as a slang and is an inferior but popular mode of expression.

However, although CPE remains the most commonly used language between linguistic groups and the most nationally understood and spoken language in Cameroon, speakers of this language often suffer stigmatization and do not enjoy the status of bilingual speakers because the state considers Pidgin English as inferior, crude and a language of an uneducated population, often reflecting the master-servant relationship of a colonial past (Ayafor 2005). Despite the attempts to stifle the popularity of CPE, Mbangwana (1989: 87) concludes that 'Pidgin English is very crucial as a communication bridge, for it links an Anglophone to a Francophone. It also links an Anglophone to another Anglophone, an educated Cameroonian to another educated one, a non-educated Cameroonian to another non-educated one, and more importantly an educated Cameroonian to a non-educated one'.

The bilingual-multilingual culture: opportunity or marginalization?

History has given Cameroonians a sublime challenge: to build a united state based on a singular course of the country, capable of constituting a model for the reconciliation and integration of the various colonial heritages and its traditional old values. This is marred by the non-respect of bilingualism in education and the public sector although the constitution makes French and English the two official languages of equal value (Kouega 1999). Public policy in Cameroon is described as best as a penchant for institutional mimicry that fails to capitalize on its multicultural heritage to be united in diversity. The aftermath of institutions of the unitary state, in its political discourses, emphasized the bilingual and pluricultural identities of the state but in reality the French political elite gradually assimilated the Anglophone cultures through subversive policies of cultural deracination. Fifty-five years after independence, Cameroon's language policies remain unique to a history of confusion, uncertainty and frustration, unlike in other multilingual countries in Europe and North America. For example, in Canada, laws like the 1969 Language Act and the 1977 Bill 101 enforce bilingualism. The Office of the Commissioner of Official Languages in Canada deals with complaints about violations of language rights (Bobda 2003). In Cameroon, no provision of any law seriously compels citizens to learn or use the other official language.

Humans naturally identify with others and this is done sometimes through the categorization of individuals into specific social groups like gender, ethnicity, race and language. As a result of this categorization, some groups become more visible and others remain less salient. Indigenous communities have become less salient compared to dominant colonial identities recognized through the mediums of French and English due to state bilingualism in Cameroon. And most visible is the sub-normalization of 'Anglophones', which has become a less salient identity when compared to a dominant Francophone identity. Schutz and Six (1996) explain the competing tensions between two languages that are used as vignettes of social categorization as a product of linguistic discrimination and prejudice of language. In this sense, prejudice is considered to refer to negative attitudes towards an individual based solely on their membership of a social group. Discrimination, however, becomes the acts towards the individual. This is what Schutz and Six (1996) refer to as linguicism which often targets oppressed and marginalized social minorities. In the case of Cameroon, the state bilingual policy and official language practice has been credited to successfully raise the status of French over English whereas both languages are politically mandated to be of equal status in 'official state bilingualism' (Jikong 2001; 2002; Ubanako 2004). The Francophone Cameroonians through education, political and public discourses, the military, law and order and high profile civil service professional seek to establish complete domination over the Anglophones by gradually assimilating the Anglophones into a monolingual French speaking Cameroon. And this stems as far back as the change of names from United Republic of Cameroon to the Republic of Cameroon.

During the referendum of 1972, English speaking Cameroon which was an independent country voted to join La Republique du Cameroun in an equal union of two distinct, independent federated states. That union gave rise to a United Republic of Cameroon which was enshrined in the constitution as two federated states uniting with each preserving its social and cultural characteristics in language, law and education among others. Any change to this union would be a constitutional change to be validated by the people of the two states in another referendum. But in 1984, the president changed the name from the United Republic of Cameroon to the Republic of Cameroon. This was interpreted as a major constitutional change without the validation of the English speaking state. It became an act of separation, which was considered to have started the social, political and cultural annexation and assimilation of the minority state of English speaking Cameroon. This and subsequent presidential decrees have continued to force the Anglophones to give up their territorial rights in all its forms. English speaking Cameroonians have had their right to education and employment greatly curtailed as most state-owned universities and professional schools are located in French speaking territory and the medium of instruction is French. The Francophone population has since 1972 dominated politics with over 90 per cent of cabinet positions, the judiciary and the military filled by Francophones. Francophones have become the Cameroonian ruling class and French is the language of public affairs. This has Anglophone resistance which considers the Francophones to have subjugated the Anglophones to the extent of denying them their political and cultural rights as a nation. This sharply contrasts with the abounding opportunities enjoyed by the Francophones who have been systematically guided through privileges and great-nation chauvinism to believe that Francophones are superior Cameroonians. Today in 2017, an Anglophone is refused service or discriminated if his/her request is made in English as this automatically presents him/her as a second-class citizen. Moreover, all schools in Anglophone are on strike, all law firms are on strike and the government interrupted internet supply for four months (from January 2017 to April 2017) as a way of curbing the coordination and flow of information in Anglophone Cameroon about the strike action.

At a speech to the nation amid the uprisings in the two English speaking regions of Cameroon, Paul Biya, the French speaking president of the Republic of Cameroon, who has been in power for 34 years having succeeded the former French speaking president Amadou Adhijo, stated that 'Cameroon is one and indivisible'. Emphasis here is on a 'one Cameroon' as one nation which is an optimistic political slogan from the dominant Francophone ruling class which simply seeks to deny the Anglophones' right to self-determination while at the same time legitimizing the superiority of the Francophones over the Anglophones. Federalism that was the basis for the 1972 reunification was abolished and Anglophones now operate a diluted Anglo-Saxon education system dictated to them by Francophone education ministers and sometimes taught to them by Francophone teachers. This education system disadvantages the Anglophone Cameroonians in high profile public service recruitment jobs and professional entrance examinations. For the few Anglophones who succeed to access these professional schools, they graduate to serve both Francophones and Anglophones in the French language because English is not the language of the Cameroon public service. The situation is equally bad in the law courts where Francophone magistrates preside over courts in the Anglophone regions and force Anglophone lawyers to present submissions in French. This is one of the grievances of the Anglophone lawyers who have been on strike since November

2016 to date calling for the reinstatement of the English speaking judiciary culture. Similarly, in health care, it is common to find a Francophone medical doctor consulting patients in French in a hospital in the English speaking region and this often leads to poor diagnoses since the medical doctor is not fluent in English. It can be concluded that 'official state bilingualism' in Cameroon is a justification for the national oppression of the Anglophone minorities and it is used to promote the assimilation of Anglophones into a 'one and indivisible' Cameroon.

Bilingualism provides opportunities to Francophone Cameroonians but it serves to hide the oppressive and assimilatory state policies that have become consistent with transforming Cameroonians into monolingual French speaking citizens. Students, teachers and lawyers who demand their territorial rights are branded by the president as extremists and some are arrested, tortured, raped and forcefully imprisoned without trial as opponents of a 'one and indivisible' Cameroon. The dominant Francophone political class gives the impression that it values the bilingual cultures of both Anglophones and Francophone Cameroon as equal but in reality the state uses overt and covert brutal strategies to destroy Anglophone institutions, render its leaders powerless and promote the superiority of French over English in a 'one and indivisible' Cameroon. In the first presidential elections held in 1992, the Anglophone leader Ni John Fru Ndi is believed to have won the elections but the narrative that emerged from the French ruling class was that he is 'Anglophone' and therefore should be perceived as threatening the very existence of the French language and 'francophonism' and all its inherent privileges. As a result, the elections were rigged to favour the French speaking incumbent. Fru Ndi was branded as 'les enemis dans la maison' who could not be president of a dominant French speaking Cameroon.

Conclusion and implications for national identity

This chapter develops a synthesis between the colonial legacy of Britain and France in Cameroon that has resulted in official state bilingualism where English and French are celebrated as visible national identities as opposed to many indigenous languages (Boum & Sadembouo 1999; Makoni & Ulrike 2003). Cameroonian speakers of English and French are able to adopt national social positions that define them either as Anglophone or Francophone. Norton (2000) stresses that language practice is connected to symbolic and cultural capital, which underpins identity. By implication, a speaker therefore speaks from a particular social position belonging to a social network and having access to symbolic resources drawn from socio-economic power and knowledge. French and English as official languages of Cameroon privilege the thought processes and knowledge of former colonial masters than the local languages that bind different tribes together in Cameroon. French and English are deemed to possess a higher value and have become the languages of the media, public service, education, the military and the judiciary whereas local languages have become more regionalized, non-standardized and almost extinct in official discourse. With this can be attributed the silent nature of local Cameroon identities. In official circles, when a Cameroonian is asked to be introduced, the question is often if (s)he is Francophone or Anglophone and not if (s)he is Ewondo, Nso, Bamoun or Bakossi. Hence to draw from the work of Bourdieu (1977), French and English are considered to have more value than local Cameroonian values. While this could be interpreted as a major course for tension and conflict, it is hardly perceived in official state discourses because the languages of instruction in Cameroonian schools, the courts, the military, the media, government, parliament and national businesses are designated to be French and English by government.

Wolf (2001) argues that the preference of colonial languages over indigenous languages leads to a de-territorialization of national identities and a reterritorialization of foreign but more powerful identities. Cameroonians first define themselves in terms of Francophone or Anglophone before their tribal affiliations. However, as has been illustrated above, the more visible form of conflict is in the application of official state bilingualism with a persistent and irreversible overt and covert marginalization of English by the French speaking political class. English language becomes a language of less value and a language of an inferior identity.

Although Cameroonians are able to take on a multiplicity of identities from tribal to national state bilingually recognized identities, linguistic capital still determines opportunities and marginalization in the country. French has been privileged by the Francophone political elite to stand out as a powerful linguistic form associated with the legitimacy and prestige of an enviable social position over English. It has become the language that wields non-negotiable political, social and economic influence in the Cameroonian context. French has more political and cultural capital and Anglophone Cameroonians need it to survive more than Francophone Cameroonians need English. Blackledge (2005) describes the dominance of one language over the other as a situation in which one language, in Cameroon, French, becomes a highly valued monetary currency that pulls everyone towards it so that they can survive professionally, socio-economically and socioculturally (Giles & Coupland 1991). When Anglophone Cameroonians are 'forced' to learn and speak French, they become part of the French community and inadvertently adopt a French identity, its values, its codes and start perceiving the world through the concepts that underpin 'francophonism'. For example, even when Anglophone police officers are posted to serve in the English speaking region, they still communicate to the Anglophones in French, eat like Francophones and issue summons in French and apply French judiciary jargons. I say 'French judiciary jargons' because according to French law, a suspect is guilty until they prove that they are innocent while in English law, a suspect is innocent until proven guilty by the courts. These police officers display assimilatory attitudes which become interpreted as further attempts to assimilate the Anglophones to become Francophone-Anglophones. Their social world becomes structured by the 'francophonism' in them and they align their thoughts with 'francophonism' which they approve as the norm and perceive 'anglophonism' as socially undesirable. As Llamas and Watt (2010) argue: 'Language not only reflects who we are, it is who we are, and its use defines us both directly and indirectly' (see also Giles & Coupland 1991). An example can be illustrated with Bamenda, which is the capital city of the North West Anglophone region and the most populated city in the two Anglophone regions. It is in Bamenda that the first political party to oppose the Francophone ruling class was launched in 1990 leading to protests, civil disobedience, ghost towns, strikes against French domination. Bamenda has become established as the symbol of Anglophone resistance. Moreover, when a Francophone refers to a Cameroonian that 'tu fais comme un Bamenda' (You are behaving like a Bamenda) the Francophone actually means that you are primitive, uncivilized, an extremist who does not know their place in society. Bamenda has become a synonym for the inferiority of Anglophone Cameroonians.

It is important not to treat Anglophone Cameroon as linguistically and ethnically homogenous (Biloa et al., (2008). Anglophones are tribally heterogeneous and they agreed in 1972 to move from an ethnic to a more civic conceptualization of national identity. Oakes and Warren (2007) consider an ethnic national identity as one which is based on common ancestry and shared cultural heritage, whereas civic national identity is manifested in a common loyalty to a territory and rooted in a set of political rights, duties and values (see also Roshwald 2006). Hence, the vote in a plebiscite in 1961 and later in a referendum in 1972 for the Southern Cameroon Anglophone state to unite with La Republique du Cameroun and form one nation was a move towards more national integration than the elaboration of regional identities (Chumbow 1980). That is why English and French were enshrined in the constitution as two national languages of equal status. It is important to point out that one weakness of the unitary constitution was the fact that local indigenous languages were neither mentioned nor protected. However, it is not the subject of this chapter. In hindsight, one wonders if mentioning or protecting the local languages in the constitution would have made any difference in an increasingly assimilatory Francophone political machinery. It is what Wardhaugh (1987) refers to as 'languages in competition'. The tension and conflict is between English and French with English and Anglophones being marginalized, whereas the constitution protects this equal status. That explains why most critical discourses about bilingualism in Cameroon often talk of 'official state bilingualism' (see Bobda 2003; Fonlon 1969; Tchoungui 1983; Kouega 2001; Anchimbe 2005). It is the state that is bilingual while its citizens are monolingually normalized in the dominance of the French language.

On another level, Francophones have started recognizing the value of English as an international window for scholarships and international jobs. A huge appetite for learning English emerged in the early 1990s when Cameroon suffered a great economic recession. The few opportunities that were reserved for Francophones could not sustain them in need and many of them started looking outwards to more affluent societies like Canada, the United Kingdom, Australia and the United States among others. That meant that learning and speaking English became a shift in language identity for the purpose of surviving abroad. Many language centres emerged in Francophone cities where English as a foreign language was taught and where preparations for English language proficiency exams were administered. That trend became an eye opener to most Francophones and those who could afford to send their children to English speaking schools did not hesitate to do so. The recognition that English is widely used in science, technology, mass media, commerce, tourism, industry, academia and the United Nations has pushed Francophone Cameroonians to send their children to English speaking schools. The surge in studies in English language has continued to reshape the identities of Francophone Cameroonians. It is important to note that this emerging trend of Francophones embracing English needs to be interpreted as an enabling factor to acquire an international currency to navigate and negotiate spaces in affluent English speaking countries abroad. It does not make provision for English as an internal currency because the French language internally provides all the openings for Francophone Cameroonians to fulfil their potential.

Internally, French remains the language of upward mobility and a visible identity. Francophone speakers are readily noticeable while Anglophones are less salient. The bilingual language culture of Cameroon provides opportunities for Francophones and marginalization for Anglophones. Most significant work places that provide important services to Cameroonians are located in Yaoundé and other French speaking cities and it is common knowledge that these services do enforce a French-only policy. The Francophone ruling class gives the impression that it values the varied ethnic and cultural backgrounds of Cameroonians through its emphasis on national integration and a bilingual policy. In reality, the policy of bilingualism is used to deny the social and cultural rights of the Anglophones that were protected in the 1972 unification constitution.

This chapter has clearly illustrated that language provides a bridge for opportunities to dominant groups and for prejudice to occur for the less salient social groups (Norton 2000). Although the 1961 Constitution of the Federal country of Cameroon clearly stated that English and French shall remain the two official languages of Cameroon of equal status, article 39 contradicted this by stating that the constitution shall be registered and published in the national gazette, the French version being the valid one. This already undervalues the English status as its official version cannot be referred to in case of any dispute. In addition, the two presidents who have ruled Cameroon from 1961 till today (2017) and their high profile associates are Francophones who do not speak English and they deliver all public, official discourses in French even when on a visit to the English speaking regions of Cameroon, or internationally to any English speaking country or in the Commonwealth of Nations. Therefore, they do not profess any example of bilingualism but rather validate the claim that official state bilingualism in Cameroon means being proficient in the French language. Furthermore all official documents are published in French and only offer poorly translated versions in English (if any). Emphasis is more on having aptly translated documents of English origin into French rather than providing accurate translations of state policies into English. Even the Franc CFA, the currency used in Cameroon, has only French renditions on it and no English translations in what is expected to be a bilingual country of two equal languages.

In 1984, the French speaking president changed the name of the country from the United Republic of Cameroon to the Republic of Cameroon, which is the name of the French speaking Cameroon before reunification of 1961. This was interpreted as removing all the traces of the English speaking country that had agreed to be united to the French speaking Republic of Cameroon. It is interpreted in Anglophone Cameroon that the change of name was an official annexation of the English speaking Cameroon state by the Francophone Republic of Cameroon. Ayafor (2005) argues that bilingualism has been an alienating rather than an integrating policy, often used by the state to keep the Anglophones in an unequal union rather than actually addressing the linguistic complexities of state bilingualism in a multilingual Cameroon.

This chapter provides historical, social and political insights into the language policy and situation in Cameroon that has empowered the Francophones as beneficiaries of official state bilingualism while at the same time marginalizing the Anglophone Cameroonians who have been 'frenchified' in a country of constitutional equal status of French and English. It highlights the genesis of the crisis, which has led to a shutdown of schools, strikes by lawyers, arrests, imprisonment and extra-judiciary killings in English speaking Cameroon where people continue the struggle for self-determinism and the fight against assimilation. The chapter does not only recommend the inclusion of indigenous languages as well as CPE in the language policy of Cameroon but also argues that the language policy should be reconstructed under the banner of multilingualism than official state bilingualism. This will help to restore an eroded culture and identity of Cameroonians in their own country.

References

Alobwede, E. (1998). 'Banning Pidgin English in Cameroon?' *English Today* 53, 14.1: 54–60.

Anchimbe, Eric A. (2005). 'Anglophonism and Francophonism: The Stakes of (Official) Language Identity in Cameroon'. *Alizés: Revue Angliciste de la Réunion* 25/26: 7–26.

Appel, R., & Muysken, P. (1987). *Language Contact and Bilingualism*. London: Edward Arnold.

Ashcroft, B., Griffiths, G., & Tiffin, H. (eds) (1995). *The Post-colonial Reader*. 2nd ed. New York: Routledge.

Ayafor, I. M. (2005). *Official Bilingualism in Cameroon: Instrumental or Integrative Policy?* Proceedings of the 4th International Symposium on Bilingualism. Sommerville, MA: Cascadilla Press.

Biloa, E., & Echu, G. (2008). 'Cameroon: Official Bilingualism in a Multilingual State'. In A. Simpson (ed.), *Language and National Identity in Africa*. Oxford: Oxford University Press. 199–213.

Bitja'a Kody, Z. D. (1999). 'Problématique de la cohabitation des langues'. In Gervais Mendo Ze (ed.), *Le français langue africaine: enjeux et atouts pour la Francophonie*. Paris: Publisud. 80–95.

Blackledge, A. (2005). *Discourse and Power in a Multilingual World*. Amsterdam/ Philadelphia: John Benjamin's Publishing Company.

Bobda, A. (1986). 'Syllable-Stress in Cameroon Standard English'. *Annals of the Faculty of Letters and Social Sciences* 2: 179–97.

Bobda, A. (1993). 'English Pronunciation in Cameroon: Conflicts and Consequences'. *Journal of Multilingual and Multicultural Development* 14.6: 435–45.

Bobda, A. (2002). *Watch Your English! A Collection of Remedial Lessons on English Usage*. Yaoundé: B&K Language Institute.

Bobda, A. (2003). 'Varying Statuses and Perceptions of English in Cameroon'. In *TRANS* 11. www.inst.at (trans/11/bobda11.htm).

Boum, N. S., & Sadembouo, E. (1999). 'L'Atlas linguistique du Cameroun: les langues nationales et leur gestion'. In Mendo Ze, G. (ed), *Le français langue africaine: Enjeux et atouts pour la Francophonie*. Paris: Publisud. 67–79.

Bourdieu, P. (1977). *Outline of a Theory of Practice*. Cambridge: Cambridge University Press.

Breton, R., & Fohtung, B. (1991). *Atlas administratif des langues nationales du Cameroun*. Yaoundé/Paris: CERDOTOLA/CREA – ACCT.hvg Ì.

Cameroon Post (2015). *President Paul Biya's Cabinet Members*. Available online: www. campost.com (accessed 12 February 2016).

Chumbow, B. S. (1980). 'Language and Language Policy in Cameroon'. In N. K. Kale (ed.), *An African Experiment in Nation Building: The Bilingual Republic of Cameroon since Reunification*. Colorado: Westview Press. 281–311.

Chumbow, B. S., & Bobda, A. (2000). 'French in West Africa: A Sociolinguistic Perspective'. *International Journal of the Sociology of Language* 141: 39–60.

Countrymeters.info (2017). *Cameroon Population 2017*. Available online: Countrymeters.info/en/Cameroon (accessed 12 January 2017).

Echu, G. (2004). *The Language Question in Cameroon*. Yaoundé/Bloomington, Linguistic Online, 18 January 2004.

Ethnologue (2006). *Languages of the World*. Available online: www.ethnologue.com (accessed 13 February 2016).

Fanon, F. (1967). *Black Skin, White Mask*. Paris: Edition du Seuil.

Fanso, V. (1989). *Cameroon History for Secondary Schools and Colleges: The Colonial and Post-colonial periods*, vol. 2. London: Macmillan.

Fonlon, Bernard (1969). 'The Language Problem in Cameroon'. *Abbia* 22, 5–40.2: 131–62.

Giles, H., and Coupland, N. (1991). *Language: Contexts and Consequences*. Minton Keynes: Open University Press.

Hoffmann, C. (1991). *Introduction to Bilingualism*. London: Longman.

Jikong, Stephen Y. (2001). 'Official Bilingualism in Cameroon: A Double-Edged Sword'. *Alizés* 19.

Jikong, Stephen Y. (2002). *Language, Thought and Discourse*. Lagos: University of Lagos Press.

Koenig, E., Chia, E., & Povey, J. (eds) (1983). *A Sociolinguistic Profile of Urban Centres in Cameroon*. Los Angeles: Crossroads Press.

Kouega, J. P. (1999). 'Forty Years of Official Bilingualism in Cameroon'. *English Today* 60.15: 38–43.

Llamas, C., & Watt, D. (2010). *Language and Identities*. Edinburgh: Edinburgh University Press.

Mackey, W. F. (1970). 'The Description of Bilingualism'. In J. Fishman (ed.), *Readings in the Sociology of Language*. The Hague: Mouton. 554–84.

Makoni, S., & Ulrike, H. M. (2003). 'Introducing Applied Linguistics in Africa'. *AILA Review* 16: 1–12.

Mba, G., & Chiatoh, B. (2000). 'Current Trends and Perspectives In Mother Tongue Education in Cameroon'. *African Journal of Applied Linguistics* 1: 1–21.

Mbangwana, P. N. (1983) 'The Scope and Role of Pidgin English in Cameroon'. In K. Edna, E. Chia and J. Povey (eds), *The Sociolinguistic Profile of Urban Centres in Cameroon*. Los Angeles: Crossroads Press. 79–92.

Mbangwana, P. N. (1989). *Flexibility and Lexical Usage in Cameroon English*. Yaoundé: University of Yaoundé.

Mbangwana, P. N. (2002). *English Patterns of Usage and Meaning*. Yaoundé: Presses Universitaires de Yaoundé.

Mbassi-Manga, F. (1973). 'English in Cameroon: A Study in Historical Contact Patterns of usage and Current Trends'. Unpublished PhD thesis, University of Leeds.

Mforteh, S. A. (2006). *Cultural Innovations in Cameroon's Linguistic Tower of Babel*. Yaoundé: University of Cameroon.

Nguyen, L., Ropers, S., Ndetiru, E., Zuyderduin, A., Luboga, A., & Hagopiana, A. (2008). *Intent to Migrate among Nursing Students in Uganda: Measures of the Brain Drain in the Next Generation of Health Professionals*. Available online: http://www.human-resources.com/content/6/1/15 (accessed 24 December 2015).

Ndille, R. (2016). 'English and French as Official Languages in Cameroon: The Intentionality of Colonial Representations and the Failure of a Cameroon-Centric Identity: 1884 and After'. *European Journal of Language Studies* 3.2: 17–34.

Ngugi, W. T. (1986). *Decolonising the Mind*. Portsmouth: Heinemann Educational Books.

Norton, B. (2000). *Identity and Language Learning: Gender, Ethnicity and Educational Change*. London: Longman.

Oakes, L., & Warren, J. (2007). *Language, Citizenship and Identity in Quebec*. Houndsmills, Basingstoke: Palgrave Macmillan.

Rosemary, L. Z. (2001). 'The Culture of Aging Individual and Societal Models in Historico-Sociological Perspective'. *Zeitschrift für Gerontologie und Geriatrie* 34.1: 2–8.

Roshwald, A. (2006). *The Endurance of Nationalism: Ancient Roots and Modern Dilemmas*. Cambridge: Cambridge University Press.

Schutz, H., & Six, B. (1996). 'How Strong Is the Relationship between Prejudice and Discrimination? A Meta-analytic Answer'. *International Journal of Intercultural Relations* 20.3–4: 441–62.

Skutnabb-Kangas, T., & Philipson, R. (eds) (1995). *Linguistic Human Rights. Overcoming linguistic Discrimination.* Contributions to the Sociology of Language 67. Berlin & New York: Mouton de Gruyter.

Stumpf, R. (1979). *La politique Linguistique au Cameroun du 1884 a 1960: Comparisons entre les administrations colonials Allemande, Francais et Britannique et le role joue par les societiesmissionaires.* Bern: Peter Langa.

Tebeje, A. (2010). *Brain Drain and the Capacity Building in Africa.* Available online: http://www.idrc.ca/EN/Resources/Publications/Pages/ArticleDetails. aspx?PublicationIS=704 (accessed 23 January 2016).

Ubanako, V. (2004). 'The Language Factor in Cameroon's Young and Pluralistic Democracy: The Case of Pidgin English'. *Geolinguistics* 30: 143–8.

Wardhaugh, R. (1987). *Languages in Competition.* Oxford: Basil Blackwell.

Wolf, H. (2001). *English in Cameroon.* Berlin: Mouton de Gruyter.

7

Refugee Communities: The Disappearance of Voice and Impact on Care and Identity

Henry Kum

Introduction

One of the most challenging questions today is why the 'refugee' has become a label of widespread scorn and ridicule. It is not only a very dreaded concept among host communities but also a contentious topicality in Western stable societies as they strive to balance human rights obligations and border controls. Refugees have been made to represent a stratum of people synonymous to human degradation where persecuted victims have become scapegoats for politicians to work out their electioneering experiments. The reluctance of countries whose people have seen an access to modest privilege to open their doors to those with immeasurable suffering helps to explain a general hostility and rejection of refugees (Smith 1998). In this chapter, it is my contention that within public spaces, refugees have been rendered within a narrow prescribed framework that erodes their voice. There is an expectation that refugees have to fit a particular set of criteria. Arendt (1958) makes a distinction between what and who a person is. A person may be identified and categorized as a woman, Jew, Muslim, asylum seeker or 'boatperson' from characteristics such as dress, appearance or context, such as on an overcrowded boat off Australia's northern coast. However, s/he can reveal who s/he is in particular, only through her/his own speech and action. The individual characteristics that distinguish each unique person can be discerned only through the revelations of that person, gained intersubjectively through interaction and engagement on a basis of equality. The 'what' of a person can only ever be an approximation of humanity, consisting of stereotypes into which individuals are grouped with little or no regard for the uniqueness of each person. To treat a person according to what rather than whom s/he is, Arendt contends, dehumanizes the person, as s/he is denied the opportunity to reveal herself/himself to the world, denied entry to the public sphere as an initiating and equal person and reduced to a representative sample of the category into which s/he has been placed. From the beginning of forced movement of people, the voice of forced migrants continues to disappear from social, political, economic and public life. Seeing refugees as passive recipients of humanitarian aid, as benefactors of host country generosity imposes normative values of people who are begging for care rather than human beings who need enabling in their quest for sanctuary.

Refugees' political lives often disappear into the background, and their 'voices' tend to become apolitical. The term 'refugee voices' becomes synonymous with the personal and human side of the story, marginalizing individual or collective self-representation. Abstracting refugees from specific political, historical and cultural milieus may ultimately lead to the silencing of refugees. While refugees flee their country as political subjects, during their journey they appear to lose political agency to become, upon arrival in host countries, the objects of migration and asylum policies, the beneficiaries of assistance or individuals with traumatic stories. This de-politicization regularly persists after they have settled in their host society. They lose their voice and increasingly become powerless. In this chapter, I use case studies to discuss instances of how the voiceless refugee is marooned into an inescapable cycle of 'silence'. In order to do this, I retrace some historical facts to buttress the point that refugeeness is not a recent concept, which as its ancient character seems to suggest is as old as the voicelessness of refugee. The erosion of refugee voices has evolved with multiple reconceptualization of who refugees are, all summing up to silence people with silent voices. I go further to illustrate insightful reflections on the impact of these silent voices on refugee identities and their sense of worth. The chapter is grounded on the theoretical underpinning of care and rights in order to posit that the absence of a voice is similar to the absence of care.

Historical context of refugee migration into the United Kingdom

By establishing a snapshot of migration trends into the United Kingdom, this section draws from history to position the erosion of voice in refugees as a result of the 'othering' that is inherent in the identities of forced migrants. Forced movement has been on the increase in recent years and people forcibly displaced because of persecution, conflict, generalized violence and human rights violations as on 31 December 2015 was estimated by the United Nations High Commissioner for Refugees (UNHCR) at 65.3 million. Of that number, 40.8 million were internally displaced persons, 21.3 million were refugees and 3.2 million were asylum seekers most of them coming from countries like Syria, Afghanistan, Iran and the continent of Africa. The exact number of immigrants is not known today but figures in 2006 put their numbers to about 191 million (UNFPA 2006; Deen 2006). Global Issues (2008) gives a break down and adds in their report that immigration has doubled in the past 50 years. It has been estimated that 119 million immigrants live in developed countries; 20 per cent (approximately 38 million) live in the United States of America alone, making up 13 per cent of its population; 33 per cent of all immigrants live in Europe and 75 per cent live in just twenty-eight countries. It is safe to posit that migrants are a growing community in many countries, for example, the richer countries of the European Union, United States, Canada and Australia. Migration now shapes virtually most national societies on the planet, playing a crucial role in how our societies are constituted and how different populations link and come together as well as how nation states form political relationships with one another. There are increasing debates both historical and contemporary about migration and these debates have an impact on the analysis of present and future patterns of migration, policy development, economic development and social development. The focus of this chapter is on refugees, which involves forced migrants fleeing from persecution and this dates as far back as the seventeenth century.

In the late seventeenth century, the word 'refugee' started gaining prominence in the political circles in England following the arrival of the Huguenots, French Protestant refugees (Rutter 2003; 2004; 2006; Greig 2009). But the ratification of the Geneva Convention of 1951 on refugees, by most countries, including the United Kingdom, meant that people fleeing their country of origin, or unable to return to it owing to a well-founded fear of persecution for reasons of race, religion, nationality, membership of a particular group or political opinion, can officially request and fight for refugee status. This change was provoked by mass displacements of people during the two world wars especially after the Second World War.

Cole (2004) identifies three periods of immigration to Western Europe since the Second World War. First, primary labour migration between 1950, and 1973–74, driven mainly by West European reconstruction. Second, secondary/family migration which accelerated in the mid-1970s; and third, that which developed in the aftermath of the end of the Cold War in 1989–90. Gedde (2003) looks at the third migration phase in the United Kingdom and comments that in Britain, economic crises in the 1970s and the 1980s, welfare state pressures and changed welfare state ideologies since the 1990s have structured people's perception of those migrants deemed to be bogus. He stretches this further by adding that it is the ways in which such migrants are categorized by institutions and organizations in the receiving countries that creates these perceptions, rather than the migrants themselves. Yet there are documented trends of systemic migration of people to the British Isles (BCAR 1969; 1980; 1981).

Hungarian refugees who were evacuated to the United Kingdom from camps in Austria in 1957 started arriving in the United Kingdom. Between 1939 and 1949, nearly 3,60,000 Polish refugees including other eastern Europeans, Jews and Belgians who were fleeing Nazi persecution arrived in the United Kingdom (Sword 1989; Rutter et al. 2007). Hungarians who, like Poles, came in the aftermath of the Second World War and later the Chileans and Vietnamese were programme refugees because their immigration status had been granted overseas and, after arrival in the United Kingdom, they were also entitled to a resettlement programme comprising housing and social welfare support. Many were resettled in reception hostels and later to large reception centres and some found work mainly in construction, mining and agricultures as well as unskilled industries experiencing a shortage of labour (Ambrozy 1984; Kunz 1985). The poor reception and coordination of the massive influx of these group of refugees led to the formation of the British Council for Aid Refugees (BCAR) in 1950 (Rutter et al. 2007). Having ratified the Geneva Convention in 1957 Britain saw the need and regard for the refugees' welfare in terms of settlement, integration and employment and BCAR started supplying flats/accommodation to the refugees especially for those that had found work (Refugee Council 2010; Rutter et al. 2007). Following the Soviet invasion of Czechoslovakia in 1968, another group of 5,000 from Czechoslovakia arrived in the United Kingdom and was received with mixed reaction; some granted temporary visas and permission to work as guest workers while others were refused sanctuary. The welcoming of these passive victims of war was becoming problematic to the host community.

The demands of expanding postwar economy meant that Britain, like most other European countries, was faced with major shortages of labour (Castles and Cossack 1985). The demand for labour was met by a variety of sources, including 5,00,000 refugees, displaced persons and ex-prisoners of war from Europe between 1946 and 1951 and a further 3,50,000 European nationals between 1945 and 1957 (Sivanandan 1976). However, the overwhelming majority of migrants who came to Britain were from the Republic of Ireland, the Indian subcontinent and the Caribbean (Miles 1986). The labour migration from the Indian subcontinent and the Caribbean proceeded by informal means with little effort made to relate unemployment to existing vacancies. Instead, it was left to the free market forces to determine the size of immigration (Sivanandan 1976; Universities UK 2005).

Those industries where the demand for labour was greatest actively recruited Asian, black and other minority ethnic workers in their home countries (Fryer 1984; Ramdin 1987). Employers such as the British Transport Commission, the London Transport Executive, the British Hotels and Restaurant Association and the Regional Hospitals Board all established arrangements with Caribbean governments to ensure a regular supply of labour (Ramdin 1987). By 1958, a decade of labour migration comprised 1,25,000 Caribbean and 55,000 Indian and Pakistani immigrants in England (Fryer 1984). They came to occupy the overwhelmingly semi-skilled and unskilled positions in the English labour market. Furthermore, they found themselves disproportionately concentrated in certain types of manual work characterized by shortage of labour, shift working, unsocial hours, low pay and unpleasant working environment.

Historical links between Britain and many colonies proved to be a major push towards immigration. Britain's links with Africa and Asia were particularly long standing. For example, there were African soldiers and slaves in the Roman imperial army that occupied the southern part of the British island for three and a half centuries before the Anglo-Saxons (the English) arrived (Fryer 1984). There has been a long history of contact between Britain and India leading to the presence of Indians in Britain (Visram 1986). India and many countries in Africa and the Caribbean had been colonized by Britain and were just becoming independent. Many people from these countries had worked in factories that helped sustained Britain in the war. After the war, wages were higher in Britain than in the colonies and it became a natural step for some of their population to migrate here. The relationship with Britain as shown above was the reason why people from these countries moved to Britain.

In the 1950s, there was a growing concern within Parliament, the media and the major political parties of the dangers of unrestricted immigration (Cole & Virdee 2005). Britain was used to ruling people with different cultures in the colonies but having them living in the United Kingdom in large numbers was a new experience. This contributed to an important shift in public policy towards migrant labour from one of support for unrestricted immigration of non-whites to one that stressed that the immigration of non-whites had to be curbed if the social fabric and cohesion of the country was not to be irreparably undermined. As a result, in 1962, an Immigration Act was introduced which had as its primary objective the curbing of non-white labour from the Indian subcontinent and the Caribbean with immigration from the Republic of Ireland unaffected (Miles & Phizacklea 1984).

With Britain being a signatory of the 1951 Refugee Convention that guarantees the right for every persecuted human being to apply for asylum, the economic factor ceased to be the only cause and type of migration to the United Kingdom (Kum 2006; Kum et al. 2008). People who suffered persistent fear of religious, social, political or ethnic persecution in their home country could apply for asylum in any safe country including the United Kingdom. In Europe from the 1980, the wind of new democracies swept through the east especially with the fall of the then Soviet Union and dictators were tested and overthrown. Human rights were preached the world over. Crises in Kosovo, the Middle East, Afghanistan, Iraq, Iran and Lebanon threatened civilian peace and stability and more people moved about in search of freedom and safety. Britain received most of those who were able to make it to the UK borders.

In 1972, the Ugandan dictator Idi Amin had expelled the entire Asian population from Uganda, blaming them of controlling the economy for their own ends. He gave them ninety days to leave the country. Most of them who already had roots and relations in the United Kingdom migrated there. Despite public hostility, the British government accepted 28,000 Ugandan Asians who held British travel documents and some 400 stateless households (Kushner & Knox 1999). In 1974 and 1975, about 10,000 Cypriots fled to the United Kingdom following the partition of the island. This group only joined a larger Cypriot community who had earlier migrated to work in the United Kingdom or had fled ethnic violence from groups that supported the independence of Cyprus. Around the same time, about 1973–76, over a million Chileans (Kay 1987) fled their homeland following the military coup that toppled the Chilean socialist government of Salvador Allende. Due to public campaigns from trade unions, the media and labour party activists, about 3,000 Chileans were admitted into the United Kingdom (World University Service-WUS UK 1974). They were granted refugee status, housed in reception centres and later resettled in housing by local committees.

This was followed by the admission of 24,000 Vietnamese between 1979 and 1992 following the fall of Saigon at the end of the Vietnam War, and a further 1,500 from camps in Hong Kong and later 10,000 more from Hong Kong (Refugee Council 1991). A second Vietnamese programme ran between 1983 and in 1988 and comprised three groups: boat rescues, members of the orderly departures programme from Vietnam (4,475 people) and family reunion cases (Duke & Marshall 1995). The third and final admission programme, administered by Refugee Action, took place in 1989 when the government agreed to admit a further 2,000 Vietnamese refugees.

The 1980s marked a turning point in both asylum migration and the government responses to asylum seekers. Before 1980s, most refugees either had come from a small number of eastern European countries, or had been admitted as programme refugees. The 1980s saw a much more diverse range of asylum seekers arrive into the United Kingdom, from African and Asian countries as well as Eastern Europe. Between 1980 and 1988, the two largest refugee groups to enter the United Kingdom were Iranians and Sri Lankan Tamils (Rutter et al. 2007). Other significant groups of asylum seekers were Iraqis, Turkish nationals (including Kurds), Poles, Ugandans, Ghanaians, Ethiopians, Eritreans and Somalis. This was essentially a migration to London between 1980 and 1997 and it was estimated that some 90 per cent of the United Kingdom's refugees lived in London (Refugee Council 1997). Asylum applications increased significantly in 1989, with 11,640 lodged that year, and continued to increase in the 1990s (Refugee Council 1997). Most of the new arrivals came from conflict zones: Bosnia-Herzegovina, Eastern Turkey, Ethiopia, Eritrea, Sierra Leone, Somalia, the Democratic Republic of Congo, Angola, Iraq, Sri Lanka, Columbia and Afghanistan.

Nevertheless, despite more complex migratory flows, total asylum applications started dropping (British Refugee Council 1989; Rutter 2003; 2006). This has been due to much restrictive legislation, in the form of restricted asylum seekers' economic and citizenship rights; new immigration rules on welfare benefits and the use of biometric passports, finger printing and high rejection rate of asylum applications (Morris 1998; Levy 1999; Rutter 2003; Refugee Council 2010). Owing to tighter immigration controls, acceptance of persons either recognized as refugees, or hence granted asylum or who were instead granted leave to remain increased during 1998 following the publication of the white paper entitled 'Fairer, Faster and Firmer – A Modern Approach to Immigration and Asylum' (National Statistics 2005). Several proposals contained in this document were implemented, as there was no need for primary legislation. Many people who applied for asylum prior to July 1993 and were still awaiting an initial decision were granted settlement from 1999 under measures aimed at reducing the asylum backlog. Decisions on applications made in the period from July 1993 to December 1995 were also considered sympathetically.

However, many people from new conflict zones like Bosnia-Herzegovina, eastern Turkey, Ethiopia, Eritrea, Sierra Leone, Somalia, the Democratic Republic of Congo, Angola, Iraq, Sri Lanka and Columbia kept on arriving in the United Kingdom. During 1994–95, Kosovar Albanians and Algerians arrived in great numbers and many were unaccompanied children. There were insufficient hostels and temporary accommodation available in London, where most asylum seekers lived. By 1997, significant numbers of asylum seekers were moved to accommodation outside London, often to poor quality hostels in seaside towns (Rutter et al. 2007). Some arrangements were also made with private property owners whose homes were mostly located in deprived outer-city estates.

From the discussion above, the United Kingdom has experienced immigration flows stretching from immigrant conquerors such as the Romans, Anglos, Saxons and Vikings and, during the quest for colonies, the British Empire expanded to include many other regions of the world (Cole et al. 2008). After the great world wars and during the political changes in the Soviet Union and Eastern Europe, more people moved to Britain and the crisis in Iraq, Syria and Afghanistan have continued to push refugee figures up. The complex immigration trends show a complex mix of identities and cultures arriving the United Kingdom and Europe and there was never any active political move to position these new arrivals as active members of the communities. Their voices were eroded and consequently their identities were compromised.

Refugees identities: dehumanization and rehumanization

Identity is a topic that has been dealt with in different forms including the discourse on migration. Once refugeeness is discussed with identity, the issue arises of 'hyphenated' identity. Identity is significant on discourse about assimilation and integration and this raises conflict within the concept of 'structural versus identificational integration' as described by Lucassen (2005). While structural integration can be measured more or less objectively by mapping social mobility, school results, housing patterns and so on, identificational integration is subjective and refers to the extent to which migrants and their offspring keep on regarding themselves as primarily different and to the extent that they are viewed as 'primarily different by the rest of society' (Tololyan et al. 2004: 2).

Theories of identity development propose specific stages, which children and adolescents progress through. Phinney (1996), for example, suggests that earlier stages known as stage one reflect a time when the identity in question is neither explored nor committed to (which he refers to as *Diffusion*), or stage two when is it accepted on the basis of others' opinions (*Foreclosure*). Some kind of discriminatory life event may push the young person into the next stage known as *Moratorium*, where exploration of, and immersion in, one's ethnicity occurs. The final stage is *Identity Achievement*, where the young person is clear and confident in his or her identity, though this does not necessarily imply a high degree of involvement with the ethnic group. A further stage is thought to be the most sophisticated, but it is not necessary that all individuals will achieve a developmental progression through the stages and research indicates that individuals can regress as well as progress through the stages. Phinney's model relates primarily to adolescence, though other models are tailored to pre-adolescent childhood and emphasize individual differences to a greater or lesser extent.

These developmental models allow critical examination of developing identities, while the broader Social Identity Theory (Tajfel & Turner 1979) can help when exploring the psychological (mental health, attitudes, beliefs) and behavioural (actions directed at group members) consequences of identification. This theoretical framework has the potential to understand the extent to which group-level behaviour is emphasized as well as the type and strength of identification that refugees report in relation to performance towards their self-image in public spaces. For example, awareness of the practices and values of the school, church, courts, hospitals, parks, shopping centres, school ethos, political institutions, rights and responsibilities of the host community can affect the way refugeeness is enacted.

With restricted voices, it becomes difficult to understand how to enact self in public spaces in a new society where refugee rights are limited, contested and mediatized. Individual identities become dormant in favour of group identities as refugeeness becomes a homogenous label. I welcome Bakhtin's (1984) theory on identity, which is further explored by Kearney (2003; 2004). In the theory, the complexity and dilemmas of crossing borders, geographically, politically and psychologically, show how complex the process of negotiating identities can be. Kearney (2003) looks at the complexity which is central to how humans maintain 'a coherent, yet ever changing, sense of self identity. It is how this connects with cultural heritage'. Goodman (1989) has written that the way we speak is an emblem of who we are and if refugees do not negotiate the social and cultural capitals of the host societies, voice becomes a symbolic gesture, at best unused and at worst silent. As refugee identities become homogenized by the host community, voice also becomes a privilege and not a right; it is controlled by the host community and rationed out conditionally. If rationed out, refugees are told how to use this in the top down approach of policy and integration expectations. Hill and Hessari (1990) reject this micro management of voice through identity homogination. Through the lens of culture, they elaborate on the fact that cultures are not as monolithic or homogenous as it is often assumed. For example, the 'blanket label "Africa" embraces many nations, cultures, religions, and languages and tries to impose a camouflaging, even patronising unity over a vast, diverse land mass' (Hill & Hessari 1990: 2). Kearney (2003) agrees with Hill and Hessari (1990) by arguing that cultures are dynamic and changing especially as they interact with histories, expectations and migration or conquest practices across borders. So for host communities to be pre-deterministic of who should belong to this boxed-in group-identity is to restrict the refugee voices; deny them the same spaces that are needed to individualize their identities and deconstruct the ascribed homogeneity believed to encompass them. To tell refugees who they are rather than to allow them spaces to act out their identities is a continuation of the erosion of their voices.

Subscription to the fluidity of identities (see postmodernist investigations of identity in Hall 1996; Brah 2007) and its multifaceted nature, viewed as being about belonging based on the recognitions of what is shared with some people and what is different with others is very important to how refugee identities are viewed. Vigouroux (2005: 254) carried out research with Francophone Africans in Cape Town, South Africa, to understand how language practice and identity repertoire are constructed among Francophone Black Africans in Cape Town. He concludes by showing that modifications of any dimensions of space can produce variations in language practice and lead to change in identities. He found out that space influences language practice and attitudes and that 'territoriality' indicates the way a speaker negotiates their position in a space. According to Vigouroux, '"[T]erritoriality" . . . thus provides a dynamic and interactional frame for understanding how different layers of context are interrelated and how they shape each other.' This adds relevance to the need to investigate the individual identities than grouping all refugees as a homogenous group who think the same, all seeking safety, unable to return and can or should claim benefits or do menial jobs. This imposes a normative value on all victims of forced migration and only the negotiated spaces for refugee voices can deconstruct this imposed normative value.

In the United Kingdom, government and community labels of the public define the refugee according to imposed normative characteristics. In a top down policy approach to refugee issues it is common to hear refugees referred to as bogus asylum seeker, failed asylum seeker, NHS destroyer, benefit cheat, health tourist, absconder, overstayer among other denigrating identities. Some right-wing media organs seek to criminalize refugee communities with derogatory media captions like 'How to destroy a nation', 'Destruction of a sense of belonging', 'Asylum seekers hit jackpot', 'Africa – World's begging bowl', 'The right to discriminate', 'How to colonize Britain', 'Foreign Invader', 'Africans are less intelligent than Westerners' and so on (*The Independent* 2008). 'Tabloid Press stokes up racism against immigrants' (Workers Power 2007). Such media captions do have a damaging effect on self-esteem of refugees and offer a stereotypical view of refugees by subverting a more accurate understanding of who they are and why they are forced to flee their homelands (Cole & Virdee 2005; Fielden 2008). This has fuelled anti-refugee rhetoric from some members of host communities who have emerged with anti-immigration ideologies within the European Union, Australia and the United States motivated by fear that immigration is out of control (UNHCR 1993; 1994). Such has been the reactions of governments in Serbia, Hungary, Macedonia, Bosnia, Romania and recently the United States of America concerning the acceptance and resettlement of Syrian, Afghan, Iraqi refugees among others, who have arrived through various borders. Therefore, in these spaces where refugees are talked about, talked down and defined rather than talked with or listened to, there is no place for their voices to counter such negative perceptions and provide a true picture of who they are. Some case studies below will further explain the tensions of refugee voicelessness and ascribed identities.

Case studies: public spaces and voicelessness

Coll (2001) in a study involving 308 Dominican, Cambodian and Portuguese refugee parents in the United States, whose children were between the ages of 6 and 12, confirmed anecdotal complaints about parents' lack of interest in their children's education. In the survey, immigrant parents overall reported a relatively low level of involvement in a range of educational participation, including meetings with teachers, setting rules about when to be home after school and establishing a place in the house for homework. The survey established that pre-immigration experiences with literacy and formal schooling, as well as aspects of the receiving communities, all influenced the differences between ethnic groups. As a result, the Portuguese who have been part of the immigration wave of that part of United States since 1800s and have a well-established community registered a higher participation rate compared to the other two immigrant groups. The immigrant groups included political immigrants (refugees) and economic immigrants but the study illustrates considerations that are necessary in creative active community groups including refugee community groups. Coll's (2001) study found that lack of participation was because refugee parents felt that they were never listened to and that their opinions did not count even when making decisions about their pre-exile conditions or about their children. The schools always knew more than the refugees and handed down value-laden judgements, which made refugee parents feel objectified rather than subjectified. The absence of voice here in school spaces affected attainment and achievement of refugee pupils.

In addition, McCollum (1996) and Bhachu (1985) explored the importance of recognizing different cultures because of persistent migration. McCollum (1996) researched with migrants in the United States and established that there is a tendency for educators at all levels to complain about today's refugee parents whom they claim are the real source of children's difficulties. In his research, he concluded that refugee parents' jobs, lack of understanding of policies, their language difficulties and values are the weaknesses that need to be addressed for effective communication, which can lead to effective social inclusion. The issues that McCollum points out above account for why refugee voices are not visible. In the same light, Bhachu (1985) looked at cultural conceptions of immigrant parents in the United States where educators tend to believe that parents should ideally be interventionists in their children's learning. He added that middle-class parents demonstrate that they value education and are concerned about their children's learning by attending meetings, volunteering for activities, helping their children with homework and ensuring their children begin school knowing their numbers and letters as preparation for school literacy instruction. In this research, McCollum is celebrating what middle-class parents are doing for their children's education and he seems to implore refugee parents to do the same. The middle-class normative values are imposed on refugee parents, who do not have the social and cultural capital, have come from a different culture and education system and may have linguistic issues. McCollum fails to create spaces for policy dialogue where refugee parents will articulate their difficulties and propose solutions for the right kind of support required. The author uses middle-class voice to silence the refugee voices. While parents from diverse cultural backgrounds may not demonstrate the expected degree of engagement with the school according to whites or middle-class values from superior ethnic groups and communities, they can show that they value and support their children in other ways like ensuring their children's regular school attendance.

Writing on cultural transmission among Italian refugee families living in Nottingham, Ganga (2004) interviewed thirty-five individuals from ten three-generational families. She found that identity was developed through a continuous exchange between the self and a variety of 'others' both within and without the immigrant group. The physical invisibility of the group played an important role in the identity building process. The importance of her discussion on identity as a continuous exchange of the self and a variety of others and the role played by religion shows the fluidity of identities across religion, gender, cultural and social grounds. Identity is a continuous exchange, a story that needs to be narrated. If refugees lose their voices and are not given the spaces to articulate their perception of self, who they are and what they stand for, they become instrumentalized as passive beneficiaries of the generosity of Western governments. In Ganga's research, the significance lies with how policy recognizes this, rather than initiating identities to be fixed and placed into boxes that can be ticked endlessly.

Ganga (2007: 45) writes about the family as a place where the older generations work hard to keep Italian traditions and language alive; but that the English school was the one site, unforeseen by the parents, where the children of immigrants start to acquire that 'hyphen' in their identity, which will require them to come to terms with some inexplicable or incoherent sides of their close ones' attitudes or behaviour, when in contact with the 'others'. Ganga's results here show how this has become difficult to achieve because the refugee is the silent recipient of the policy and discourse on integration, on multiculturalism without having the space to actively contribute. Refugee's voicelessness exposes them to become victims of assimilation.

Hopkins (2007) interviewed young Muslim refugees who had become British citizens living in Glasgow and Edinburgh about their feelings with respect to their Scottish and Muslim identities. Hopkins's informants used different markers to identify their Scottishness; such as 'place of birth, length of residence, a commitment to place as well as upbringing and accent'; one of his informants said: 'Everything is Scottish about me . . . Yeah, I'm a practising Muslim, and I practice Islam, but that doesn't mean I'm not Scottish. I do all the things that other Scottish people do. I play football, I go out.' Another informant used the imagery of a 'blue square', which formed the title of Hopkins's paper, showing how he feels that his Muslim identity and his Scottishness are intertwined:

I don't think there's a tension at all . . . I'm Scottish Muslim because I'm Scottish and I was born in Scotland. So it's my culture, it's my background, it's my home.

Muslim is my goal. Being Muslim is my philosophy or my belief system. It doesn't contradict my nationality in any way because they deal with different questions, you know. It's like being a . . . blue square . . . A blue square, it's blue and it's a square. Its being a square doesn't interfere with it being blue. It's being blue doesn't interfere with it being a square. (68)

Another of his informants, however, felt that others could never see him as Scottish:

The first thing is my colour, and secondly my accent . . . thirdly if I was to abandon my Muslim morals and things, yeah, and I was to become like totally westernised, I still wouldn't be accepted by you lot as I'll still be seen as an outsider, you know what I mean. It's the same in Scotland; you've got to be white to be Scottish. (72)

Hopkins raises the fact that the feelings of 'otherness and difference' can be either 'enforced upon refugees through others or through personal choice' and states that 'being Scottish still has strong connections with whiteness, and either secularism or other religions' (73). I agree with Hopkins that 'otherness and difference' can be 'enforced through others' but I disagree with his conclusion that 'otherness' can be enforced through personal choice. The refugees may choose to embrace the identity of the host community but such a choice is irrelevant because choice goes with rights. If they do not have the rights that nationals of the host community enjoy, they cannot express the informed choice of belonging. They may agree to belong but their hosts who deny them those rights may not consider them as belonging. The last interviewee articulates this view and they do not have the voice to articulate and enforce the desire to belong and enjoy the rights of belonging. The process of migration undermines what Alheit and Dausien (2002: 15) refer to as their 'biographically acquired landscape of knowledge' and as the case studies above illustrate, refugees are forced to learn new behaviours, understand new rules and adapt to new values and another type of social organization. This is necessary in order to empower them with a voice capital although this does not usually amount to that because of the contested rights of refugees. Castel (2003), Lyn and Lea (2003), Bloch (2002) and Zetter (2007) agree that much of these contested rights are related to the homogenous identification of refugees which creates negative association and reinforced by political and popular discourses, which represent refugees as a burden to an overstretched welfare system, as a security threat and as a feared other threatening national identity and social cohesion. These negative associations show the imbalance between refugee care and their rights as a result of the erosion of their voices.

Refugee voice, refugee care and refugee rights: worlds apart

Two related themes are discussed in this section as a response to contest popular discourse on how human rights pattern refugee care. This section argues that care is a right to people in need and if refugees are fleeing persecution, they are a vulnerable community in need of care. The absence of voice reinforces a particular contemporary problem, although not entirely new, of the degradation of the idea of refugeeness. This in effect predicts the limits of care. The reconciliation of justice and care as an inclusive impartial moral value can and needs to be protected by the voices of the actors involved. Smith (1998) has argued that a reconciliation of the tensions between the conflicting claims of justice and care is important, if a sense of empathetic engagement is to have any implications for the quality of collective social life of vulnerable or marginalized people in need. As he explains, in many Western states the absence of such a sensibility creates the stark marginalization and exclusion of many vulnerable groups, especially refugees who depend on the very Western communities for care and protection. Therefore, it is not difficult to see how the ethic of care that rejects the false dichotomy between justice and care can have substantive implications for the everyday lives of marginalized groups like refugees. Citing Barry (1995) and O'Neill (1996), Smith argues that impartial justice and Gilligan-inspired care can be reconciled in that they function at different orders or levels of moral deliberation – there is a set of rules of justice at the general level, but there is also room for care in shaping one's life. Justice is about seeking supporting institutions and policies that reject injury and suffering so that caring activities are enabled. Can justice and care as rights of refugees be protected where they are rationed out to refugees who have no say in what is handed down to them? We all need care in life: a disabled person, a mentally ill person, a child, the elderly, a sick person, a servant and even a master. Care goes with voice, which underpins justice and rights. However, in the world today, refugee identities are devalued and they are assimilated to function as victims without any social and political spaces because they lack a voice to be heard and to articulate this persistent injustice. That voice is absent in their personal circumstances, in political circles where policies are adopted about them and in the media where host community sentiments are whipped up against refugeeness in a far from objective manner rendering them to be represented as victims only.

Tronto (1993) and Clement (1996) posit a similar response: in their writings, justice is connected to care, solidarity, compassion and empathy. Both justice and care, it is argued, are involved in how people live their lives. Both are about the inclusion of different perspectives on situations; justice cannot be reduced to care and vice versa, for each is required for the other. Thus, justice connected to care does not accept the status quo unquestioningly, but seeks progressive change 'on the basis of an enlarged and continuously enlarging moral sphere that seeks to respect and engage the largest number of moral viewpoints possible' (Gleeson and Kearns 2001). Recognition of value pluralism (Berlin 1990; 2002), however, does not mean the abandonment of general principles or the rejection of progressive policy change that has real effects on the inclusion of marginalized groups (like refugees) in society. The fact that refugees on seeking sanctuary in civilized communities where freedom of expression is a right are immediately cramped into detention centres is seen by many as a rejection of their voice and power. They are represented by legal practitioners who are devoid of compassion about persecution and sometimes are often deported to the same countries where wars and conflict are the persecuting forces. This is because their plight lacks narrative spaces and their stories are either unheard or untold. The context of expression requires an understanding of what it means to seek sanctuary and also what it means to be at the mercy of the person who is listening.

Furthermore, a focus on care could provoke policy changes about the justice of the treatment of refugees. In this way, care and justice are not seen as competitors, but as allies in the formation of democratic and inclusive practices and policies. As Clement (1996) asserts, care helps us recognize our justice obligations to others (regardless of whether they are close or distant from us). Thus, the capacity to empathize with others who suffer requires something more than a simple focus on relationality (found in feminism and communitarian discourses); it requires renewed political economies and institutional arrangements grounded in justice. This is to advocate a concept and practice of an enlarged and constantly enlarging justice through the reconceptualization of an ethic of care. An ethic of care, then, expands the consideration of justice obligations to others, a process that produces new and unexpected moral imaginaries of 'caring communities' (Gleeson & Kearns 2001). This should form the pinnacle of democratic citizenship as an instrument of care. In addition, democratic citizenship functions better with the expansion of justice to recognize those who are the 'others', those who are not privileged to be 'us' and coming from societies that devalues their right to democratic expression of self through voice. It involves accepting that refugees are different but in need of the same values that sustain our thinking of freedom and liberty as instruments of justice. It requires negotiating their care and caring with them rather than caring for them in a top down approach where their voices are stifled.

In another development, in exploring the relational aspects of care and the question of how far we should care, Sevenhuijsen (1998; 2000) examines the ethic of care as a principle of modern citizenship and suggests that care can be seen as providing a more universalistic set of ethical principles for public life rather than being defined as intensely personal. Thus, drawing together different strands of the ethics of care, a new remoralization of care, that is, care as an inclusive moral issue (Kabeer 2005) is utilized in conjunction with notions of caring as a humanitarian practice (Sevenhuijsen 2000; Tronto 2001). This reconceptualization highlights the right of each citizen to be able to give and receive care. More specifically, Knijn and Kremer (1997) argue that citizenship should be reconceptualized so that every citizen will be a caregiver sometime in their life: all human beings were dependent on care when they were young, and will need care when they are ill, handicapped, frail or old. Care is thus not a women's issue but a moral humanitarian issue. Although this approach to caring as a humanitarian practice is clearly contextualized within the boundaries of modern nation-states and citizenship which reflects winners and losers in the political game (Tronto 2001), there is no reason why human beings should be responsible (as caregivers) only to those with whom we share citizenship rights (or have shared understandings). There is no need why 'the other' should be stripped of the power of their voice and have care rationed out to them in measurable proportions because they are the 'other'. If this is not checked, care ceases to be a humanitarian moral issue and polarises the societies, between those who have the right to care (us) and those who should be deprived of care (refugees). It becomes an antipodal society of 'them' and us', which contrasts with justice and democratic citizenship and inclusivity. And to break the stigma of 'us' versus 'them', the others need to be empowered by listening to them, acknowledging their humanity and sense of social and cultural identities and providing them with the right democratic spaces to belong, to be heard and to regain a sense of worth which has been lost through flight.

Both Knijn and Kremer's as well as Tronto's accounts do not unseat the image of the citizen within classical definitions of citizenship in modern nation states. However, Kershaw (2005) argues that human rights are above any responsibility connected to citizenship rights, the point being that those to whom one may be accountable (morally or legally) need not be members of one's own legal community. So Western states need not only care for their citizens but also those in need like refugees and this comes across as a fundamental human principle. That right to expression needs to be challenged by deconstructing and challenging right-wing, mediatized anti-refugee discourse and giving them the voice to display the values inherent in their respective identities.

Morris (2001) also makes an appeal for an inclusive ethics of care built on the concept of human rights. As she writes:

> We need an ethics of care which is based on the principle that to deny the human rights of our fellow human beings is to deny our own humanity... Most importantly we need an ethics of care which, while starting from the position that everyone has the same human rights, also recognizes the additional requirements that some people have in order to access those human rights. (15)

Clearly, such an ethics of care differs from the ethics of care proposed by feminist moral philosophers working in the tradition of Gilligan, Noddings and Tronto. For Morris, an ethic of care is a measure of justice based on access to care as a human right. The political recognition of caring – that is, the practice of caring as political citizenship (see also Kershaw 2005) – raises the issue of rethinking the meaning(s) of the politics of care. For instance, caring as a democratic practice forms the basis for an approach that rejects the discrimination of individuals (refugees and others) by those in authority (policymakers, immigration officers, etc.) on grounds of their ethnicity. This approach creates openings for a public dialogue that recognizes the visible labour contributions that refugees make to the prosperity of many American, Australian, Canadian and European countries, as opposed to the lack of rights and recognition accorded to them by the state (Fortier 2005; Zembylas 2010). An active political discussion about the changing nature of care opens up a number of possibilities within which to develop renewed institutional policies and practices concerning immigration. Refugees may not even have the required capitals to recognize where their voices could be articulated and by not recognizing this difference, host communities and governments are turning a blind eye by compromising the spaces necessary for self-expression. By not recognizing the handicaps refugees face at the level of language, difference in education, cultural practices, gender interpretations among others, policymakers cannot develop the right policies to empower refugee voices. The ability to recognize that refugees may have additional requirements to access rights in a specific country means that governments can help to identify mechanisms that enhance those additional requirements as enablers for refugee voices. There is a difference between equality and equity. While equality requires everybody to be provided equal opportunities and a level playing field to function, equity recognizes that those with additional needs require more resources proportionate to their needs in order to enable them to fulfil their potentials. In addition, a look at the torture, suffering and unsafe cross-border corridors that refugees negotiate to reach safety, added to interrupted education, work and family life, strengthens the case that they have additional requirements to access rights in receiving communities. They need the spaces to articulate what those additional needs are.

Most industrialized countries seems to make an effort in the direction of Geras (1995) and Corbridge (1993) who invite humans to empathize with one another especially those who are disadvantaged like refugees. And as Singer (1995: 222) earlier suggested, '[W]e can see that our own sufferings and pleasures are very like the sufferings and pleasures of others, and that there is no reason to give less consideration to the sufferings of others, because they are others'. Tronto (1993; 2001) sustains this line of reasoning further by stating that care should be institutionalized because a right to care (like all welfare rights) is linked to social responsibility and not only to individual duty. In addition, the right to be heard, the right to a voice and the right to self-expression are all parts of the social responsibility that must be supervised by every government worthy of a democratic culture. The lived experiences of refugees, their experiences of integration in the host communities, whether good or bad, need to be articulated for effective integration and social policies.

These authors all agree on care as inseparable from human nature and this leads to the conclusion that the politics of care could provide useful guidance on how humans, countries and political blocs like the EU could interrogate their policies and approach to refugee crisis. Cohen et al. (2000: 40) consider 'research as a tool for advancing knowledge, promoting progress and enabling humans to relate more effectively to their environment, accomplish their purposes and resolve conflicts'. An interrogation of the policy context of the United Kingdom, EU and all democratic societies on refugee voices provides a platform for further political debates on how to relate to the ever-increasing refugee crisis affecting Europe and the world.

Conclusion

The voices of forced migrants, exiles and refugees are rarely heard in most contexts, except to reinforce their passivity, vulnerability and 'neediness' as humanitarian aid recipients in an undefined space between nation-states. This chapter, through a historical snapshot of immigration into the United Kingdom and refugee crisis, indicates that immigration is as old as human civilization. In addition, the perennial problem of fleeing migrants has remained that of the disappearance of voice. Through a series of case studies, the chapter draws from different research projects in many parts of the world to show the effect of the absence of refugee voice on the construction of identities and on the interpretation of self. The competing tensions surrounding refugees are determined by people outside their voices concerning what they would have been known to represent if they had voice. One should posit the argument that the care refugees receive is related to the disappeared voices that should represent them. In order to elaborate on this argument, I delve into the philosophical and theoretical underpinning of the ethic of care with Kantian moral philosophy and in the context of rights, Justice and democratic citizenship. This discussion helps to explain why refugee voices or expressions of the displaced and dispossessed are crucially necessary as a means of understanding the effects of displacement in terms other than those of the nation-state. The frequently silenced voices of refugees who exhibit adaptability, resilience, longing and resistance in the grey zones and borderlands between states and state bureaucracies are challenged in this chapter as instruments promoted by anti-immigration rhetoric from some right-wing politicians and media houses that work against them. This denigrates the care that refugees receive.

The chapter concludes with the need not only for articulation but also for dialogue/conversation; the difference between having voice and being heard – soliciting refugees' voices is one dimension, but genuinely listening to what those voices say is a much deeper phenomenological process. It is recognized that dominant discourses marginalize or even exclude refugee experiences and often as 'the other'. The discussion here acknowledges that the vulnerability of refugees is a key factor in understanding how readily they are excluded from or integrated into dominant narratives. The willingness of state authorities to promote specific refugee narratives raises important questions about the means by which refugee voices can be heard. The refugee voices that can be likely heard are those that celebrate the generosity of the host countries as welcoming to desperate forced migrants in search of sanctuary. Nevertheless, the actual accounts of the exclusionary realities, racism and discrimination that refugees go through as they try to forge a sense of individual and collective identity are silenced. Speech and action are fundamental dimensions of the human condition and distinguish us from other animals. If we are deprived of the opportunity to speak and act, and to engage with other human beings on a basis of equality, we are denied an essential aspect of our humanity.

When someone's speech and action are not recognized, s/he is treated and judged, not according to who s/he is (through his or her words and deeds), but according to his or her membership in a category. This refusal to recognize someone's individuality is a refusal to recognize a fundamental aspect of his or her humanity and is profoundly dehumanizing. When Arendt (1958) speaks of the individual, it is not the preexisting abstract autonomous individual of Enlightenment thought, upon which modern politics is based, but rather, she is referring to an ontologically intersubjective and interdependent individual. The self for Arendt is the self of a human community that is formed through and cannot exist without interacting in the world. The power of speech and action is not only a capacity for self-revelation, consisting of the disclosure of a pre-formed and complete self to a waiting world, but is simultaneously self-constituting. Humanity is fundamentally plural, and plurality is an inescapable and a desirable dimension of humanity. Refugees who have remained passive actors in the political games of governments and the media are recognized in this chapter as social actors who can also become narrating subjects; who challenge portrayals of refugees as passive, vulnerable, needy victims or threatening outsiders and whose accounts refer to personal, lived and first-hand experiences of persecution, displacement and exile. The chapter argues by appealing to host governments to provide active public spaces for 'speaking refugees' rather than maintaining the status quo of 'listening refugees'.

References

Alheit, P., & Dausien, B. (2002). 'The Double Face of Lifelong Learning: Two Analytical Perspectives on Silent Revolution'. *Studies in the Education of Adults* 34.1: 3–22.

Ambrozy, A. (1984). *New Lease of Life; Hungarian Immigrants in Victoria, Assimilation in Australia*. Adelaide: Dezsery Ethnic Publication.

Arendt, H. (1958). *The Human Condition*. Chicago: University of Chicago Press.

Bakhtin, M. (1984). *The Problems of Dostoevsky's Poetics*. Manchester: Manchester University Press.

Barry, B. (1995). *Justice as Impartiality (a Treatise on Social Justice)*, vol. 2. Oxford: Clarendon Press.

Berlin, I. (1990). *The Crooked Timber of Humanity*. Oxford: Oxford University Press.

Berlin, I. (2002). *Liberty*. Oxford: Oxford University Press.

Bhachu, P. (1985). *Parental Educational Strategies: The Case of the Punjabi Sikhs in Britain*. Research paper 3. Centre for Research and Ethnic Relations. University of Warwick.

Bloch, A. (2002). *Refugees' Opportunities and Barriers in Employment and Training*, Department for Work and Pensions Research Report 179. Norwich: HM Stationery Office.

Brah, A. (2007). 'Non-binarised Identities of Similarity and Difference'. In M. Wetherell, M. Lafleche and R. Berkeley (eds), *Identity, Ethnic Diversity and Community Cohesion.* London: Sage.

British Council for Aid to Refugees (BCAR) (1969). *One Year Later: A Report on Czechoslovak Arrivals.* London: British Council for Aid to Refugees.

British Council for Aid to Refugees (BCAR) (1980). *Annual Report.* London: British Council for Aid to Refugees.

British Council for Aid to Refugees (BCAR) (1981). *Background History of the British Council for Aid to Refugees.* London: British Council. For Aid to Africa.

British Refugee Council (1989). *Asylum Statistics, 1980–1988.* London: British Refugee Council.

Castel, S. (2003). 'Towards a Sociology of Forced Migration and Social Transformation'. *Sociology* 37.1: 13–34.

Castles, S., & Cossack, G. (1985). *Immigrant Workers and Class Structure in Western Europe.* Oxford: Oxford University Press.

Clement, C. (1996). *Care, Autonomy, and Justice: Feminism and the Ethic of Care.* Oxford: Westview Press.

Cohen, L., Manion, L., & Morrison, K. (2000). *Research Methods in Education.* 5th ed. London: Routledge.

Cole, M. (2004). 'Brutal and Stinking and Difficult to Handle: The Historical and Contemporary Manifestations of Racialisation, Institutional Racism, and Schooling in Britain'. *Race, Ethnicity and Education* 7.1: 35–56.

Cole, M., & Maisuria, A. (2008). 'Racism in Post 7/7 Britain: Critical Race Theory, Marxism and Empire: What Is the Role of Education?' In D. Kelsh, D. Hill and S. Macrine (eds), *Teaching Class: Knowledge, Pedagogy, Subjectivity.* New York: Routledge.

Cole, M., & Virdee, S. (2005). 'Racism and Resistance from Empire to New Labour'. In M. Cole (ed.), *Education, Equality and Human Rights.* 2nd ed. London: Routledge/Palmer.

Coll, G. (2001). *Parents' Involvement in Their Children's Education: Lessons from Three Immigrant Groups.* New Haven, CT: Yale University.

Corbridge, S. (1993). 'Marxism, Modernities, and Moralities: Development Praxis and the Claims of Distant Strangers'. *Environment and Planning D: Society and Space* 11: 449–72.

Deen, T. (2006). *Pros and Cons of International Migration.* Latin America and the Caribbean: Inter Press Service (IPS).

Duke, K., & Marshall, T. (1995). *Vietnamese Refugees since 1982,* Home Office Research Study 142. London: HM Stationery Office.

Fielden, A. (2008). *Local Integration: An Under-reported Solution to Protracted Refugee Situations. New Issues in Refugee Research paper No 158.* Geneva: UNHCR Evaluation and Policy Analysis Unit.

Fortier, A.-M. (2005). 'Pride Politics and Multiculturalist Citizenship'. *Ethnic and Racial Studies* 28: 559–78. Taylor & Francis Online.

Fryer, P. (1984). *Staying Power: The History of Black People in Britain.* London: Pluto Press.

Ganga, D. (2004). *Intergenerational Identity Shift among Italian Immigrants in the Nottingham Area.* Sheffield: University of Sheffield (unpublished PhD).

Ganga, D. (2007). 'From Potential Returnees to Settlers: Nottingham Older Italians'. *Journal of Ethnic Migration Studies* 32.8: 1395–413.

Geddes, A. (2003). *The Politics of Migration and Immigration in Europe.* London: Sage.

Geras, N. (1995). Solidarity in the *Conversation* of *Humankind*: The *Ungroundable Liberalism* of Richard Rorty. London: Verso.

Gleeson, B., & Kearns, R. S. (2001). 'Remoralising Landscapes of Care'. *Environment and Planning D: Society and Space* 19: 61–80.

Global Issues (2008). Available online: Globalissues.org/Human Rights/racism/ immigration.asp// opinionreflecthypeespeciallyduringelectiontime (accessed 20 May 2009).

Goodman, K. (1989). Unpublished Lecture Given at the Institute of Education, London. Cited in Kearney, C. (2003). *The Monkey's Mask. Identity, Memory, Narrative and Voice.* Stoke-On-Trent, UK; and Sterling, USA: Trentham Books.

Greig, P. (2009). 'Huguenots Identity in Post Medieval London'. *Assemblage* 10.09: 7–15.

Hall, S. (1996). 'What Is This Black in Black Popular Culture'. In D. Morley and K. Chen (eds), *Stuart Hall: Critical Dialogues in Cultural Studies.* London and New York: Routledge.

Hill, D., & Hessari, R. (1990). *Practical Ideas for Multicultural Learning and Teaching in the Primary Classroom.* London: Routledge.

Hopkins. P (March 2007). 'Blue Square, Proper Muslims and Transnational Networks. Narratives of National and Religious Identities among Young Muslim Men Living in Scotland'. *Ethnicities* 7.1: 61–81.

Kabeer, N. (ed.) (2005). *Inclusive Citizenship.* London: Sage.

Kay, D. (1987). *Chileans in Exile: Private Struggles, Public Lives.* Basingstoke: Macmillan.

Kearney, C. (2003). *The Monkey's Mask: Identity, Memory, Narrative, Voice.* Stoke-On-Trent, UK; and Sterling, USA: Trentham Books.

Kearney, C. (2004). 'Inventing Mythologies: The Construction of Complex Cross Cultural Identities'. *European Educational Research Journal* 3.3: 603–25.

Kershaw, P. (2005). *Carefair: Rethinking the Responsibilities and Rights of Citizenship.* Vancouver: UBC Press.

Knijn, T., & Kremer, M. (1997). 'Gender and the Caring Dimension of Welfare States: Toward the Inclusive Citizenship'. *Social Politics* 4 (Fall): 328–61.

Kum, H. (2006). 'Obstacles to Refugee Parents Participation in Their Children Education in English School'. Dissertation submitted in part fulfilment for the award of a MA degree in Education to the University of Northampton (unpublished).

Kum, H., Menter, I., & Smyth, G. (2008). *Refugees into Teaching in Scotland (RITeS)*, Research Report. West Forum Wider Access.

Kunz, E. F. (1985). *The Hungarians in Australia*. Melbourne: AE Press#.

Kushner, T., & Knox, K. D. (1999). *Refugees in an Age of Genocide: Global, National and Local Perspectives during the Twentieth Century*. London: Frank Cass.

Levy, C. (1999). 'Asylum Seekers, Refugees and the Future of Citizenship in the European Union'. In A. Bloch and C. Levy (eds), *Refugees, Citizenship and Social Policy in Europe*. Basingstoke: Macmillan.

Lynn, N., & Lea, S. (2003). 'A Phantom Menace and the New Apartheid: The Social Construction of Asylum Seekers in the United Kingdom'. *Discourse and Society* 14.4: 425–52.

Lucassen, L. (2005). *The Immigrant Threat: The Integration of Old and New Migrants in Western Europe since 1880*. USA: Library of Congress Cataloguing-in Publication Data.

McCollum, P. (1996). *Immigrant Education: Obstacles to Immigrant Parent Participation in Schools*. Online at: http://www.questia.com/PM/qsr (retrieved on 14 March 2009).

Miles, R. (1986). *State, Racism and Migration: The Recent European Experience*. Amsterdam: Centre for Economic and Political Studies, 23.

Miles, R., and Phizacklea, A. (1984). *White Man's Country: Racism in the British Politics*. London: Pluto Press.

Morris, J. (2001). 'Impairment and Disability: Constructing an Ethics of Care That Promotes Human Rights'. *Hypatia* 16.4: 1–16.

Morris, L. (1998). 'Governing at a Distance: The Elaboration of Controls in British Immigration'. *International Migration Review* 32.4: 949–73.

National Statistics (2005). *Control of Immigration*. Statistics, United Kingdom 2004 (accessed on 23 August 2005).

O'Neil, O. (1996). *Toward Justice and Virtue: A Constructive Account of Practical Reasoning*. Cambridge: Cambridge University Press.

Phinney, J. (1996). 'When We Talk about American Ethnic Groups, What Do We Mean?' *American Psychologist* 51: 918–92.

Ramdin, R. (1987). *The Making of the Black Working Class in Britain*. London: Gower.

Refugee Council (1991). *Vietnamese Refugee Reception and Resettlement: 1979–88*. London: Refugee Council.

Refugee Council (1997). *Helping Refugee Children in Schools*. London: Refugee Council.

Refugee Council (2010). *Chance or Choice: Understanding Why Asylum Seekers Come to the UK*. Available online: www.refugeecouncil.org.uk (retrieved on 18 April 2010).

Rutter, J. (2003). *Working with Refugee Children*. York: Joseph Roundtree Foundation.

Rutter, J. (2004). *Refugees: We Left because We Had To*. London: Refugee Council.

Rutter, J. (2006). *Refugee Children in the UK*. Buckingham: Open University Press.

Rutter, J., Cooley, L., Reynolds, S., & Sheldon, R. (2007). *From Refugee to Citizenship: Standing on My Own Two Feet. A Research Report on Integration,*

Britishness and Citizenship. London: Metropolitan Support Trust and the Institute of Public Policy Research.

Sevenhuijsen, S. (1998). *Citizenship and the Ethics of Care: Feminist Considerations on Justice, Morality and Politics*. London and New York: Routledge.

Sevenhuijsen, S. (2000). 'Caring in the Third Way: The Relation between Obligation, Responsibility and Care in Third Way Discourse'. *Critical Social Policy* 20.1: 1–37.

Singer, P. (1995). *How Are We to Live? Ethics in an Age of Self-Interest*. Amherst, NY: Prometheus Books.

Sivanandan, A. (1976). 'Race, Class and the State: The Black Experience in Britain'. *Race and Class* 17: 347–68.

Smith, D. M. (1998). 'How Far Should We Care? On the Spatial Scope of Beneficence'. *Progress in Human Geography* 22.1: 15–38.

Sword, K. (1989). *The Formation of the Polish Community in the UK*. London: School of Slavonic Studies, University of London.

Tajfel, H., & Turner, J. C. (1979). *An Integrated Theory of Intergroup Conflict*. In W. G. Austin and S. Worchel (eds), *The Social Psychology of Intergroup Relations*. Monterey, CA: Brooks-Cole.

The Independent (2008). 'Fury at DNA Pioneers Theory: Africans Are Less Intelligent Than Westerners'. Available on http://www.independent.co.uk/news/science/fury-at-dna-pioneers-theory-africans-are-less-intelligent-than-westerners-394 (accessed 14 February 2010).

Tololyan, K., Waltraud, K., & Alfonso, C. (eds) (2004). *Diaspora, Identity and Religion. New Directions in Theory and Research*. London and New York: Routledge.

Tronto, J. (1993). *Moral Boundaries: A Political Argument for an Ethic of Care*. London: Routledge.

Tronto, J. (2001). 'Who Cares? Public and Private Caring and the Rethinking of Citizenship'. In N. Hirschmann and U. Leibert, *Women and Welfare: Theory and Practice in the United States*. Piscataway, NJ: Rutgers University Press. 65–83.

UNFPA (2006). *State of World Population 2006. A Passage to Hope-Women and International Migration*. Available online: www.unfpa.org/swp/2006/english (retrieved on 18 February 2008).

UNHCR (1993). *The State of the World's Refugees: The Challenges of Protection*. London: Penguin.

UNHCR (1994). *Refugee Children: Guidelines on Protection and Care*. Geneva: UNHCR.

Universities UK (2005). *A Review of Black and Minority Participation in Higher Education*. Available online: www.aimhigher.ac.uk (21 June 2006).

Vigouroux, B. C. (2005). 'There Are No Whites in Africa: Territoriality, Language and Identity among Francophone Africans in Cape Town'. *Language and Communication* 25: 237–55.

Visram, R. (1986). *Ayahs, Lascars and Princes: Indians in Britain 1700-1947*. London: Pluto.

World University Service (WUS UK 1974). *Reception and Resettlement of Refugees from Chile*. London: World University (UK).

Workers Power (2007). *Workers Power*. Available online: http://www.workerspowere. com/index.php?id 128,1127,0,0,1,0.

Zembylas, M. (2010). 'The Ethic of Care in Globalized Societies: Implications for Citizenship Education'. *Ethics and Education* 5.3: 233–45.

Zetter, R. (2007). 'More Labels, Fewer Refugees: Remaking the Refugee Label in an Era of Globalisation'. *Journal of Refugee Studies* 20.2: 172–1.

8

Subalternity, Language and Projects of Emancipation: An Analysis of Dalit Literature

Joseph Mundananikkal Thomas

Introduction

This chapter is essentially an analysis of what has come to be known as 'Dalit Literature' (*Dalit Sahitya*, in Marathi and other Indian languages). The authors of such literature are people belonging to communities designated as dalit by the protagonists themselves. 'Dalit' as a term takes its meaning from the context of stratification of society in large parts of the Indian subcontinent, namely, caste. Caste has been the predominant system of social stratification prevalent in India for many years. The term 'caste' refers to two separate but interrelated concepts such as *varna* and *jati*. *Jati* refers to particular bounded communities in local areas which are largely endogamous with their own notions of commensality within themselves and with other *jati*s. It provides the most basic communitarian identity to most Indian citizens.

Varna, however, refers to the pan Indian scheme for categorization of *jati*s into five broad categories. Among these the first four categories are termed the *chaturvarna* (four groups) which consist of the categories of *Brahman* (traditionally the priestly class), *Kshatriya* (the warrior class), *Vaishya* (the trader class) and *Shudra* (the menial class). In addition to these categories, there is a fifth category which does not have a fixed name. This category consists of the people outside the fourfold division mentioned above. In a specific sense dalits (along with tribals) are traditionally categorized as the fifth category (*panchma*). This implies that people belonging to dalit *jati*s are outside the very organization of the caste structure. Because of this they have been called 'out castes'.

*Jati*s designated as dalits have been subjected to various forms of discrimination and civil disabilities and exclusions. In the traditional structure of Indian villages, their dwellings were outside the main village where people of other *jatis* dwelt. They have been 'outcastes' in such a geographical sense as well. Disabilities such as prohibition in the use of public wells, public roads and temples were in full force in many parts of India. Though there have been significant changes in these practices of exclusion over the years, especially after independence from the British, many of such practices still remain entrenched across the length and breadth of India.

Due to the prohibitions imposed on them in the traditional caste order, they have been called 'untouchables'. During the colonial period, the term 'depressed classes' was used to include dalits. From the year 1935, ever since the government of India commenced the practice of making a schedule of all the *jatis* who are categorized into the fifth category, another term originated, that of 'scheduled castes'. The legal and administrative term in vogue in contemporary India is 'scheduled castes'.

At the height of the movement for freedom from the British, Mohandas Karamchand Gandhi (Mahatma Gandhi) had initiated many movements in several parts of India for the removal of untouchability as a practice. To bring about a semantic transformation in the term used to refer to the untouchables, he coined the word *harijan* (literally 'people of God'). Article 17 of the Constitutions of India refers to the abolition of untouchability and related practices. Eventually untouchability as a practice was constitutionally banned by the Indian State through an Act of the Indian Parliament in the year 1955. Taking cognizance of extreme forms of atrocities unleashed on dalit communities, the Indian Parliament enacted 'The Scheduled Caste and Scheduled Tribes (Prevention of Atrocities) Act' in the year 1989. The government of India has also put in place measures of compensatory discrimination known as 'reservations' by making specific provisions for the dalits (along with tribals and other social groups who are victims of backwardness) in terms of certain percentage of reservation in employment and seats in educational institutions in the public sector. Despite these provisions, practices of exclusion still persist in different parts of India. In some areas they have metamorphosed into newer forms of discrimination.

At a basic level endogamous *jatis* remain the bedrock of social organization as well as identity in India's villages. Though there is marked diversity and mobility in the urban areas, in many ways one can notice an extension of *jati* identities and practices of exclusion and discrimination. On the psychological level, the *jati* becomes a major component of one's sense of self. For those belonging to the dalit *jatis* this would translate itself into an internalized sense of disability buttressed by the experience of victimhood through generations.

From a sociocultural point of view, dalit literature takes its inspiration from the earlier writings of people from a dalit location and from the writings and politics of leaders from the movements against Brahmanism[1] as an ideology. The most significant of such movements was initiated by Dr Bhimrao Ramji Ambedkar[2] (1891–1956) who gathered inspiration from earlier leaders, particularly Jotirao Phule.[3] Ambedkar belonged to the Mahar *jati*, one of the preeminent untouchable *jatis* in the state of Maharashtra. At every phase of life, he was subjected to various practices of exclusion and ill-treatment at the hands of people belonging to higher castes. He articulated coherently hitherto one of the most powerful critical treatises on the caste system, epitomized in his *Annihilation of Caste*, the text of a lecture which he was to have delivered at Lahore in the year 1935. In that treatise he made a pointed argument saying that the entire architecture of caste stands on the sanction given by Hindu religious texts. Therefore, one cannot imagine a reversal unless the religious texts are questioned and challenged. In effect, his argument pointed to the idea that exit from caste system is possible only by destroying its very foundation, that is, the religious scriptures.

This treatise of Ambedkar followed his attempts at reform of the caste order. From 1925 CE onwards, he led many movements for the emancipation of dalits such as temple entry movements, movements towards access to water from public wells and prevention of other instances of civic discrimination. His efforts met with stiff and vehement resistance from the high caste Hindus. Consequently in the year 1935 he made a declaration that he was born a Hindu of which he had no choice but would not die a Hindu as he has a possibility of choice on the matter. From then, his efforts were geared towards the possibility of conversion for him as for other dalit *jatis* in India to another religion. His efforts materialized into the conversion event of 14 October 1956 when Dr Ambedkar, along with his wife and around 4,00,000 people, mostly dalits, converted to Buddhism at Nagpur, Maharashtra, in the presence of Mahasthavir Chandramuni, the seniormost Buddhist monk in India at that time. This gave rise to the growth of a distinct religious identity for dalits, namely, Buddhism which is today referred to in popular parlance as Neo-Buddhism or Navayana Buddhism.[4]

Over the years, even though conversion to Buddhism has been largely confined to those who belonged to the Mahar *jati*, it inaugurated a template open to all dalit *jatis* to emulate. Subsequently, instances of dalit communities in different parts of India converting to Buddhism have occurred in recent years. However, the most potent transformation associated with Babasaheb Ambedkar is the way he has become the preeminent icon for dalit emancipation across India. He has come to symbolize the most powerful of sentiments towards dalit assertion and has become the central axis on which projects of dalit emancipation are foisted. His persona is combined on the one hand with his status as the architect of the Constitution of India as well as his contributions as a statesman par excellence and on the other with his iconic struggle and contribution towards emancipation of dalits. References of him abound in dalit literature.

Dalit literature

Historically, dalit literature[5] grew as a distinct genre of Marathi literature comprising of works of poetry, plays, short stories, life-stories, folk songs and novels, and got wide acceptance for its specificity.[6] It is a literary-cultural movement, promoting the growth of a composite dalit identity. The dalit 'littérateurs' perceived a close connection between literature and the society at large. Their initial revolt against mainstream Marathi literature represented a rejection of the social order from which that literature originated. 'They considered it their duty to expose the actual conditions of Indian society, to shatter the complacent illusion of middle-class Hindus, and to reveal the empty façade which scarcely concealed the unrealised dreams and broken promises of Indian Independence' (Gokhale 1993: 311).

The predominant theme of dalit literature is the break with the past and the transformed sociocultural situation of the dalits. They engage with the horrors of the past and the promise of the present. Social justice and the transformation of society resound as important themes in some of the dalit writings. Dalit literature took upon itself to show the ugly face of varna ideology. A major portion of dalit literature thus 'was devoted to scathing denunciations of Hinduism, derision directed at Hindu gods and goddesses, contempt for its irrationality and superstitions, and hatred for its principle of caste. The language used was often deliberately provocative, blasphemous, and even obscene, designed to flaunt their rebellion and shock the orthodox' (Gokhale 1993: 312).

At the same time dalit literature contains strands that portray sentiments of 'comportment'.[7] Dalit writing revolutionized Marathi literature with down-to-earth phrases and language which mirrored the stark reality of lower caste existence in the villages and cities of Maharashtra. The city, especially Bombay, is represented in dalit literature as both a locale of possibilities and a site of squalor and struggle. The poems and short stories penned by dalit writers gave vivid details about dalit life-worlds, ranging from the deprived sections of urban dalit populace of the slums to the world of the dalits working in offices in Bombay.

Dalit literature found a niche for itself in the wider domain of Marathi literature.

As early as 1970, Dalit literature was accorded a place in the Marathi Sahitya Sammelan (Marathi Literary Conference), with a panel discussion on the subject. Dalit works are regularly reviewed in Marathi newspapers as well as in English language publications. With the Ford Foundation awards that Daya Pawar and Laxman Mane received, international recognition was also conferred on Dalit literature. Thus the movement has been able to acquire a stature as a serious literary-cultural form at the same time that its creators are accorded recognition as arbiters of literary-cultural values which is an unprecedented event in Indian cultural history. (Gokhale 1993: 328)

Since 1950 there have been various dalit literary organizations. The literary journal called *Asmitaadarsh* has remained a prominent forum for the publication of dalit literary works. Of late numerous publishing houses are springing up among the Buddhists of Maharashtra.

At one level, dalit literature is steeped in notions attributable to European Modernity. There is an emphasis on scientific outlook, rationality and a concern with pedagogy of the masses. Dalit literature is equally about the dalit life-world and its attended complexities and plural ways of engagement.[8] Here too, one can notice the tension between the idiom of the universal and that of the particular. For example, one of the points of debate among the dalit writers was on the focus of their writing. While one group argued that they need to address the larger domain of the dalits, another group wanted a specific Buddhist literature.[9] A majority of dalit writers are Buddhists[10] and the Buddhist theme like sentiments of devotion towards Babasaheb and the Buddha abound in some of their writings.[11]

Among works specifically belonging to a Buddhist idiom, there are popular songs that 'deify' both the Buddha and Babasaheb. These are found mostly in the pamphlets distributed at the sites of importance to the Buddhists. In her study of the songs of the Buddhists from Vidharbha region of Maharashtra, I. Y. Junghare (1988) writes of the various images of Babasaheb that are portrayed. She talks about two processes that are evident in those songs: a process of 'ascension' by which Babasaheb is raised to a level akin to that of the divine and the process of 'descent' which positions Babasaheb like an 'avatar' (94). She has also demonstrated that folk poetry such as the *palna*[12] and the *ovi*[13] also engage with the theme of the heroism of the Buddha and Babasaheb.

T. J. Gajarawala (2013) places dalit literature in the larger context of writings of social realism. She argues that as a protest literature, it shows remarkable continuity with literature of social realism both in European and Indian languages. 'Despite its oppositional and exclusionary stance, however, dalit literature has been irrevocably shaped, and indeed produced, by the critique of the very non-dalit sphere it excoriates. These upper-caste literary forms function as oppositional parameters, in dialectical fashion; dalit literature should therefore be read as constructing an antigenealogy' (4). Basing herself largely on developments of dalit literature in Hindi language, Laura Brueck (2014: 21) suggests that it represents 'cultural performance' representing the emergence of a counter public which seeks to forge into a larger canvas of the 'dalit' all the marginalized communities privileging their life-world and their experiences. One may characterize dalit literature as an expression of 'subaltern counterpublic'.[14] The works of dalit writers need to be read as negotiations on defining the contours of the counterpublic with claims of authentic experiences of life which were hitherto represented largely by the non-dalit writers.

What follows is a more detailed analysis of the themes related to dalit literature.

Dalit

The term 'dalit' (originally from Marathi language) literally means 'broken'.[15] Today in academic circles this term is used in a specific sense to refer to communities that were formerly called as 'untouchables' and 'depressed classes'. In some ways the word 'dalit' corresponds to another technical term currently in vogue in India, namely, 'scheduled castes'.[16] In addition to this, the term 'dalit' has also been employed by different people to refer to all the communities and groups who are marginalized or 'subaltern' as victims of the hegemonic social structure. There has been a move on the part of some political parties and movements to employ the term in conjunction with '*bahujan*' (literally, diverse peoples) to refer to all the marginalized and subaltern groups. There are also a few communities in India who are in the category of scheduled caste but have expressed the view that they don't want to be referred to as '*dalit*' as it refers to a state of victimhood. The term was popularized by the *Dalit Panthers*, a movement of dalit revolutionaries in the city of Mumbai which originated in the year 1972 and was modelled on the Black Panthers movement.

However, it is argued by academics and activists alike that the term 'dalit' holds within it a dual focus: a focus on subalternity as in brokenness as well as a focus on awakening from the state of brokenness. The term takes its semiotic accent from the social movements of dalits across India, particularly in Maharashtra. Commenting on this connection, P. Constable (1997) argues that the present power of dalit literature needs to be understood in the context of the historical movements of dalits, particularly the Mahars[17] of Maharashtra. He situates the setting that inspired dalit consciousness in the latter half of the nineteenth century in Maharashtra to the work of Gopal Baba Valangkar[18] and the organization that he gave shape to, namely, *Anarya Dosh Pariharik Mandal* (Association for the solution of the disabilities of non-Aryans).

Dalit subalternity

The term 'subaltern' gained currency in its relation to postcolonial literature. The subaltern came to be understood in terms of colonialism and its histories of erasure. The Subaltern Studies Collective brought to the fore a corpus of literature which sought to interrogate the moments of erasure and let the subaltern speak. While the dominant canvas on which subalternity is imagined is that of colonialism, the canvas on which dalitness is imagined is that of caste and its ramifications, particularly the lived experience of inclusion by exclusion which defines the dalit subject. Dalit settlements are outside the boundaries of villages. Dalits in that sense become the other of all that non-dalits are. Dalit is part of the wider society, and yet his/her being part of the society is by being outside of it, by being the other. This is the subalternity of dalitness which gets reflected in the writings of dalits. 'The dalit's subaltern status is inherited from birth and sanctioned by sacred authority. It is eternal and unalterable' (Alok Mukherjee in Limbale 2004: 3).

From a historical point of view, dalit subalternity has had a dual pronged engagement with colonial rulers. On the one hand, they recognized the violence of the colonizers and made common cause with anti-colonial struggles but at the same time, they engaged with colonial regimes in order to enlist their help in ameliorating the tyranny of caste. Dalit subalternity positions itself at the intersection of particularity and representation. It privileges the particular experience of the dalit subject whose experience is singularly carved out and explicated. At the same time, the experience of one subject is pictured as representing the generalized dalit experience where, in the term, dalit stands for its most extended and plural of meanings, enveloping the range of subalternity occasioned by structures of caste, class, the non-indigenous as against the indigenous and patriarchy.

Dalit literature as subaltern writing

Dalit literature (*Dalit Sahitya* in Marathi) is used to refer to the corpus of writings of dalits with particular focus on the dalit life-world. The writings of the dalits are full of vivid descriptions of the settings, the villages and the slums along with the narratives of experiences filled with comportment. They grasp the reader with counter narratives of powerlessness, victimhood as well as stories of aspiration and assertion. The genre spans into various forms such as life narratives,[19] biographies, poems, short stories, novellas, novels and drama. It celebrates the vivacity of the dalit life-world. As mastery of the English language was not accessible to the dalits due to various reasons, both structural and situational, their writings have been largely in the regional languages containing therein particularity of both form and content, language and experience. Arjun Dangle, one of the earlier dalit writers, has this to say of dalit literature: 'Dalit literature is not simply literature . . . dalit literature is associated with a movement to bring about change . . . At the very first glance, it will be strongly evident that there is no established critical theory or point of view behind them [dalit writings]; instead, there is new thinking and a new point of view' (quoted in Limbale 2004: 2). Essentially dalit literature is literature of protest rooted in anti-caste politics propelled by a clear sense of dalit consciousness. Initially the writings of the dalits were not accorded the status of literature as the latter term was used exclusively for elitist writings. Gradually as the popularity of the writings by the dalits grew, there was increasing recognition. At the present time, the writings of the dalits are not only acknowledged as literature but they are also widely read by the literary public. Celebrated publishing houses are today concentrating on publishing English translation of the works of dalit writers from many of the Indian languages. Speciality publishing houses concentrating particularly on dalit literature have also sprung up.[20] The popularity of dalit literature in the Indian subcontinent can also be gauged by the invitation extended regularly to dalit writers for participation in the iconic Jaipur Literary Festival year after year.

Theorizing dalit literature

Though his writings are necessarily read in the genre of postcolonial literature, some concepts developed by Homi Bhabha (1994) come handy in making sense of dalit literature. For instance, dalit literature can be located in the domain of 'cultural difference' that Homi Bhabha refers to in his works. In the way it has marked a niche for itself in opposition to what has been hitherto certified as literature of the high culture, dalit literature consciously positions itself at the 'ambivalence of cultural authority'. Bhabha calls this act as the moment of enunciation or the third space of enunciation wherein the traditional forms of authorized cultural production are put through a process of interrogation by the emerging new forms of cultural resistance. Or rather, dalit literature represents 'the disruptive temporality of enunciation' because it problematizes the unitary renderings of nation produced by the hegemonic discourses of nationality and nationhood in postcolonial India.

As Homi Bhabha argues rebellion, mobilization and resistance can be the most poignant when they are enunciated in cultural production, in the form of what he calls 'discursive temporality' and 'negotiation'. Negotiation is a term that Bhabha (1994: 26) uses to refer to forms of political 'iteration' which seek to name oppositional elements without being subsumed into the rationality of transcendence. The 'other' represents itself, not in essentialized binaries but in hybrid renderings wherein the poignancy of otherness laced with interrogations of socio-political circumstances makes itself heard in cultural production that can be singled out for its authenticity of experience.

Dalit literature can be situated in the 'in-between' spaces (interstitial perspectives) that Homi Bhabha refers to. For him these are liminal spaces located between the narratives of the 'originary' subjectivities on the one hand and the moments of the articulation of cultural difference on the other. It is within these in-between spaces that new senses of the self become possible with new strategies for selfhood aligned with modes of collaboration and contestation leading to novel ideas about society itself. Such articulations constitute ongoing processes of negotiation with dominant and other subaltern cultures. Dalit literature in that sense can be placed as part of the project of a reconstruction of society itself. 'Social differences are not simply given to experience through an already authenticated cultural tradition; they are the signs of the emergence of community envisaged as a project – at once a vision and a construction – that takes you "beyond" yourself in order to return, in a spirit of revision and reconstruction, to the political conditions of the present' (Bhabha 1994: 3). For Bhabha, such art of reconstruction engages with time in novel ways. It forges a new relationship between the past and the present wherein the past is configured as an 'in-between' space that 'innovates' and 'interrupts' the performance of the present (7). In the case of dalit literature, there is this imagining of the new present with its possibilities of emancipated subjectivities, which make sense in relation to the bondages of the past.

The social realism that reverberates in the writings of dalits is akin to 'the affective experience of social marginality' that Bhabha (1994: 172) talks about and which 'forces us to . . . engage with culture as an uneven, incomplete production of meaning and value, often composed of incommensurable demand and practices, produced in the act of social survival'.

Thematic presentation of selections from dalit literature

Rejection of Brahmanism and Manusmriti

Generally, dalit literature gives painful details of dalit lives and engages in a questioning of the social structure that sanctions violence against them at all levels. The hegemonic ideology of Brahmanism represented by texts such as the Manusmriti (The Code of Manu) is castigated in the most virulent language by the dalits. Brahmanism broadly refers to the corpus of ideas, legal codes and systems of practice that legitimizes discrimination on the basis on caste. The term takes its origin from the word 'Brahman' which denotes the caste legitimized as highest of all castes in the hierarchy of castes. Manusmriti is a code of law which contains modes and sanctions related to inter-caste living and contact. As a text which legitimized the most inhuman of the oppressions that dalits have endured over generations in India, Manusmriti has come in for particular opposition not only in the writings of the dalits but also within the larger dalit movement. One of the high points of the movement for emancipation of dalits spearheaded by Babasaheb Dr B. R. Ambedkar was at the event in which he and his followers burned the pages of the Manusmriti, which had come in for severe criticism even before Dr Ambedkar. For instance, Kondaji Ramji known as Pandit Kondiram, a dalit had written a poem and added it to the famous petition submitted to the British by Valangkar in the year 1894 CE. In this poem Kondiram singled out Manusmriti as the text that sanctioned the indignity of the Mahars and argued for an escape from the Hindu caste order through the means of bhakti[21] to personalized deities. Among the various verses that make up the poem, he writes of the condition of the Mahars, '[L]ive in a hut which you must build outside the village! That is what the Brahmans write in this books' (Constable 1997: 320).

Eleanor Zelliot (1996: 283) presents in translation a selection of short couplets from dalit writers who have commented on Manu ('the Brahmanical law-giver'):

(a) A couplet by dalit poet Waman Nimbalkar:

> O heirs of Manu! For millennia we have watched our own
> naked evening. In half a dozen huts on the village
> boundary our countless bodies have been burning, set afire by your feeble
> thoughts.

Through these lines, Nimbalkar seeks to portray the existential condition of the dalit subject whose dwellings are outside the boundaries of the main village and whose bodies are bearing the brunt of caste oppression sanctioned by the text of Manu (Manusmriti).

(b) By Shashikant Lokhande:

> When you try to heat the bread of your sweat or pull up
> the lungoti (loin cloth) of your pain they slash at your buttocks,
> your breast, your hand, they bind on your neck the
> burden of Manusmriti

Here dalit poet Lokhande alludes to instrumental use of violence by the upper castes that keep the caste system in place where the dalit becomes the principal victim.

(c) By Daya Pawar:

> By the mixture of our blood
> Manu's wall will be demolished brick by brick.

Daya Pawar is one of the most popular dalit writers. In this couplet he expresses the general theme that runs through dalit writings: the assertion of resolve to break the system legitimized by the code of Manu.

Engagement with bhakti tradition

Gopal Baba Valangkar at the turn of the twentieth century advocated bhakti as a way for dalits to take the shackles of untouchability off their shoulders. He was himself devoted to the bhakti tradition of the Ramanandi sect. He found doctrinal justification for the ignominy of untouchability in the vedas and other Hindu texts and put forward bhakti as a way out of the quagmire. He pointed out that in the bhakti tradition, what matters is one's inner purity and not the ritual status given by the custodians of the structures of society. He also singled out the maxim of equality that reverberated in the works of the bhakti saints. The

name of Chokhamela, the bhakti saint who is said to have belonged to the Mahar
jati was pointed out by Valangkar as an example of egalitarianism that reigns in
the bhakti tradition. The persona of Chokhamela is again invoked by other dalit
writers over the years in a clear indication of the dalit connection with the bhakti
tradition.

One can notice strong traces of protest in some of the verses (*abhangas*) of
Chokhamela. For instance, one verse reads thus:

> In the beginning,
> at the end
> there is nothing but pollution.
> No one knows anyone who is born pure.
> Chokha says, in wonder,
> who is pure? (Zelliot 1996: 270)

Chokhamela is revered as a saint-poet of the particular bhakti tradition popular
in the state of Maharashtra called the *varkari sampradaya*. While the other bhakti
saints of the tradition belonged to higher castes, predominantly the Brahman
varna, Chokhamela is said to have belonged to the untouchable *jati* of Mahar.
Even as a saint in the tradition of bhakti, there is no question of erasure of his
caste status. The above mentioned lines echo his lament as an untouchable who
is stigmatized as impure. He asks in a philosophical sense whether there is any
human being in the world who is actually born pure.

Centrality of Babasaheb Dr B. R. Ambedkar

Babasaheb Dr B. R. Ambedkar, who relentlessly fought for annihilation of caste
by launching movements on multiple fronts culminating in his conversion to
Buddhism along with his followers in 1956, is a central figure in most of the
narratives of the dalits. In writings and speeches he examined with a critical
lens and from the standpoint of someone hailing from the untouchable caste
the history, myths and sacred texts of Hinduism thereby carving out space for
dalit assertion. The dalit life narratives emanating from across India, particularly
from the state of Maharashtra (from where Babasaheb hailed), bear the imprint
of his intervention in Indian society. A marked departure from being victims
to claimants of rights and harbingers of assertion and resistance is evident in
dalit life narratives. Many of them depict the pre-Ambedkarite era as one of
victimhood and the post-Ambedkarite era as one of resistance and assertion.

The following poem by Namdeo Dhasal is representative of the many works by dalits which honour Babasaheb:

It was Friday
An arithmetic book a slate
and one piece of chalk
mother with eagerness brought from the bazaar
She was very tired that day
In the light of the brass lantern
she made me massage her hands and feet.
Then she said,
'Baba – until I fall asleep
take a look at this book
I never learned but you do this
To start your education
make B for Babasaheb.
He was far more beautiful than Lord Ganesh.
So don't trace
Shri Ganesh.
The lord of the people is never ugly
He is from among the True/holy/beautiful
Babsaheb Ambedkar
is true, holy, beautiful
Otherwise this book has no meaning'

(Zelliot 1996: 312)

Namdeo Dhasal is one of the founders of the Dalit Panther movement which took shape in Bombay (now Mumbai) in the year 1972. His writings have been very revolutionary and have remained inspirational for a whole generation of dalit activists. Here in this poem he articulates the unique space that Babasaheb Ambedkar has in the dalit life-world. It specifically refers to the stress on education which was a cornerstone of the dalit movement led by Babasaheb. For instance, the slogan that he coined for the movement read, 'Educate, Organise, Agitate'.

Buddhist conversion and new life

Dalits who consider themselves Buddhist post the conversion event of 1956 when Babasaheb Ambedkar and his followers embraced Buddhism write about the new life in Buddhism and the sense of liberation it gives them. Some of the dalits have written poems and other works of literature on being a Buddhist.

Here is a poem by Bhagwan Sawai:

Then the primordial man within me exclaimed
I will lay a stone on my chest
and carve on it
images of my sorrow
songs of pain
that bear witness to my wounds
and welcome tomorrow's sun.
Tathagata
I've come to you
my sorrows interred in my bones
bringing my darkness within the radius of your light
Take me within your fold, away from this darkness
Out there, I've worn myself out, slogging in their carnival
losing my self-identity.
Tathagata
Ask no questions, questions are alien to me,
I do not know myself
Out there, there was nothing but darkness and rocky muteness
So transmigrate into me from that picture
in flesh and blood, into my effusive being.

(Dangle 1992: 29)

Bhagwan Sawai is one of the dalit writers. In this poem he portrays the Buddha (Tathagata) as the giver of refuge. The emphasis is on the experience of pain and powerlessness in the social order and his looking up to the light of the Buddha for deliverance. The Buddha was pictured by Babasaheb Ambedkar as a person who showed the way to an enlightened life. Sawai's poem here evokes the Buddha as a saviour from the ills of suffering and bondage.

Language

One of the dominant characters that strike a reader of dalit narratives is its difference in the language that is used. The expressions are direct and evocative and reflective of both the pathos as well as the sense of revolt that comes out of dalit imagination. For instance, here is a selection from a poem by Arun Kamble (translated by Gauri Deshpande into English):

Bone-chewing grampus
at the burning ghat:
permanent resident
of my own heart:
with the weight of tradition
behind his back
yells: Saddling bastard
I tell you,
stutter with our tongue!
Picking through the Vedas,
buttering his queue,
the Brahmin teacher at school
bellows: Speak my pure tongue
whoreson!

Now you tell me which speech
am I to tongue? (Quoted in Zelliot 1996: 279)

Arun Kamble juxtaposes the earthy language of the dalit with that of the Brahman. Implicit in the rendering is the utter disdain the Brahman holds for the language of the dalit.

Dalit versus non-dalit literature

It is also a rhetorical device on the part of dalit writers to promote a sustained distinction of dalit writing from the non-dalit one. The debate on the specific genre of dalit literature has thrown up many responses. One of the responses is that dalit literature embodies specific experiences of life and hence is directed towards specific audiences implying that dalit writers are not addressing a universal audience. It is added to this response that the particular audience that is intended by the writers has a bearing on the literary and aesthetic styles that they adopt. However, Laura Brueck argues that it will be an incomplete treatment of dalit literature if we stop with this characterization. Her analysis throws up novel areas of adaptations from which dalit writers have ventured into developing narrative styles of resistance and protest. The tropes that dalit writers employ portray multiple forms of assertion of their personhood as against the portrayal of abjectness that envelops the dalit characters in literature produced by the non-dalits.[22]

Dalit women

Within dalit literature there are now voices of dalit women who not only voice their protest against caste oppression but also stand up against the tendency among dalit writers and activists not to address issues of patriarchy within the dalit fold.[23]

We get a sense of the tenor of dalit women's writing from the themes that they have explored therein. Most of these writings are again autobiographical in nature. The ignominy of humiliating experiences are recounted in great detail by many of the writers. The harsh experience of life that has become part of a dalit women's world is explicated in all its vividness by Jyoti Lanjewar in the following poem titled 'Why Were You Born?'

And why were you born
in this ghetto
of rotten lampposts
dust-choked streets
and stumps of trees
with elephantiases
why were you born?

No shelter here
not even a hoarding
or a cement column
and behind barbed wires
flowers bloom
for maggots and worms;
Shoemakers are barefoot
why were you born?

Shoemakers are barefoot
why were you born?
and barbers hirsute,
toothless dentists tout
used false teeth;
even thorns make a point
so why were you born?

Here horses are redundant
and elephants retired;
recruitment has begun
to enlist men into stables
for dragging humanity along.
Why were you born? (Quoted in Deo & Zelliot 1994: 47–8)

The writings of the women dalits also resound with the sense of defiance and assertion demonstrated by dalit women of grit against the systemic acts of violence which has marked their everyday lives. For instance, in her memoir *Aydan*, Urmila Pawar recounts the experience of humiliation she suffered within the school and how in the strong retort of her mother, she found strength of will and experienced a transformation of self. She talks about the way her father, at his deathbed, instructed her mother to educate the children so that they would be able to escape the humiliations of being dalit. One day, despite the insistence of her mother, Urmila was reluctant to go to school because of the treatment that she habitually received at the hands of the teacher. He used to make her sit in the last row, insist on her sweeping the floor of the classroom after the class was over and pick up dung from the courtyard. One day when she refused to clear the dung from the yard, the teacher hit her hard and ordered her not to come to the school again. The mother noticed the swollen cheeks of her dear daughter and confronted the teacher in public. Urmila quotes her mother in her work, *A Childhood Tale*:

> 'Look here, I am not a respectable woman. I live under a tree, by the roadside. With my children like an exile. Why? So that they can study . . . become important people, and you harass a girl like this?' Aai (mother) was speaking ungrammatically, incorrectly. In a loud voice she threatened Guruji (teacher), 'Look here, after this if your finger so much as touches my daughter, I will see to it that you will never walk on this road . . .'
>
> After that day many things became easier . . . collecting dung and Guruji's beating were no longer part of my fate and destiny. But the main thing was that I began to see my mother as a tremendous support. And my life got some direction. (Pawar 2002: 54–5, as quoted in Chakravarti, U. 2013: 140).

In an analysis of the oral poetry and paintings of dalit women, Gopal Guru introduces the idea of 'labouring intellectualism'. He situates the language of resistance of dalit women in their oral poetry, not in the written word. Here orality becomes the major medium through which a language of resistance takes shape. His analysis demonstrates that the oral poetry of dalit women contains a critique of the dominating structure of caste as well as self-critique of the dalit self. The context of labour done collectively has produced the distinct genre of dalit women's oral poetry in Marathi known as *ovi* (folk poetry sung at harvesting time) (cf. Guru 2013: 59–61).

Within debates in feminism, strong arguments have been made about the unique location of dalit women and the need for according their experiences a specific space in the wider feminist discourse in India. Such debates pinpoint the need to foreground caste as an important factor in feminist analysis and praxis. They lament the way movements of the labouring communities mobilized primarily on class lines as well as movements of women bordering on ideas of eco-feminism have excluded the life-world and experience of dalit women.

Within the dalit fold itself, women have implicated men by pointing out the different forms of patriarchy. Gopal Guru (1995: 2548–50) explains that dalit women have expressed reservations about the way dalit men have overwhelmingly captured the dalit political space and the prominent space in dalit literature.

Conclusion

The diverse registers that envelop the larger corpus of dalit literature today attest to the fact that dalit writing has entrenched itself into a discursive field with both a passionate interrogation of the claims of representation on the part of the non-dalit writers and an assertion of plural literary representations of dalit personhood in all its vitality, vigour, spirit of resistance and revolt.

Dalit literature has brought into the literary public a deeper awareness of the dalit life-world. The inanity of the life of the dalits is something that people belonging to the high caste would rather not talk about. In intellectual and academic circles, there have always been efforts to camouflage the stark realities of the life of the dalits with idioms and images. Dalit literature has exploded into the public sphere with real life experience, in earthy language giving the reader a ringside view of the life lived on the margins of the social order. It has called into question the contemporary Indian's propensity to argue away the stranglehold of caste or talk about caste by other means such as 'hygiene' and 'merit'. It has not only brought the violence of caste to centre stage but also developed a language and a voice for dalit emancipation and assertion. In addition, dalit literature imparted global visibility to the life-world of the dalits as translations of dalit life narratives were not only published internationally but also the protagonists were invited to international forums to comment on their life and their work.

Dalit literature sought to forge a larger dalit identity among the various dalit *jatis* by interrogating the logic of hierarchy among the various 'them' who traditionally conceived of themselves in a scale of graded inequality based on notions of which of them was more pure and more impure. Dalit literature in that sense gave wider currency to 'dalit' as an overarching identity of all former untouchable *jatis*.

Notes

1 The ideology that privileges the hierarchy of *jati*s as per the fourfold division is broadly termed as Brahmanic ideology. The most pointed juridical text associated with Brahmanic ideology is that of Manusmriti (the code of Manu) whose origin is generally attributed to ca. 100 BCE.

2 Reverently referred as 'Babasaheb' (an honorific title for one's ancestor/father).

3 Jotirao Phule was the leader of anti-Brahman movement in the western Indian state of Maharashtra. He along with his wife Savitribai Phule is credited with the starting of the first school for women and untouchables in India. The schools were set up around the year 1850 in the city of Pune (then known as Poona). He is now referred to as Mahatma Jotiba Phule.

4 Navayana Buddhism of Babasaheb Ambedkar can be positioned along with similar movements in different parts of the world which fall under the rubric 'socially engage Buddhism'. For more details on this, cf. S. B. King, *Socially Engaged Buddhism* (University of Hawaii Press, 2009). It can also be seen in continuation of other movements in late colonial India where people belonging to untouchable *jati*s opted for modern interpretations of Buddhism. For instance in Southern India, there was a movement among the Paraiyar caste called Sakya Buddhism spearheaded by a leader named Pundit Iyothee Thass. Navayana Buddhism represents a Buddhist identity interpreted for modern times, or rather a modern rendering of tradition. One of the major events at the ceremony of conversion which inaugurated Navayana Buddhism was the twenty-two vows that Babasaheb Ambedkar presented before his followers. Prominent of among them are the explicit denial of the theological and ritual foundations of Hinduism that legitimize the practice of caste.

5 According to Dangle, the term 'Dalit Literature' was coined at the first ever Dalit Literary Conference in 1958, which passed a resolution defining the term. See Dangle (1994 [1992]: xi).

6 Though the beginnings were in the state of Maharashtra, within Marathi language, the specific form of writings known as dalit literature spread to other Indian languages. Today there is a corpus of writing designated as dalit literature in almost all Indian languages.

7 D. Ganguly (2005) deals with this theme in her analysis of Marathi Dalit Literature. She reads dalit literature from the point of view of experiences taking place in the everyday life-world of the dalits, not as products of an ideological battle. 'Comportment is not quietism or a resigned acceptance of one's place in an unjust world order. It is rather an orientation towards all that is life-giving in a slippery, treacherous, aggressive, sorrowful, oppressive, unjust world. It points to truths that are larger than the pedagogical truths of either the social sciences or those of

political activism'. She focuses on those works of dalits which address the issue of oppression in 'non-pedagogical and non-ideological terms', not overtly conscious of 'contributing to transforming the social order' (177).

8 Within the literary movement, Gokhale (1993) finds three different groups of dalits. The first group comprises of well-established dalit writers with an institutional presence. They are recognized by the other Marathi litterateurs and most of them hail from middle-class backgrounds. The second group is younger, more radical and organized, and is more oriented towards action. The third group is that of the older, less-educated folk poets, who represent a continuity from the tradition of *jalasa* and whose work is more accessible to the dalit masses (299).

9 As a consequence, a plurality of themes has developed. According to an estimate made by J. Gokhale, the dateline probably being in the late 1980s, there were three main groupings of dalit writers. The first group is that of Dalit Sahitya Sansad headed by Baburao Bagul. The second the Asmitaadarsh group of G. Pantawane and the third the Bauddh Sahitya Parishad initiated by Bahusaheb Adsul. Each of these groups holds its conferences in different parts of Maharashtra (see Gokhale 1993: 328–9).

10 There are also prominent non-Buddhist dalit writers. For example, a very popular dalit writer Annabhau Sathe belonged to the *Matang* community and his poems and other writings contain strong sentiments of revolution.

11 For example, two poems of this variety are included in the anthology of dalit literature in English titled *Poisoned Bread*. They are: *Tathagatha* authored by Bhagwan Sawai, and *Yashodhara* by Hira Bansode. See Dangle (1994 [1992]: 29–30; 31–2).

12 Lullabies.

13 'Verses, a distich of a particular measure in vernacular language, and the light air sung by women while grinding, lulling infants etc' (Poitevin 2002: 373).

14 *Subaltern counterpublic* is a term developed by Nancy Fraser (1990). She explains it thus: '[T]hey are parallel discursive arenas where members of subordinated social groups invent and circulate counterdiscourses, which in turn permit them to formulate oppositional interpretations of identities, interests and needs' (67).

15 According to Sharmila Rege, renowned academician and pioneer of studies on the dalit-feminist standpoint, the word 'dalit' was first coined by Babasaheb Dr B. R. Ambedkar in the year 1928 CE in his writings in the journal *Bahishkrut Bharat* (India of the ex-communicated). Cf. Rege (2006: 11).

16 'Scheduled castes' refer to caste groups which are categorized as such in the schedule prepared by the central as well as the state governments primarily marking them eligible for benefits of compensatory discrimination in public educational institutions and undertakings.

17 The Mahar is a caste group (*jati*) belonging predominantly to Maharashtra state. They constitute the largest *jati* in terms of population among all the *jatis* of the former untouchables.

18 Gopal Baba Valangkar is considered a pioneer in the assertion of dalits in demanding rights from the British administration. In a petition that he submitted to the British in 1894 he demanded of them to ensure equal civil rights and employment to untouchable communities. The 'Valangkar Petition' is considered as a benchmark in the evolution of dalit consciousness in western India.

19 The particular accent of dalit literature has been in the form of *testimonio* as commented upon by writers such as Sharmila Rege (cf. Rege 2006). Rege talks of dalit literature as posing an 'epistemological challenge' (1). She considers dalit life narratives as *testimonio*s 'which forge a right to speak both for and beyond the individual and contest explicitly or implicitly the 'official forgetting' of histories of caste oppression, struggles and resistance' (13).

20 For instance, Navayana Publishing House, based at New Delhi.

21 *Bhakti* (literally translated as devotion) refers to a range of religious movements that spanned the length and breadth of present day India. These movements were anti-Brahmanic in the sense that they insisted on the devotee's personal relationship with a deity as central to religious belief. The promoters of bhakti movement are generally called sant (saint) and held views of equality of all persons before deities thereby directly attacking ritual-ortiented Brahmanic priesthood.

22 Two characters gleaned from writings of non-dalit writers referring to the dalit subjects that Laura Brueck mentions are: (a) the character of Velutha in *God of Small Things* by Arundhati Roy and (b) the personality of Mangal in Premchand's novel *Dudh ka Daam* (the price of milk).

23 Laura Brueck particularly mentions the example of Kusum Meghwal, a dalit woman writer who has stood up to the tendency on the part of the dalit writers to silence the voices of dalit women when they address the violence of patriarchy that they encounter at the hands of dalit men. Cf. Brueck (2014: 178).

References

Bhabha, H. K. (1994). *The Location of Culture*. London and New York: Routledge.

Brueck, L. (2014). *Writing Resistance: The Rhetorical Imagination of Hindi Dalit Literature*. New York: Columbia University Press.

Chakravarti, U. (2013). 'In Her Own Write: Writing from a Dalit Feminist Standpoint'. *India International Centre Quarterly* 39.3,4: 134–45.

Constable, P. (1997). 'Early Dalit Literature and Culture in Late Nineteenth and Early Twentieth Century Western India'. *Modern Asian Studies* 31.2: 317–38.

Dangle, A. (ed.) (1992). *Poisoned Bread: Translations from Modern Marathi Dalit Literature*. Bombay: Orient Longman.

Deo, V., & Zelliot, E. (1994). 'Dalit Literature – Twenty-Five Years of Protest? Of Progess?' *Journal of South Asian Literature* 29.2: 41–67.

Fraser, N. (1990). 'Rethinking the Public Sphere: A Contribution to the Critique of Actually Existing Democracy'. *Social Text* 25/26: 56–80.

Gajarawala, T. J. (2013). *Untouchable Fictions: Literary Realism and the Crisis of Caste.* New York: Fordham University Press.

Ganguly, D. (2005), *Caste, Colonialism and Counter-Modernity: Notes on a Post colonial Hermeneutics of Caste.* London and New York: Routledge

Gokhale, J. (1993). *From Concessions to Confrontation: The Politics of an Untouchable Community.* Bombay: Popular Prakashan.

Guru, G. (1995). 'Dalit Women Talk Differently'. *Economic and Political Weekly* 30.41 & 42: 2548–50.

Guru, G. (2013). 'Labouring Intellectuals: The Conceptual World of Dalit Women'. *India International Centre Quaterly* 39.3,4: 54–68.

Junghare, I. (1988). 'Dr. Ambedkar: The Hero of the Mahars, Ex-Untouchables of India'. *Asian Folklore Studies* 47: 93–121.

Limbale, S. (2004). *Towards an Aesthetic of Dalit Literature: History, Controversies and Considerations,* trans. A. Mukherjee. Hyderabad: Orient Longman.

Poitevin, G. (2002). *The Voice and the Will: Subaltern Agency: Forms and Motives.* New Delhi: Manohar Publishers and Distributors & Centre de Sciences Humaines.

Rege, S. (2006). *Writing Caste/Writing Gender: Reading Dalit Women's Testimonies.* New Delhi: Zubaan, An Imprint of Kali for Women.

Zelliot, E. (1996). *From Untouchable to Dalit: Essays on the Ambedkar Movement.* New Delhi: Manohar Publishers.

Mandarin Chinese in Education and Society in Xinjiang

Mamtimyn Sunuodula

Introduction

The passage and coming into force of 'Law of the People's Republic of China on the Standard Spoken and Written Chinese Language' (also known as 'Law on National Common Language') in 2000 and 2001 marked the beginning of a new era in language planning and policy in China (Budao 2001; People's Republic of China 2001; Xu 2001). The law placed a renewed emphasis on Mandarin Chinese as the national 'common language' of China and provided a legal framework for language planning and policies to promote and enforce the standard language nationally. This was followed by provincial and local implementation directives and policy guidelines issued by governments at subnational levels (Kumul City Government 2006; XUAR Government 2004). While the law and the subnational level directives and guidelines reinforced the ongoing efforts to promote and enforce Mandarin Chinese as the standard spoken dialect in areas where other Chinese spoken dialects are in use, the effects on the areas with predominantly non-Han populations, many of whom are educated and proficient only in their mother tongue, have been far greater. One such area is Xinjiang Uyghur Autonomous Region (XUAR, or Xinjiang hereafter), which has the official autonomous region status with the main local language being Uyghur, recognized as a regional official language, along with the national majority language, Mandarin Chinese (People's Republic of China 2001; XUAR Government 2002). The Xinjiang government began implementing what it dubbed as 'bilingual' (Baker 2006: 213–26) education policy in which Mandarin Chinese replaced the minority languages as the medium of instruction and Chinese writing instead of minority scripts at all levels of minority education, pushing the minority languages into being a mere school subject. The XUAR government described it as 'leap frog development' (跨域式发展) in ethnic education (Gu 2010; XUAR Government 2011a), while some critics used the familiar term 'great leap forward' (R. Ma 2009), invoking memories of China's disastrous industrialization campaign which took place in the late 1950s. The change came in the backdrop of rapid increase in population mobility, high economic growth, social transformations and growing individual, ethnic and regional disparities. In this chapter, I will examine the following:

1. How the current and historical language policies in Xinjiang relate to the Chinese state-building projects, especially in its ethnic and linguistic peripheries.
2. The local dynamics of language practices and agency of local actors in producing, reproducing and transforming their linguistic habitus, often in opposition to the what is ascribed for them by the state and its agents.
3. The ways in which current language policies represented, articulated and implemented and the manner in which we understand the underlying forces and counter-forces within the framework of relations of power.
4. The (in)effectiveness of the state's policies in achieving the stated goals and how we understand the gap between the goals and actual outcomes.

Unified language and Chinese state-building

In his widely cited work, James Scott (1998) notes the importance of language in state knowledge, control, authority and maintenance and reproduction of its power over its subjects. This is how he put it:

> The great cultural barrier imposed by a separate language is perhaps the most effective guarantee that a social world, easily accessible to insiders, will remain opaque to outsiders. Just as the stranger or state official might need a local guide to find his way around sixteenth century Bruges, he would need a local interpreter in order to understand and be understood in an unfamiliar linguistic environment. A distinct language, however, is a far more powerful basis for autonomy than a complex residential pattern. It is also the bearer of a distinctive history a cultural sensibility, a literature, a mythology, a musical past. In this respect, a unique language represents a formidable obstacle to state knowledge, let alone colonization, control, manipulation, instruction, or propaganda.
>
> Of all state simplifications, then, the imposition of a single, official language may be the most powerful, and it is the precondition of many other simplifications . . .

One can hardly imagine a more effective formula for immediately devaluing local knowledge and privileging all those who had mastered the official linguistic code. It was a gigantic shift in power. (72–3)

Scott asserts that modern nation-state is deliberate political construct based on centralization, including the centralized single language. The increasingly forceful promotion of Mandarin Chinese over the past decade and through it a linguistic centralization over the diverse population of Xinjiang is not only about the learning of Mandarin Chinese and achieving communicative competence in the language by non-Chinese speaking peoples, it is, more importantly, also about setting Mandarin Chinese as the norm and the bearer of superior civilization (Bourdieu 1991; Harrell 1995) and devaluation of local knowledge.

Learning of Mandarin Chinese by minority language speakers has frequently been represented in the media, political and so-called expert discourses as bringing to indigenous peoples of Xinjiang more than five thousand years of Chinese civilization, Confucian values, Chinese literature, contemporary popular culture, economic progress and access to scientific knowledge (Guan 2001; L. Wang 2001). China's political leaders envisage it as part of a wider political project to make Uyghur culture and Uyghur people 'legible' within a scheme that they consider universal, inevitable and grandly utopian. They see Mandarin Chinese medium education as superior and more sophisticated in quality than minority language medium education and mean to inculcate political loyalty among Uyghurs towards the state and assume identity positions that make them identify with the Chinese motherland and an imagined Han-centric nation. The process of linguistic centralization requires Uyghurs not only to have the necessary proficiency in Mandarin Chinese, but also to embrace majority Han culture, for example, Han mythologies that claim ancestry from the mythical Yan and Huang emperors (Hu 2010).

Whereas the basic competence in Mandarin Chinese and loyalty to the Communist Party had once defined participation in political and economic life for some Uyghur elites, a full command of the language and embrace of Chinese cultural norms is now demanded from every Uyghur in order for them to qualify for participation in the economy, politics, education and social structures which are dominated by the majority Han. The implicit logic is to define a hierarchy of languages and cultures, devaluing the Uyghur language and culture to an inferior status in the public domain, such as education and government. At the apex of this implicit hierarchical order are the Han culture and Mandarin Chinese and the embodying institutions such as schools, universities and businesses in Han dominated cities and provinces. Competency in Mandarin Chinese and Han cultural norms has become the focal point of total political power in Xinjiang upon which physical mobility, economic advancement, political patronage, public services and education system are all hinged, as well as a pointer to the path of social advancement and material success. The project offers both coercion and inducements promising to reward those who comply with its logic and to penalize those who ignore it (Scott 1998: 72–3).

Uyghur language, a key code to Uyghur history, sensibilities and ethnic identity, has now become the logical focus of the Chinese government's modernist ambitions and linguistic centralization project. For Uyghurs, the Uyghur language is an emblem of their identity, which is often deeply felt. As Mandarin Chinese has been made at once powerful and exclusionary (Hill 2004) through state institutions, mediating access to sought after resources, privileging its legitimate speakers, the Uyghur language faced economic and political devaluation and marginalization.

But the learning of Mandarin Chinese is not a simple process that involves memorization and reproduction of vocabulary, grammar and standardized meaning, that is, the abstract linguistic code (Schieffelin 2007: 140–1). As Bakhtin (1981) reminds us, activities of passing ideas from one language to another is not and has never been neutral. Not only are they imbued with language ideologies and culture-bound textual practices, in the context of Xinjiang, issues of power are never far from the surface. As Bakhtin puts it: 'Language is not a neutral medium that passes freely and easily into the private property of the speaker's intentions; it is populated – overpopulated – with the intentions of others. Expropriating it, forcing it to submit to one's own intentions and accents, is a difficult and complicated process' (294). In the following sections, I will discuss the issues of Chinese state-building, language centralization and local responses in Xinjiang within the framework of norm setting, authority and power relations.

Mandarin Chinese as a school subject in Uyghur education

After Xinjiang was incorporated into the People's Republic of China in 1950, the Uyghurs were recognized as one of the fifty-five minority nationalities in China and, in 1956, Xinjiang was named the Xinjiang Uyghur Autonomous Region (XUAR), one of five province-level administrative units in the country to be designated as an autonomous region, in recognition of the dominant demographic position of the Uyghur population (CCP Central Committee Archival Research Office and CCP XUAR Committee 2010). The Uyghur language was legitimized as an official regional language, along with Mandarin Chinese. In the first decade prior to 1959, most primary school pupils followed the system of learning Uyghur and using it as the medium of instruction. Chinese was not taught till they reached secondary school (Ouyang and Liu 2009).

Expansion of Uyghur schools continued after 1949. There were 182,427 (20% enrolment rate) Uyghur and other ethnic minority students studying at 1,335 primary schools and there were only 4,191 at secondary level and 185 at university level (XUAR Local History Editorial Office 1985: 496). In 1952, there were 40 middle schools in Xinjiang employing 540 Uyghur and other ethnic minority teachers (XUAR Local History Editorial Office 2007: 659). The education system only managed to produce a few people who were sufficiently proficient in Mandarin Chinese to act as translators and interlocutors between the Han officials and local Uyghurs (XUAR Local History Editorial Office 2000: 604–607). Many Han who migrated to southern Xinjiang had to learn to speak in Uyghur as they found themselves to be in the absolute minority in linguistic terms and population size (Ouyang and Liu 2009).

After Mandarin Chinese was made an optional school subject in 1950 at Uyghur middle schools, along with Russian (XUAR Local History Editorial Office 2000), the position of Chinese language was gradually strengthened (A. Wang 2012). As very few Uyghurs attended school and even fewer went on to study at secondary school, the actual impact of Mandarin Chinese education, especially on those living in rural southern Xinjiang, was minimal. For those rural Uyghurs, Uyghur language is the only one they know and with which they communicate, mostly with each other. There was also a shortage of qualified Chinese language teachers and lack of suitable teaching material and adequate learning resources that contributed to the poor learning outcome.

At the second XUAR Secondary Education Congress in 1956, specific Chinese language requirements were put forward for Uyghur schools. It stipulated that Uyghur middle schools must offer four to six hours of Mandarin Chinese lessons per week and students must learn at least 2,500 Chinese characters, as well as acquire basic competency in oracy by the end of three-year middle school education. It also demanded that students learnt further 2,000 characters at high school level and achieve competency in scientific language so that they can be educated in Mandarin Chinese at tertiary level (Benson 2004; Ouyang and Liu 2009). This was a very ambitious goal, if not a totally unrealistic one. Among the 56,000 characters in modern Chinese, the most commonly used 2,400 characters make up 99 per cent of all characters used in Chinese publications. Considering the large number of characters, it is a challenging task for anyone to learn it regardless of their cultural background, or ethnic origin (Sun 2006). Accordingly, the Uyghur students were expected to reach the same level of literacy and oracy in Mandarin Chinese as the native Mandarin Chinese speakers.

It was not clear how many Uyghur students at Uyghur medium schools succeeded in achieving what was required of them, but considering the linguistic ecology, availability of qualified teachers and resources to support the learning as well as resistance from at least some sections of the Uyghur society who saw the move as a threat to their traditional way of life, it is not difficult to see that, for most Uyghurs, the document remained only on paper without bringing about the desired effects. Many Uyghurs also hold the view that they are the indigenous and rightful owners of the territory of Xinjiang and the Han migrants to the region should learn to speak Uyghur, rather than demanding that the Uyghurs speak Mandarin Chinese (Smith Finley 2013: 34; Tsung 2014).

In 1957, Uyghurs were offered the choice to attend Chinese language schools, but the take up was negligible. However with the rapid increase in Han migration to Xinjiang from late 1950s, the number of Uyghurs who chose to send their children to Han schools has increased, especially after the Cultural Revolution. But considering the relatively high number of Uyghurs from well-educated backgrounds being located in a major city with nearly 80 per cent of the population being Han, the take up of places in Han schools by Uyghurs appears not high. This can be an indication of Uyghur attitude to Han education and their strong desire to maintain Uyghur language and culture through education in Uyghur language, despite the lure of economic and political advantages for being educated in Chinese schools.

However, the lack of interest or resistance by Uyghurs in sending their children to Chinese schools did not stop the government from stepping up its efforts to strengthen the teaching of Mandarin Chinese, or investing in new Chinese language textbooks, at Uyghur schools.

The teacher training institutions in Xinjiang started recruiting Han students from Inland cities and provinces to be trained as Mandarin Chinese teachers. At one such institution, over a thousand students were being trained in 1966. They were recruited to several different strands, including majoring in Uyghur language. By 1965, the number of Uyghur secondary schools and the number of teachers increased to 339 schools and 3,709 Uyghur teachers, but the figures were still very small compared with the total population – 300 Mandarin Chinese teachers across Xinjiang in 1965 teaching in Uyghur and other non-Chinese language instruction schools (Ouyang and Liu 2009).

After ten years of disruption and destruction to the education system in Xinjiang, the ending of the Cultural Revolution in 1976 and its official repudiation provided a window for the exertion of Uyghur political strength (Hill 2004). Despite the official rhetoric about the importance of achieving Mandarin Chinese competency, a degree of local autonomy in Xinjiang can also be seen in some aspects of regional language and education policies. The number of teachers teaching at Uyghur medium schools increased fourfold between 1976 and 1997, an indication of rapid expansion of Uyghur medium education during this period. The latitude given to the regional authorities and those at subregional level in how and to what extent they implement policies emanating from the national level has increased. What is clear, from the numbers and education qualifications of Mandarin Chinese language teachers employed at Uyghur schools, is that systematic, long-term Mandarin Chinese language education programmes of proven effectiveness were poorly funded in Uyghur majority areas.

Against the backdrop of the restoration of the traditional Uyghur written script and a relatively liberal period for Uyghur language in education after the Cultural Revolution, policies related to language provision for Uyghurs continued to emphasize the importance of teaching Chinese to Uyghur pupils. The XUAR government issued a document in 1977 entitled 'The Directive on Strengthening the Mandarin Chinese Teaching at Minority Schools' requiring that Mandarin Chinese be introduced as a core subject from Year 3 of primary schools at ethnic minority schools. In 1984, the XUAR CCP Committee put forward a goal of achieving universal proficiency in both Mandarin Chinese and Uyghur language in education by 1995 (Ouyang and Liu 2009). A further government document issued in 1985 asserted that within five years schoolteachers and administrators in the region were required to use Chinese in all formal domains, such as classrooms and meetings. All secondary school leavers were required to have competence in Chinese.

From 1987, the investment on resources devoted to the teaching of Mandarin Chinese began to be accelerated. An additional 500 vacant teachers' positions were diverted from other subject areas to Mandarin Chinese teaching posts at Uyghur schools annually on the government's order (XUAR Local History Editorial Office 2007: 603). By 1988, the number of Mandarin Chinese teachers at Uyghur schools reached 5,661, of which 2,958 were secondary school teachers. The total number increased to 7,337 in 1990 and by 1999, the number of Mandarin Chinese teachers at schools reached 13,776 (Ouyang and Liu 2009) and, again in 2005, the number increased to 19,989 (Y. Wang 2009).

The level of proficiency in Mandarin Chinese among the Uyghurs remained low, despite the general increase in the level of education and drives to achieve universal compulsory education. An official survey conducted in 1986 showed that only 4.4 per cent of the Uyghurs reported that they were fully communicative in Mandarin Chinese, with 90 per cent reporting that they did not have the basic communicative competence in the language (CASS Institute of Ethnology and Anthropology 1994).

Education in Mandarin Chinese: a new phase-ethnic minority language policy discourse

In contemporary Chinese political, media and academic discourses, it is normal to consider minorities as backward or inferior in any aspect, including their languages and cultures, compared with the superiority and advancement of the majority Han (J. Ma 2013: 219; Postiglione 2007: 99). The pejorative perception of ethnic minorities, and by extension the languages they speak, is apparent in much academic and political discourse about them. The following examples illustrate how widespread and influential such discourses are:

> Improving the quality of labour force is the most important precondition for infrastructure development. The first problem to resolve is the language barrier. When the cadres in Inland[1] areas do mass ideological persuasion work (i.e. propaganda), they can at least be understood by the masses after a few repeats. But in Xinjiang, that won't work because of the language barrier makes it impossible to communicate. Moreover, the ethnic minority languages have great limitations; some new terms are impossible to explain in minority languages, this is particularly evident in the age where information technology is highly developed. Therefore, the first task we need to do now is to have the schoolteachers to teach in Mandarin Chinese. But, it is not sufficient for the teachers who teach in Mandarin Chinese to understand only Chinese, we must build an army of teachers who can understand both Mandarin Chinese and Uyghur languages at the same time. Secondly, we need to attach importance to improving the quality of ethnic minority cadres. The simple and straight psychological characteristics of ethnic minorities are very advantageous for communicating and building trust and understanding with them.' (L. Wang 2001)

Wang was the party secretary of the CCP XUAR Committee for more than a decade from 1994 to 2010' as well as a member the CCP Central Politbureau.

> With the great economic transformation and the massive movements of people and goods, more and more people form ethnic minority areas began to realize that 'for them, in order to integrate into the world, they must first integrate into the nation, in order to integrate into the nation, the language barrier must be overcome'
>
> As citizens of China, they must deepen their sense of mission and responsibility towards the motherland. They can only foster identification with the culture of the motherland through understanding the Chinese culture which goes back to time immemorial, and understanding the history of development of ethnic groups. (Turahun 2010)

Turahun is an ethnic Uyghur government official who was charged with implementation of the 'bilingual' education policies.

> In the long historical process, Han ethnicity has been the unifying core to which all other different ethnic groups yearned for. This is because Han people possessed a superior natural conditions and stable geographic entity, strong state power, advanced economy and abundant culture. Meanwhile, Han people, like an ethnic melting pot with its characteristic inclusivity, accepted and integrated those ethnicities and their culture and continuously radiated in all directions and grew bigger and bigger like rolling snow ball. (Guan 2001)

Guan Yanpo is a professorial fellow at the Institute of Ethnography and Anthropology in the Chinese Academy of Social Sciences, specializing in the history of ethnic relations in China.

As evidently shown in those sample quotations from powerful political figures and prominent intellectuals, a body of discourse about different value of languages in China has ideologically been shaped by these actors and in turn the discourse has shaped the government's language policies towards ethnic minority languages. In the broader context, the government's political discourse of ethnic integration in education and the position of Uyghur language in its linguistic stratification are interdependent (Y. Chen 2008).

Policymakers as well as majority of the Han population in China believe that national minorities lack proper education and the state should take measures to enhance the chances of minority students being able to participate in the kind of 'regular' education that already exists among Han students, that is, the education in Mandarin Chinese as opposed to minority language education (Hansen 1999: 6–8; Harrell 1995). The socially and politically constructed categories of regular 'education' for Han majority as opposed to 'ethnic education' for non-Han peoples form constructed structural inequalities (C. Wang and Zhou 2003). 'The ideology of inequality is legitimized by the conviction that the dominance of the center is truly helping and thus is to the benefit of the culturally inferior peoples' (Hansen 1999: 243). Language education policies are planned, devised and implemented in Xinjiang within the context of paternalistic and hierarchical approach to ethnic relations (Sautman 1998).

Bilingual education policy

Of the many language policies officially promulgated in the history of Xinjiang, it can be argued the one that has caused the most far-reaching consequence for the fate of Uyghur language and culture is the region-level document promulgated by the Xinjiang government on the promotion of 'bilingual' education. The 2004 'bilingual education' document stipulates that Mandarin Chinese be made the primary or the sole language of instruction in elementary and middle-school classrooms (A. Feng and Sunuodula 2009). A further document issued in 2005 expands the scope of the policy to preschool education (Turahun 2013). 'Bilingual education' has come to mean that Mandarin Chinese is *the* medium of instruction from kindergarten onwards and minority languages are to be relegated to a school subject where it is offered (Ma 2009).

The small-scale experimental 'bilingual' classes with Uyghur and Mandarin Chinese languages as the language of instruction were set up in 1992 with the ostensible aim of improving the quality of minority education and the proficiency of Uyghur students in Mandarin Chinese. By 2000, there were around 4,000 students receiving 'bilingual' education in Xinjiang and the figure increased to 36,000 in 2004 (Y. Wang 2009: 224). Xinjiang University, the top university in the region, had long maintained two faculties, one for Chinese language and one for Uyghur language instruction. In 2002, the government ordered that all classes except Uyghur literature would be taught in Chinese, and professors accustomed to lecturing in Uyghur were given a year to brush up their Mandarin (Millward 2007: 345).

Since 2004, the campaign was pushed to an unprecedented new level. The pace of 'bilingual' education reform greatly accelerated and the language of instruction switched from Uyghur to Mandarin Chinese in all basic education. The changes were implemented within a short space of time, leaving schools, the teachers and the students unprepared, resentful and often confused (R. Ma 2009; Turahun 2013). In 2006, the number of Uyghur students who were receiving 'bilingual' education jumped to 1,45,000, more than fourfold increase in two years' time (Y. Wang 2009: 224).

The stated aim of the programme has had a number of strands, which evolved over time, but it is clear the overriding priority is a political one and it is ideologically driven. Initially, it was dubbed as a human resource development issue to improve the chances and competitiveness of Uyghurs by improving their proficiency in Mandarin Chinese through intensive Chinese language education, but this was quickly overtaken by political consideration. A ten-year planning document issued by the XUAR government in 2011 sets out the rationale and objectives of the 'bilingual' education drive:

> China is a multiethnic country. Mandarin Chinese and standard Chinese writing is the National Common Language. Learning and mastering of the National Common Language is beneficial for the strengthening of different ethnic groups' sense of belonging to the Chinese motherland and their Chinese national identity. It is also beneficial for the promotion of interethnic communication and exchange among the youth from different ethnicity and benefits their all-round development for the rest of their lives. Advancement of 'bilingual' education with the National Common Language at its core supplement by ethnic minority languages in Xinjiang is a strategic measure to raise the quality of ethnic minority education and develop ethnic minority multilingual talents who are proficient in both Mandarin Chinese and an ethnic minority language. This is an inevitable necessity for deepening the implementation of the Great Western Development Strategy, building a harmonious socialist society and to realize Xinjiang's leapfrog development. It is a pressing demand for protecting the ethnic and national unity, common prosperity, development and progress of all ethnic groups and achieving long lasting peace and stability in Xinjiang. The Party and the State attach great importance to the development of ethnic minority 'bilingual' education in Xinjiang and consider the advancement of the 'bilingual' education as strategically important measure for achieving Xinjiang's long lasting peace and stability and leapfrog development. As an important task in realizing the leapfrog development of education in Xinjiang, the 'bilingual' education is placed in an strategically important place. (XUAR Government 2011b)

While the statement is careful to avoid using the term 'official language' for Mandarin Chinese, it nevertheless confirms the position of Mandarin Chinese as the core and dominant language in education, society, economic and political life, universally applicable to all diverse peoples of China. Likewise, it also explicitly states that the ethnic minority language is supplementary, regardless of the geographic location, demographic composition, diverse linguistic and cultural traditions. By restating the obvious that China is a multiethnic country and describing Mandarin Chinese as the 'common' language for all peoples, it suggests that it is an obligation for all Chinese citizens to be proficient in Mandarin Chinese. As Scott (1998: 72–3) pointed out, this created a hierarchy of languages and cultures in China with Mandarin Chinese and Han culture being imagined at the apex of that hierarchical order. It is also telling that, in political discourse and official statements, the politically loaded construct 'bilingual education' has totally different meaning for the majority Han and minority peoples like the Uyghurs. For Uyghurs, it meant to be fully proficient in Mandarin Chinese and Han cultural norms to catch up with the Han, while the Uyghur language plays an auxiliary role in their lives. For the Han, it is largely conceptualized as being proficient in English and Mandarin Chinese and becoming globally competitive and culturally cosmopolitan, rather than putting an effort to learn Uyghur or other ethnic minority languages (A. Feng 2007).

It is stated in the passage that the learning of Mandarin Chinese by Uyghurs would improve their quality, help them to catch up with the modern world and become more civilized. Implied logic in this statement is that the goal of learning Mandarin Chinese language is not only to become communicative in the language, rather the language itself embodies a more advanced civilization and higher quality than Uyghur language and culture. By mastering the Mandarin Chinese language, Uyghurs become more ideologically and politically acceptable only if they also recognized the superiority of the Mandarin Chinese language and inferiority of their own Uyghur language.

In specific terms, it meant the fluency in Mandarin Chinese has been made one of the defining requirements in order for Uyghurs to qualify for a job, to participate in the economy and political life and become a qualified Chinese citizen. The link between development, modernization and fluency in Mandarin Chinese is viewed as direct, inevitable and scientific conclusion. By this insertion the Party-state is attempting to establish an absolute regime of truth in which Mandarin Chinese and Han cultural practices are the authorized and legitimate norms by which all other languages and cultures in Xinjiang are ideologically judged, economically evaluated and politically assessed, while at the same time signifying those minority languages and cultures as backward, unrefined and not fit for a modern world.

Countless propaganda articles in government controlled or mediated national, regional and local newspapers and other media outlets have been published praising the benefits of the 'bilingual education' for the Uyghurs and singing the achievements of the 'bilingual education' campaign. Numerous so-called bilingual education experts have been assembled, or sprung up by themselves seeking a political opportunity or an economic reward, to justify the switch of the language of instruction in education at Uyghur schools from Uyghur to Mandarin Chinese. The phrase 'bilingual education' has become a buzzword for political figures and they lined up one after the other stressing the importance of learning Mandarin Chinese by Uyghurs and praising the benefits of 'bilingual' education.

'Bilingual education' has come to mean the promotion of Chinese through an education system in which Chinese is taught both as a school subject and used as the medium of instruction for other subjects, regardless of the special status of Uyghur as a minority language (A. Feng 2005; Schluessel 2007; XUAR Office for Bilingual Education Steering Committee 2012).

The document sets out 2020 as the goal to achieve a comprehensive all Mandarin Chinese medium education system from age 5 onward for Uyghurs and other ethnic minorities, ending the support for the Uyghur language medium education across all parts of Xinjiang. According to the document, 2020 is also the target date for all Uyghur high school graduates to achieve full proficiency in the National Common Language (i.e. Mandarin Chinese). The document adds that Uyghur language will be supplementary, but it doesn't specify any required standards and assessment targets or how that might be achieved (XUAR Government 2011b).

The conceptualization of 'bilingual education' as Mandarin Chinese medium education replenished by a few hours of Uyghur language classes a week has posed unprecedented challenge to the position of the Uyghur language in political, economic, social and cultural spheres and for the Uyghurs living in Xinjiang who use Uyghur as their primary language (*Economist* 27 June 2015). The most directly affected have been the students and staff at minority language medium schools and other educational institutions. They are now required to become fluent (or near fluent), within a short space of time, in both spoken and written Chinese. The teachers also have had to switch from Uyghur to Chinese in conducting their teaching (R. Ma 2009). The symbolic effect of this change on Uyghur ethnic, social and cultural identity is just as great as the economic and tangible impacts.

School mergers and changes to teaching staff

Large-scale school-merging campaigns were launched in 2004, with an ostensible aim of creating a better Chinese language environment by requiring Chinese medium schools and Uyghur medium schools to move under the same roof (CCP XUAR Committee and XUAR Government 2005; XUAR Local History

Editorial Office 2005: 323), and effectively placed under Han school leadership. Where schools previously had almost all Uyghur employees in predominantly Uyghur populated areas and created precious little white collar employment opportunities for well-educated Uyghurs, they now faced with increased squeeze by Han teaching staff as they are favoured by Han school heads and school management. Between 2000 and 2007, a 71 per cent increase in the number of merging schools could be observed, from 461 up to 791. Experienced Uyghur teachers who had difficulty in switching the language of instruction to Mandarin Chinese were assigned to menial jobs while a few lucky ones were assigned to teach Uyghur language, which has now become a school subject.

While the official rhetoric states that achieving competency in both Uyghur and Mandarin Chinese languages is the goal of the current Mandarin Chinese education drive, it is clear in practice that only minimal level of Uyghur language provision is offered as a school subject, at some schools where Model 1 'bilingual' education curriculum is adopted. Uyghur is not even offered as an optional subject at schools which have chosen Model 2 curriculum, which follows the national curriculum standards. This has led to many Uyghur schoolteachers who were experienced in teaching academic subjects in Uyghur but were judged not to be proficient to conduct their teaching in Mandarin Chinese, using strict set of tests in Mandarin Chinese, and other criteria such as political loyalty to the CCP, to be deemed no longer fit for teaching jobs. Their expertise in academic subjects, pedagogical experience and training became worthless (XUAR Government 2011b; XUAR Government Education Department 2011; XUAR Government Education Department and XUAR Government Human Resources Department 2015).

Now new teachers who are recruited from non-Mandarin Chinese native speaker background must reach the appropriate level in the National Mandarin Chinese Language Graded Test for Ethnic Minorities. 'New teachers whose mother tongue is Mandarin Chinese will receive training in the minority language to enable them to gain basic communicative competence in the language and adapt to the requirements of "bilingual" education' (XUAR Government 2011b). While the document sets out specific, stringent and hard to achieve Mandarin Chinese test requirements for Uyghur language speaking candidates for teaching jobs, it only sets vaguely defined training and basic competence in minority languages for Mandarin Chinese speaking candidates, without specific test targets. Furthermore, the document specifies a number of preferential employment terms and conditions for those Han candidates who come to Xinjiang from the Inland to teach.

The document also makes explicit the position of Mandarin Chinese in relation to Uyghur language in bilingual education. It states that the aim is to 'develop a bilingual education where the national common language (i.e. Mandarin Chinese) is central and Uyghur language is secondary' (XUAR Government 2011b).

Uyghur response: case studies

Language policy discourses in Xinjiang consistently present justifications and rationales, which distinguish Mandarin Chinese from the other languages as the language of modernity, economic progress and national unity and tacitly approve it as a measure of the level of civilizing Uyghur and other ethnic minorities. Language education policies explicitly represent Chinese medium education for Uyghurs as the only means by which to increase their human capital, job opportunities and political loyalty to the state and improve their human 'quality'. However, the political and administrative decisions taken cannot explain fully how the boundaries of the linguistic field are set or changed on the ground. The impact and outcomes of the language policies and discourses are contingent on them being legitimized by the society and recognition by the Uyghur students, as well as the degree of complicity and acceptance by the wider Uyghur society.

Presented here is the research data relating to Mandarin Chinese collected at multiple research sites in Xinjiang over a period of three years using a mixed methods approach. The qualitative interview data was gathered at a university using semi-structured interviews with Uyghur university students following ethnographic interviewing method. The aim was to solicit the students' views on different language practices and reflect on their own language practices and linguistic ideological dispositions at home, at school and in wider society. The qualitative data is supplemented by a quantitative research conducted at a later date at four high schools in four different locations. The research sites were chosen on the basis of linguistic demography, rural-urban difference, languages of instruction in education and types of institutions, as well taking into consideration the accessibility from both logistical and political perspectives. The analysis of data follows the emerging themes from the data and is conducted within Bourdieu's framework of capital, market and power.

Value of Mandarin Chinese as economic capital

Learning and achieving proficiency in Mandarin Chinese by Uyghurs is portrayed in political, media and academic discourses as a crucial part of human resource development in Xinjiang (L. Wang 2001). Current Mandarin Chinese – Uyghur 'bilingual' education policy and practices, which place Mandarin Chinese in an all-powerful position – is consistently defended with utilitarian economic and political justifications rather than cultural or other reasons. As professional and technical jobs, by definition, require higher education and higher education in Xinjiang is only conducted in Mandarin Chinese since the early 2002, Mandarin Chinese has a gatekeeping function which allows, or prevents, choice of continued education and, thus, future job opportunities for the individual and fulfilment of labour market needs for the society.

As a result, Mandarin Chinese has become the language of political power and prestige, socioeconomic mobility and advancement.

Data shows (Table 9.1) that over 90 per cent of the civil servant vacancies required proficiency in Mandarin Chinese in Xinjiang in 2010, in contrast to only 10 per cent required proficiency in minority languages, including Uyghur language. The ethnicity requirement specify 60 per cent from Han ethnicity who make up 40 per cent of Xinjiang's population and from 27 per cent minorities, who make up 60 per cent of Xinjiang's population. The unspecified default 10 per cent can be added to Han ethnicity, as this is what happens in practice. Considering language and ethnicity quotas include Chinese speaking Hui Muslims and others, such as Xibe and Mongolians who are more closely assimilated into Chinese language and culture than Uyghurs, they stand better chance of being successfully qualified as civil servants than Uyghurs and it can be speculated that the actual figure for Uyghurs can go even lower. It is an indication of how powerful the Mandarin Chinese language and its legitimate speakers, Han, has become in Xinjiang. Comparative figure for Tibet shows a more favourable picture for Tibetans than what we see for minorities in Xinjiang.

Analysis of my quantitative questionnaire responses and qualitative interview data below shows how Uyghur students view the changing fortunes of capital and value ascribed to different languages in Xinjiang's multilingual linguistic market and how they intend to invest their time and resources on different languages based on the students' understanding of the material and symbolic value and capital associated with each language.

Table 9.1 Ethnicity and language requirements specified in civil servant recruitment examination in Xinjiang, Tibet and Inner Mongolia in 2010

a. Xinjiang Uyghur Autonomous Region

No. of vacancies	Language requirement		Ethnicity requirement			
	Mandarin Chinese	Uyghur	Unspecified	Han	Minorities	Two ethnicities	Unspecified
1973	1385 (70.2%)	209 (10.6%)	379 (19.2%)	1196 (60.6%)	541 (27.4%)	43 (2.18%)	193 (9.78%)

b. Tibet Autonomous Region

No. of vacancies	Language requirement		Ethnicity requirement	
	Unspecified		Han	Ethnic minorities	Unspecified
1986	1986		23 (1.16%)	58 (2.92%)	1905 (95.92%)

c. Inner Mongolia Autonomous Region

No. of vacancies	Language requirement		Ethnicity requirement	
	Unspecified	Chinese / Mongol Bilingual	Unspecified	Ethnic minorities (Ewenki, Daur)
3408	3235 (94.93%)	173 (5.07%)	3397 (99.68%)	11 (0.32%)

Source: Tursun (2010). *The Protection of Minorities in Court Proceedings: A Perspective on Bilingual Justice in China.*

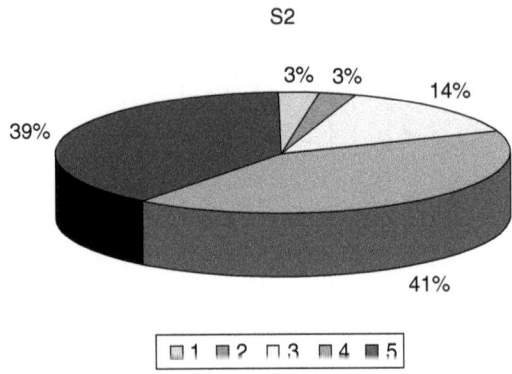

Figure 9.1 Student response to the importance of learning Chinese at school.
Source: Sunuodula and Cao (2015).

Following is the response to one of the questions asked in the questionnaire survey (Figure 9.1):

Statement: Chinese language teaching and learning should be further enhanced in my school.

The scale: 1 = strongly disagree, 2 = disagree, 3 = neutral, 4 = agree, 5 = strongly agree

As the chart shows, a significant majority of respondents (80%) supported the learning of Mandarin Chinese language at school. This demonstrates that majority of Uyghur students are willing and keen to improve their Chinese language skills and recognize the growing dominance and market value of Mandarin Chinese in the linguistic marketplace of Xinjiang. They are willing to invest their time, financial resources and effort to learn Mandarin Chinese so that they can gain the economic capital valued by the Han dominated economy and polity in order to prepare themselves for the employment market. Here is the observation of one of the teachers interviewed: 'They are very hard working. They get up very early and spend all day studying. You don't know how much energy they put into study (Mandarin Chinese).' Qualitative data from the student ethnographic interviews and responses to open-ended questions on the quantitative questionnaire confirm the conclusion from the quantitative data analysis. In both cases, the Uyghur students show strong extrinsic orientations about learning Mandarin Chinese, that is, not seeing it as means of identity and affiliation, rather for financial reward and communication (Bourdieu & Passeron 1990: 116). Following are some of the students' comments about learning Mandarin Chinese:

'Mandarin Chinese is very important for me to find a job.'

'I want to be a teacher in the future. It is a must that I learn Mandarin Chinese well.'

'My parents wish me to learn Mandarin Chinese well.'

'Mandarin Chinese is our national language. We have to learn it to communicate with others outside Xinjiang.'

'I will take College Entrance Exam in Mandarin Chinese, so I will need to study it hard.'

This shows the current Chinese medium education is socializing these students into the acts and stances associated with being successful in the job market, rather than socializing them into the acts and stances associated with what they are politically expected to be by the state.

Perception of threat to mother tongue

While the Uyghur students showed keen interested in learning Mandarin Chinese in order to improve their life chances where Mandarin Chinese occupies an unassailable dominance, many interviewees also showed anxiety about the rapid increase of the majority Han population and its growing economic and socio-political dominance on the region, diminishing status of Uyghur language in official discourse, negative influence on their education of being educated in a language that they did not fully grasp and about their own future for lacking Mandarin Chinese competence. The following are some typical answers from the Uyghur university students interviewed:

I am more worried about the great influx of Han immigration into Uyghur areas. This trend will have greater impact than the language assimilation policy. (Uyghur male, fifth year in journalism)

Mandarin Chinese is a difficult language to learn. I am required to write my thesis in Mandarin Chinese. There is little originality and creativity in it because I don't have deep enough knowledge of Mandarin Chinese to fully express myself. What is happening is language assimilation, not bilingual education. Most lectures are about politics, Han China's history and culture. I can't relate myself to what was taught about Qing history. (Uyghur male, first year MA in humanities)

I am very concerned about the overwhelming influence and pressure to learn Mandarin Chinese. Uyghurs are least knowledgeable in Mandarin Chinese compared with most other minority nationalities in China. I am not sure if I will be able to progress to Master's degree course when I finish my BA. (Uyghur male, fifth year in social sciences)

I used to be able to compose poetry and short stories in Uyghur and had a lot of creative imagination when I was at school. My mother tongue is the essential tool for me to think and create and it can never be replaced. I am now becoming a passive learner because I lack proficiency in Han language and I am not able to think creatively in Han language. I am losing interest in the subjects as I am not able to understand, digest and internalize the knowledge I have learned using Han language. (Uyghur male, fifth year in journalism)

Decades of rigorous, top-down promotion of Mandarin Chinese language education does not seem to bring about desired outcomes. The data as a whole suggest that the strong influence of the majority culture and the government policy to promote it cause anxiety leading to resistance which may well be the major hurdles for Uyghur students to acquire the Chinese language they wish to acquire (Dörnyei 2003).

The responses to the quantitative question on the position of Uyghur language in education show an overwhelming support for strengthening its position in schools. It is interesting to note that the responses received from the students who were enrolled at the Inland boarding schools, where there is no provision of Uyghur language and surrounded by Chinese linguistic and cultural landscape, were even stronger than students studying at schools in Uyghur majority areas.

Economic and symbolic value of Mandarin Chinese in Uyghur society

Policymakers interviewed were strongly supportive of the forceful promotion of Mandarin Chinese in Xinjiang. They believe that teaching Mandarin Chinese to Uyghur students will lead them to better employment and greater economic benefit. Uyghur language is also important, but with a lower ranking in comparison with Mandarin Chinese. As one official at the Xinjiang Education Department put it:

It is a choice between development and culture. If Uyghur people hope to raise their incomes and improve their living conditions, they must learn to speak Mandarin Chinese. It is a basic tool for them to participate in the country's economic development. It is unavoidable that minority language and culture will be affected to some extent. But they have to make the choice.

They appeared to be concerned with the lack or shortage of qualified teachers who, in their definition, ideally would be Uyghur teachers and can perform teaching tasks in Mandarin Chinese. They claimed it was the biggest challenge for carrying 'bilingual' education. As one put it: 'To improve our education, the precondition is the quality of teachers. We are in great demand of bilingual teachers who can teach in Mandarin Chinese. Good teachers won't stay. Natural environment is bad here and salary is not high.' They all agreed that teaching Uyghur students in Mandarin Chinese would lead them to better employment prospects and greater economic benefits and Uyghur language and culture are collaterals worth sacrificing for the sake of economic benefit and modernization of Xinjiang and China as whole. Such views were particularly evident in data from the two Han officials who expressed that Uyghur language is also important, but with a lower ranking in comparison with Mandarin Chinese.

In comparing empirical evidence obtained in several different minority populated regions in China, Feng and Sunuodula (2009) propose an analytical cycle for the process of minority language education policymaking (Figure 9.2). The evidence showed that the education in different regions had different degrees of integration into the national curriculum and that language education policies and practices differed from region to region, depending on the flexibility of the national policies in accommodating different conditions on the ground and interpretation of national policies by the local actors in accordance with the local priorities.

The stark difference in the implementation of two different sets of language education policies in Xinjiang, that is, the processes of implementing Uyghur language education policy and the Chinese language education policy, showed the dynamic relationship among the key actors and factors in a clear picture. For the policy process with the aim to promote Chinese language

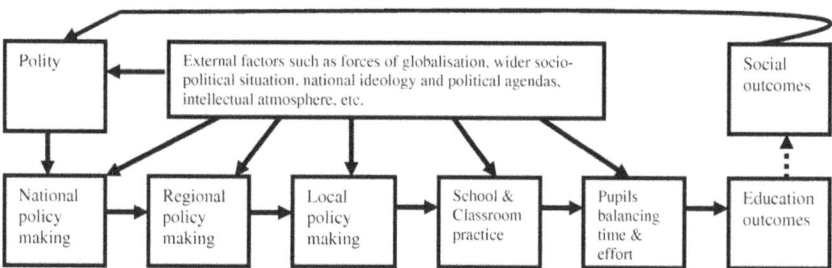

Figure 9.2 An analytical framework for minority educational policies in China. The dotted line between educational and social outcomes suggests a weak link between the two as social outcomes would usually derive from the entire society with schools forming only part of that society (Feng & Sunuodula 2009).

in education, all actors specified in the model are fully mobilized to play their respective roles. The literature and the data show that policymakers at regional, prefectural and county levels tend to carry the state policy exceedingly far by overemphasizing the promotion of Chinese, whereas parents and pupils make use of the system to balance the benefits and time and resources invested on it.

Autobiographical account of an Inland Xinjiang Senior Class student

Adil is one of the thousand students of the first cohort of Inland Xinjiang Boarding Class, which the government initiated in 2000. When he left Xinjiang in 2000, he was still a child aged 14. After four years of boarding school education at a prestigious high school located in one of the major trading centres in southern China several thousand miles away from his isolated hometown in southern Xinjiang and, surrounded completely by Han cultural and linguistic environment, he then goes on to enrol onto a degree programme at a university in another major coastal city in southern China where he spends four more years studying business management. On his graduation, he decides to take his chances and stays in the city and manages to find a job in a private company there, rather than returning back to Xinjiang to work. Very quickly, he becomes a successful and key employee of the company. After a long period of living in eastern China, his Mandarin Chinese is fluent and even carries the traces of slight southern Chinese accent.

Excerpts from Adil's Autobiographical Account

As Inland Xinjiang Senior Class students, we are the real sufferers. In fact, everyone wanted return to Xinjiang, but from an ideological viewpoint we couldn't adapt to and accept the conditions in Xinjiang, and Xinjiang also couldn't accommodate us.

The biggest question was employment. Everyone wanted to live and work in Urumqi. But, there is no hope of being able to get into one of the big national companies. I have not heard of any Uyghur who was able to succeed in getting a job in these big companies in Xinjiang. The Uyghurs had the following four types of employment options: civil servant, local government worker, special police and specially appointed temporary teacher. There was a great demand for temporary teachers as Xinjiang was implementing the 'bilingual education' policy and there were severe lack of qualified teachers. Any Inland Xinjiang Senior Class graduate can be competent in that job.

My friends from the Inland Xinjiang Senior Class had all returned to Xinjiang. I learned that one of them became a local policeman in Urumqi after graduating from a top university in China and another one found a job as prison guard after being unemployed for more than a year. These are the ones with good family connections. To pass the civil service recruitment exam, one must first have good family connections. Passing the written test is only a formality. Our 'Class Flower' took the civil service test in her hometown and she came first in the written test result, but she failed at the interview stage. So, she is now employed as a temporary teacher at a county school. Civil service positions were also tight in Xinjiang. Because there aren't much good employment opportunities there, one couldn't even think about starting up a business enterprise.

While studying in the Inland, we all had plans and ambitions, but after returning to Xinjiang, nothing was up to us. For those of us graduated in my cohort, we were made to feel that the state attached great importance to us as the students of first Inland Xinjiang Class and we had great expectations. But, after we graduated we felt we were almost forgotten. Not only did we grow fluent in Mandarin Chinese language, we also became fully knowledgeable in Han culture and social norms, which is still a very difficult task to overcome for the vast majority of ordinary Uyghurs. Chinese language education at the local schools is useless, there were no Han speakers in their living environment and the Han language they learn is impossible to use for communication. But we grew up in Inland Han society and are used to the way the Han people think. So, I always believe that people like me will have great opportunities in the future.

Two or three outstanding students in our cohort found employment in Beijing and stayed there. Perhaps they are also faced with the same questions that I am facing now. In the Inland, it wasn't so difficult for us to find employment. Despite the ethnic differences and misperceptions, the discrimination against the Uyghurs is still less in the economically developed areas of eastern China than in Xinjiang. The environment is fairer and the opportunities are more equal. But, it is not our hometown and there are many inconveniences living there and I miss my family.

Conclusion

Modern Uyghur education and formation of unified Uyghur linguistic market

Education, both formal and informal, plays a decisive role in the process that leads to the construction, legitimation and imposition of an official, or a formal, language. Through education the pupils are inculcated with the ideology of legitimate language and 'the similarities from which the community of consciousness which is the cement of the nation stems' (Bourdieu 1991: 48). But the education does not exist in a vacuum. It is situated within a web of cultural, social and ideological beliefs and practices that shape both educational practices and the way that these practices are interpreted (Friedman 2010).

With the introduction and expansion of modern education in Xinjiang from the early part of the twentieth century, the parallel education system, that is, the state-sponsored formal education versus the schools set up and run by Uyghur community organizations, continued. The Chinese warlord governors Yang Zengxin, later Jin Shuren, continued with the policy of state supported education in Chinese using the old Confucian style content and pedagogical methods more or less unchanged (W. Ma 2006). They even saw modern education for the Uyghurs as a threat to their despotic minority rule and obstructed its expansion (Millward 2007: 173–4). This has further alienated the newly emerged Uyghur intelligentsia as well as wider public, moving them further apart from the state education system, which was conducted in Chinese (Y. Wang 2009).

Harrell (1995) points out that the success of civilization projects depends not only on the efforts of the civilizing centre, but also on the degree of complicity and acceptance of it by the conceived peripheral peoples who are the objects of these projects. And, in Xinjiang's case, we can clearly see that the complicity and acceptance by Uyghurs of the Confucian civilizing project directed against them was minimal leading to an almost total failure of the project. In Bourdieu's (1991: 56) terms, the linguistic domination can occur only if a unified linguistic market and its social conditions exist with 'unequal distribution of the chances of access to the means of production of the legitimate competence, and to the legitimate places of expression'. Only then, the group that possesses the legitimate linguistic competence, such as Chinese, is able to impose it as the only legitimate language in formal linguistic markets. As long as the social and cultural basis for the production and reproduction of Uyghur language and a language ideology that considers and receives Uyghur as the norm exists, the top down efforts to change it are often doomed to fail (Billig 1995).

The modern education system established by progressive Uyghur intellectuals and wealthy businessmen in the first half of twentieth century, which was modelled on education systems in Turkey or Soviet Central Asia, laid the foundation for the expansion of literacy among the Uyghurs and the formation of a standard Uyghur language. Some of the individuals educated at these schools later became the leaders of Uyghur nationalist movements who established the two short-lived independent East Turkestan Republics (1933–34, 1944–49) and became key figures in the debate about the unified Uyghur language and national identity (Millward 2007: 171–5; Thum 2014: 171–4). This has had profound effect on the development of modern Uyghur ethnic and national self-consciousness and the development of modern Uyghur language and literature.

By the time when Xinjiang was incorporated into the newly established People's Republic of China in 1950, the Uyghur education was well established and widely spread among the Uyghurs, especially those living in urban areas, and it was incorporated into the state education by the new communist government (Benson 2004). The Uyghur medium education rapidly expanded in the following decade and again after the Cultural Revolution in 1976, in line with the state's goal of increasing literacy rates and education levels for the production of efficient workforce. This has created mechanisms for cultural and linguistic homogenization of Uyghur population and social conditions that make it possible for them to identify as members of the imagined Uyghur community (Anderson 1991: 6). Uyghur education and Uyghur language became the bedrock of modern Uyghur ethnic identity through which the identity itself is performatively realized. Among the many symbolic resources available for the cultural production of identity, language is the most flexible and pervasive (Bucholtz and Hall 2004). The individual novices are socialized into speaking Uyghur language and acquiring Uyghur ways of speaking, acting and being in the world that are recognized as legitimate within the Uyghur community (Friedman 2010). For most Uyghurs, speaking in Uyghur language is a natural, automated, unconscious or semi-conscious act, which formed the basis of their linguistic habitus that linguistically predispose them in their social interactions. The Uyghur medium education created the social conditions for the production and reproduction of a standard Uyghur language and unification of linguistic market within the Uyghur community, in parallel with the state-sanctioned official language, Mandarin Chinese. This has created a formidable resistance in defence of Uyghur language practices against the state efforts to promote the national majority language, Mandarin Chinese.

Mandarin Chinese as the 'common language' and symbolic domination

After more than a century from the introduction of state-sponsored Chinese medium education for Uyghurs in Xinjiang and the state's continuous efforts in assimilating the Uyghurs culturally and linguistically through education and political measures, the gap between the state's goal and linguistic and cultural practices of Uyghurs in reality remained as wide as ever. In fact, as statistically shown in this chapter, there was little progress in the number of Uyghurs who are considered to be proficient in Mandarin Chinese, let alone those who acknowledge Mandarin Chinese and idealized Han culture as the norm. It is too complex to trace an exhaustive list of explanations for this, but the individual Uyghur linguistic habitus and the collective social institutions that have been shaped and shaping the Uyghur linguistic and cultural practices remained strong, playing decisive roles in the endless reproduction of their linguistic predispositions and cultural habitus.

It is evident that most Uyghur interviewees in my qualitative research, as well as the respondents to my quantitative questionnaires, are well aware of the conditions they live in and are eager to improve their Mandarin Chinese competence in order to improve their life chances. They are also strongly supportive of maintaining or strengthening of the teaching of Uyghur language in their education, which has been in steep decline in recent years. What they perceive negatively in terms of language ideological orientation is not the learning of Mandarin Chinese and achieving the required communicative competence in the language; rather it is the efforts to culturally and linguistically assimilate them into the Han norms and practices and attempts to devalue the Uyghur language, by implication the Uyghur identity, in the all aspects of public life, a situation which Bourdieu (1991: 46) calls 'linguistic domination'.

Language and power

As Bourdieu (1977) informs us, language is a social practice rather than an abstract system which can be exchanged between users of different languages. It is a practice that is not distinct from other forms of everyday social activity. Practice is habitual social activity, the series of actions that make up our daily lives and being in the world. Thus through repetition and reproduction of Uyghur language, along with other Uyghur social practices, the Uyghur's way of being in the world, which Bourdieu called habitus, is shaped. Similarly, Bakhtin

(1981) reminds us that every utterance that we spell out is overloaded with the intention of others, past, present and imagined.

Thus the legitimate competence in Mandarin Chinese is far more than the competence in the language code, whether it is the spoken Mandarin Chinese or the literacy in Chinese writing. The linguistic relation of power is not solely dependent on the linguistic competences present at the time of exchange. 'The weight of different agents depends on their symbolic capital, i.e. on the *recognition*, institutionalized or not, that they receive from a group' (Bourdieu 1991: 72; emphasis in the original). Bourdieu defines legitimate competence as 'the statutorily recognized capacity of an authorized person – an authority – to use, on formal occasions, the legitimate (i.e. formal) language, the authorized, authoritative language, speech that accredited, worthy of being believed'. In other words, the legitimate competence of a language includes, but is not limited to, the abstract notion of language and deeply embedded within the sociohistorical conditions.

We see clearly from the qualitative and quantitative data presented in this chapter the predicament of Uyghur students on a scale of not being competent in Mandarin Chinese to being fully communicative in the language and aspects of Chinese culture. The data clearly demonstrates the unequal power relations between Uyghur language and Mandarin Chinese in a rigidly regulated hierarchical social and political structure as well as in the current Mandarin Chinese education drive. While the students on the lower end of the scale struggle to obtain the linguistic competence in Mandarin Chinese demanded of them by the language policy, the biographical account of a successful Uyghur who became fluent in Mandarin Chinese language and socialized into Chinese culture throughout his education tells us that Mandarin Chinese communicative competence is part of a larger unequal process in which power is distributed unequally. Here, only the legitimate speakers are imbued with the symbolic capital that makes them 'accredited, worthy of being believed' (Bourdieu 1991: 72), which is a necessary condition for equal power and status.

'Symbolic capital' consists of resources that may be drawn upon to build social and economic success (Bucholtz and Hall 2004). In order to make a symbolic profit in the linguistic market measured by the dominant language, the capacity to speak a language is not sufficient as most people have the biological capacity to learn it. As Bourdieu (1991: 55) puts it: 'What is rare, then, is not the capacity to speak, which, being part of our biological heritage, is universal and therefore essentially non-distinctive, but rather the competence necessary in order to speak the legitimate language which, depending on social inheritance, re-translates social distinctions into the specifically symbolic logic of differential deviations, or, in short, distinction.' Thus, the social distinction authorized as legitimate by the society and often rendered invisible, along with competence in the standard language, is crucial for individuals to succeed in increasing their linguistic capital in the social hierarchies.

By acknowledging the centrality of power relations in the linguistic exchange between Uyghurs and Mandarin speakers in Xinjiang, my focus is to shift the emphasis from examining the merits of languages in the abstract to the actual predicaments of their speakers (May 2012b: 4). Official languages are social and political constructs that are 'created' out of the politics of state-making, and not the other way around (Billig 1995: 13–36). There is nothing 'natural' about the status and prestige attributed to particular majority languages and, conversely, the stigma that is often attached to minority languages, or to dialects (May 2000). The emphasis on cultural and linguistic homogeneity within nation-states and the attendant hierarchizing of languages are neither inevitable nor inviolate. In short, national identity, its parameters and its constituent elements, including the standard or 'common' language, are social, ideological and political constructs, rather than based on natural, primordial characteristics of a particular group (May 2012a: 8).

The current Mandarin Chinese medium education policy process is more about differential power relations than anything else, rather than being about 'modernization' and 'aiding' the economic development of Uyghurs, as is often constructed in political, media and academic discourses. Bourdieu's (1982; 1991) notions of 'linguistic markets', 'symbolic capital' and linguistic domination provide an explanatory framework for my discussion – particularly with regard to the differential status and value accorded to majority and minority languages. The ascendancy of Mandarin Chinese is principally achieved by its legitimation and institutionalization within the increasingly monolingual and monocultural Chinese nation-state and the subsequent marginalization of Uyghur and other language varieties. The formation and bolstering of the nation-state based on Mandarin Chinese as the norm is, more than anything else, responsible for the marginalization of Uyghur and other minority languages and perpetuating the linguistic (and wider) inequalities experienced by Uyghur language speakers (May 2012b).

Note

1   Inland (Neidi in Chinese) is used in Xinjiang to denote the areas of China east of Xinjiang, especially the provinces where population is predominantly Han.

References

Anderson, B. R. O'G (1991). *Imagined Communities: Reflections on the Origin and Spread of Nationalism*. London: Verso.

Baker, C. (2006). *Foundations of Bilingual Education and Bilingualism*. 4th ed. Clevedon, Buffalo: Multilingual Matters.

Bakhtin, M. M. (1981). 'Discourse in the Novel'. In Michael Holquist (ed.), *The Dialogic Imagination: Four Essays*. University of Texas Press Slavic series. Austin: University of Texas Press. 259–422.

Benson, L. (2004). 'Education and Social Mobility among Minority Populations in Xinjiang'. In S. Frederick Starr (ed.), *Xinjiang: China's Muslim Borderland*. Armonk, NY: M.E. Sharpe Inc. 190–215.

Billig, M. (1995). *Banal Nationalism*. London: Sage. 194 p.

Bourdieu, P. (1977). 'The Economics of Linguistic Exchanges'. *Social Science Information* 16.6: 645–68.

Bourdieu, P. (1991). *Language and Symbolic Power*. Cambridge: Polity. 302.

Budao (2001). ' "Guojia Tongyong Yuyan Wenzi Fa" de banbu he shixing dui shaoshu minzu de yiyi (Significance of "Law of the People's Republic of China on the Standard Spoken and Written Chinese Language" on Ethnic Minorities)'. *Yuyan Wenzi Yingyong* (2): 10–11.

CASS Institute of Ethnology and Anthropology (1994). *Zhongguo shaoshu minzu yuyan shiyong qingkuang (Language Use Survey of China's Ethnic Minorities)*. Beijing: Zhongguo Zangxue Chubanshe.

CCP Central Committee Archival Research Office and CCP XUAR Committee (2010). *Xinjiang gongzuo wenxian xuanbian: 1949–2010 (Selected Documentary Collection on Xinjiang Affairs: 1949–2010)*. Di 1 ban ed. Beijing: Zhongyang wenxian chubanshe. 815.

CCP XUAR Committee & XUAR Government (2005). 'Jiakuai jingji fazhan, zengjin minzu tuanjie, nuli shixian Xinjiang ge minzu gongtong fanrong jinbu (Accelerate Economic Development, Strengthen Ethnic Solidarity and Strive for Realisation of Common Prosperity and Progress for All Ethnic Groups)'. Available online: http://www.seac.gov.cn/art/2005/7/25/art_3093_69841.html%3E (accessed 27 June).

Chen, Yangbin (2008). *Muslim Uyghur Students in a Chinese Boarding School: Social Recapitalization as a Response to Ethnic Integration*. Lanham, MD: Lexington Books. 211 p.

Dörnyei, Z. (2003). 'Attitudes, Orientations, and Motivations in Language Learning: Advances in Theory, Research, and Applications'. *Language Learning* 53.S1: 3–32.

Economist (27 June 2015). 'Tongue-Tied: Teaching Uighur Children in Mandarin Will Not Bring Stability in Xinjiang'.

Feng, Anwei (2005). 'Bilingualism for the Minor or the Major? An Evaluative Analysis of Parallel Conceptions in China'. *International Journal of Bilingual Education and Bilingualism* 8: 529–51.

Feng, Anwei (2007), 'Introduction'. In Anwei Feng (ed.), *Bilingual Education in China Practices, Policies, and Concepts*. Clevedon: Multilingual Matters. 1–10.

Feng, Anwei, & Sunuodula, M. (2009). 'Analysing Minority Language Education Policy Process in China in Its Entirety'. *International Journal of Bilingual Education and Bilingualism* 12: 685–704.

Friedman, D. A. (2010). 'Becoming National: Classroom Language Socialization and Political Identities in the Age of Globalization'. *Annual Review of Applied Linguistics* 30: 193–210.

Gu, Mingyuan (2010). 'A Blueprint for Educational Development in China: A Review of "The National Guidelines for Medium- and Long-Term Educational Reform and Development (2010–2020)"'. *Frontiers of Education in China* 5. 291–309.

Guan, Yanbo (2001). 'Zhongguo gudai shi shang de minzu ronghe wenti (shang) (The Question of Ethnic Fusion in Ancient History of China: Part 1)'. *Lishi Jiaoxue* (8): 22–5.

Hansen, Mette Halskov (1999). *Lessons in Being Chinese: Minority Education and Ethnic Identity in Southwest China*. Seattle; London: University of Washington Press. xxi, 205 p.

Harrell, S. (1995). 'Introduction: Civilizing Projects and Reaction to Them'. In Stevan Harrell (ed.), *Cultural Encounters on China's Ethnic Frontiers*. Seattle: University of Washington Press. 3–36.

Hill, A. M. (2004). 'Language Matters in China: An Anthropological Postscript'. In Minglang Zhou and Hongkai Sun (eds), *Language Policy in the People's Republic of China: Theory and Practice since 1949*. Boston; London: Kluwer Academic Publishers. 33–8.

Hu, Jintao (2010). 'Xinjiang Gongzuo Zuotanhui zhaokai, Hu Jintao, Wen Jiaobao fabiao zhongyao jianghua (Xinjiang Work Conference Opened, Hu Jintao and Wen Jiaobao Made Important Speeches)'. Beijing: Xinhuanet.

Kumul City Government (2006). 'Hami shi Renmin Zhengfu Ban'gongshi guanyu yinfa Hami shi shi yi wu qijian shuangyu jiaoyu jiaoxue guihua de tongzhi (Kumul City Government Office Pronouncement on Bilingual Education Planning for the 11th Five Year Planning Period)'. *China Legal Education Network* (updated 2006): http://www.chinalawedu.com/news/1200/22598/22615/22792/2007/1/wc8831334441917002166232-0.htm%3E (accessed 11 July).

Ma, Jianxiong (2013). *The Lahu Minority in Southwest China: A Response to Ethnic Marginalization on the Frontier*. Routledge contemporary China series. London; New York: Routledge. xv, 252 p.

Ma, Rong (2009). 'The Development of Minority Education and the Practice of Bilingual Education in Xinjiang Uyghur Autonomous Region'. *Frontiers of Education in China* 4: 188–251.

Ma, Wenhua (2006). *Xinjiang jiaoyu shigao (History of Education in Xinjiang)*. Urumqi: Xinjiang Renmin Chubanshe.

May, S. (2000). 'Uncommon Languages: The Challenges and Possibilities of Minority Language Rights'. *Journal of Multilingual and Multicultural Development* 21.5: 366–85.

May, S. (2012a). *Language and Minority Rights: Ethnicity, Nationalism and the Politics of Language.* 2nd ed. New York; London: Routledge. xiv, 434 p.

May, S. (2012b). 'Multilingualism and Language Rights'. In Carol A. Chapelle (ed.), *The Encyclopedia of Applied Linguistics.* Oxford, UK: Blackwell Publishing Ltd.

Millward, J. A. (2007). *Eurasian Crossroads: A History of Xinjiang.* New York: Columbia University Press. 440.

Ouyang, Zhi, & Liu, Ge (2009). 'Xinjiang zhong xiao xue shaoshu minzu Hanyu ji shuangyu shizi duiwu fazhan licheng yu peixun xianzhuang yanjiiu (Research on the Historical Trajectory and Current State of Ethnic Minority Mandarin Chinese and Bilingual Teacher Development and Training in Xinjiang)'. *Xinjiang Shifan Daxue Xuebao (Zhexue, Shehui Kexue ban)* 29.3: 94–10.

People's Republic of China (2001). 'Law of the People's Republic of China on Regional National Autonomy'. 20th Meeting of the Standing Committee of the Ninth National People's Congress ed., National People's Congress; Beijing: National People's Congress.

Postiglione, G. A. (2007). 'School Access in Rural Tibet'. In Emily Hannum and Albert Park (eds), *Education and Reform in China.* Critical Asian scholarship. London; New York: Routledge. 93–116.

Sautman, B. (1998). 'Preferential Policies for Ethnic Minorities in China: The Case of Xinjiang'. *Nationalism and Ethnic Politics* 4.1–2: 86–118.

Schieffelin, B. B. (2007). 'Found in Translation: Reflexive Language across Time and Texts in Bosavi, Papua New Guinea'. In Miki Makihara and Bambi B. Schieffelin (eds), *Consequences of Contact Language Ideologies and Sociocultural Transformations in Pacific Societies.* Oxford: Oxford University Press. 140–65.

Schluessel, E. T. (2007). ' "Bilingual" Education and Discontent in Xinjiang'. *Central Asian Survey* 26: 251–77.

Scott, J. C. (1998). *Seeing Like a State: How Certain Schemes to Improve the Human Condition Have Failed.* New Haven: Yale University Press.

Smith Finley, J. (2013). *The Art of Symbolic Resistance: Uyghur Identities and Uyghur-Han Relations in Contemporary Xinjiang.* Brill's inner Asian library. Leiden; Boston: Brill. 453.

Sun, Chaofen (2006). *Chinese: A Linguistic Introduction.* Cambridge, UK; New York: Cambridge University Press. xiv, 234 p.

Thum, R. R. (2014). *The Sacred Routes of Uyghur History.* Cambridge, MA: Harvard University Press. vii, 323 pages.

Tsung, L. (2014). 'Trilingual Education and School Practice in Xinjiang'. In James Leibold and Yangbin Chen (eds), *Minority Education in China: Balancing Unity and Diversity in an Era of Critical Pluralism.* Hong Kong: Hong Kong University Press. 161–86.

Turahun, E. (2010). 'Jiada shuangyu jiaoyu lidu yiyi shenyuan: Erkenjiang Tulahong weiyuan tan shuangyu jiaoyu (Stepping Up the Intensity of Bilingual Education Has Far Reaching Significance)'. *Xinjiang Ribao (Xinjiang Daily)*, 9 March, p. 1.

Turahun, E. (2013). 'Jiji tuijin shaoshu minzu shuangyu jiaoyu, gong zai dangdai, li za qianqiu (Active Promotion of Ethnic Minority Bilingual Education: Pain for Now but Gain for Generations to Come)'. *Xinjiang Ribao (Xinjiang Daily)*, 9 September, sec. Zhuanti baodao (Special report).

Wang, Ashu (2012). 'Xinjiang shuangyu jiaoyu zhengce de dangdai yanjin (Evolution of Bilingual Education Policy in Xinjiang)'. *Xinjiang Shehui Kexue* 2013.3: 119–22.

Wang, Chengzhi, & Zhou, Quanhou (2003). 'Minority Education in China: From State's Preferential Policies to Dislocated Tibetan Schools'. *Educational Studies* 29.1: 85–104.

Wang, Lequan (2001). 'Xibu Da Kaifa gei Xinjiang dailai jiyu (Western Development Brings Opportunities to Xinjiang)'. *Zhongguo Jingji Shibao (China Economic Times)*, 13 March, sec. Yaowen (Main news) p. 3.

Wang, Yang (2009). 'Dui Wei Hanyu jiaoxue yanjiu (Research on Teaching Mandarin Chinese to Uyghurs)'. PhD (East China Normal University).

Xu, Jialu (2001). 'Lishi shang di yi bu guanyu yuyan wenzi de falu (First Language and Literacy Law in History)'. *Yuyan Wenzi Yingyong* no. 2: 3–5.

XUAR Government (2004). 'Guanyu dali tuijin 'shuangyu xuexi' jin yi bu jiaqiang yuyan wenzi gongzuo de yijian (Proposal for Rigorous Promotion of "Bilingual Learning" and Further Strengthening of Language and Literacy Planning Work)'. *Zhengfu Gongbao* 2004: 20–3.

XUAR Government Education Department (2011). 'Yiwu jiaoyu jieduan shuangyu jiaoyu kecheng sheji fang'an (Curriculum Plan for Bilingual Education at the Compulsory Education Stage)'. in Education Department (ed.). Urumqi: XUAR Education Department.

XUAR Government Education Department & XUAR Government Human Resources Department (2015). 'XUAR General Regulations on Open Recruitment of Contract 'Bilingual' Teachers in 2015'. Available online: http://www.xjedu.gov.cn/xjjyt/jyzt/tgjszp/zxxjszp/zpxx/2015/87684.htm%3E (accessed 6 July).

XUAR Local History Editorial Office (1985). *Xinjiang nianjian 1985 (Xinjiang Yearbook 1985)*, ed. Ying Zhong. Xinjiang nianjian; Urumqi: Xinjiang Renmin Chubanshe. 708.

XUAR Local History Editorial Office (2000). *Xinjiang tongzhi: di 76 juan: Yuyan wenzi zhi (Xinjiang gazette: Volume 76: Language Gazette)*, 76. Wulumuqi: Xinjiang Renmin Chubanshe.

XUAR Local History Editorial Office (2005). *Xinjiang nianjian (Xinjiang Yearbook): 2005*. Wulumuqi: Xinjiang Nianjianshe. 598.

XUAR Local History Editorial Office (2007). *Xinjiang tongzhi: di 74 juan: Jiaoyu zhi (Xinjiang Gazetter: Volume 74: Education)*, 74. Wulumuqi: Xinjiang Jiaoyu Chubanshe.

XUAR Office for Bilingual Education Steering Committee (2012). *Xinjiang shaoshu minzu shuangyu jiaoyu zhengce jiedu (Xinjiang Ethnic Minority Bilingual Education Policy Explained)*. Wulumuqi: Xinjiang ren min chu ban she. 114.

Part Four

Pedagogical Discourse

Editor's introduction

In this pedagogical section, education is seen as a source of empowerment contrasting with education as a structural reproduction of existing power arrangements. This entails arguing in favour of education as a cultural dynamic rather than predominantly economic with cultural ownership by its participants who are actively engaged in the construction of pedagogical discourse in the classroom, whether these be teachers or students.

Chapter 10 focuses on student and teacher discourses in the foreign language classroom and Chapter 11 on teachers' developmental discourse.

Chapter 12 concludes by arguing against economic instrumentalism in pedagogy as a predominant force or the 'banking system' of Paolo Freire and in favour of education as primarily an agent for social change for intercultural understanding in the contemporary world.

10

Cultural Discourses in the Foreign Language Classroom: Economic Opportunity, Instrumental Motivation or Cultural Understanding

David Evans

Introduction

In this chapter foreign language classroom pedagogy is seen to be traversed by different and often competing discourses such as socio-economic, bureaucratic, disciplinary/regulatory, developmental, locally based community/family and cultural-intercultural. It demonstrates the connectedness between some of these classroom discourses and larger societal discourses through ideological power in the construction of student learner identities. The chapter is able to establish such connections through classroom based observations and student interviews. I acknowledge previously covered theoretical concepts explored in Chapters one and two such as heteroglossia (Bakhtin 1981; Wertsch 1991) and symbolic capital (Bourdieu 1991) and, as a consequence, we will see that classroom participants in the research are traversed by different voices, some of which are more powerful than others.

We will see a dominant economic voice for language learning and also witness an alternative cultural voice for a positive regard towards alterity and difference. In this chapter I argue that the voice or discourse that promotes cultural empathy towards alterity and cultural understanding should be promoted because this inhabits the language itself rather than existing as an external instrumental motivation.

The chapter consequently argues that a foreign language is not English in translation but is constituted by a different culture within the spoken and written foreign language. Therefore one can only understand a culture through learning the language which both constitutes and expresses the culture of 'otherness'. In doing this, some students understand that they are able to explore and develop their own identities by engaging with the alterity of a different language and culture.

The theoretical base for this chapter lies in the relationship between language, culture and ideology, and I argue here that individuals construct their identities at the intersection of different and often competing discourses. It is also important to consider, as Lave and Wenger (1991) point out, that learning and identity are bound up in the same process. According to one's discursive learner identity, modern foreign language learning can be a practical holiday activity, an economic activity for employment prospects, an activity for cultural discovery, an intercultural reflection on difference, a technical word/sentence based grammatical activity, a literary activity or finally a combination of many of the above. I argue that pedagogical activity cannot exist in isolation from wider social structure and that educational undertakings are always sociocultural and framed by sociocultural ideologies.

Fairclough (1989; 1993) argues that cultural discourses help to shape individual identities within a dialectical relationship to non-discursive formations of society such as financial, socio-economic institutions and modes of production. Discourse therefore is more than language.

Foucault (1972) talks about discourse as ways of being in social practice and, therefore, the foundation of our being in the world is shaped by discourse. Foucault's 'discursive formations' establish the rules that determine what can be stated about the social world and what cannot. Discourse is then more that linguistic utterances, it is also about silence in terms of what cannot be said and encompasses those who have voice and those who, often as a consequence, do not. In this respect discourse is permeated with notions of power. This is particularly relevant in an educational context in terms of control over curriculum content, types of assessment and teaching methods.

Foucault argues furthermore that the way we use discourse as a social practice governs the type of knowledge we construct for ourselves and so different discursive practices would have resulted in different types of knowledge. Discourses are then social ways of being that 'systematically form the objects of which they speak' (Foucault 1972: 57) There is then a sense that collectively we talk ourselves into knowledge. Indeed educational/pedagogical knowledge practices have changed over time from being largely regulatory and disciplinary in the past with an emphasis on physical punishment to a contemporary liberal developmental construction where pupils are now students. Now, students co-construct knowledge and express student 'voice' more democratically as opposed to the rigorous didactical passivity of former times. This is an example of pedagogical knowledge that has changed over time as education has been constructed differently over time. This is because epistemologically, knowledge is often now viewed as sociocultural phenomena to be constructed rather than inert static phenomena to be uncovered, as though it is passively awaiting discovery. These are philosophical differences concerning the nature of knowledge and the position of the 'knower' and indeed come to be translated into pedagogical practices.

Seen in this light, modern foreign languages (henceforth MFL) as well as other subjects have different meanings and interpretations from different positions occupied by different stakeholders, although these stakeholders may not have equal access to structures of power.

A Socio-economic educational discourse

I have adapted Fairclough's (1989) socio-economic model of discourse to the way in which the ideological construction of classroom pedagogy can be constructed in the Figure 10.1 below.

The adaptation I have made is to place the MFL classroom as the setting for interactive level of discourse production at the centre of a circular model where orders and types of discourse are labelled. The rationale for this is to show the manner in which MFL discursive meanings are subject to the same socio-economic and cultural forces as other social phenomena.

The rationale behind this diagram is to show the 'situatedness' of classroom pedagogy and the classroom itself within larger social structures. Therefore the classroom does not exist in isolation from wider discourses and to a large extent the wider structures find their representation within patterns of classroom interaction. An example of this is in the notion of social order, implicit in the larger Orders of Discourse which can be seen in the exercise of a regulatory power discourse within the classroom. Oral (2013: 96) argues that second language pedagogical research has mainly ignored regulatory discourse thereby treating the classroom as autonomous and isolated from wider society and as she maintains 'insulated from socio-political concerns and power relations'. Regulatory discourse, as Oral points out, interacts with teacher/student relations in terms of issues such as student autonomy, treating learners as active students

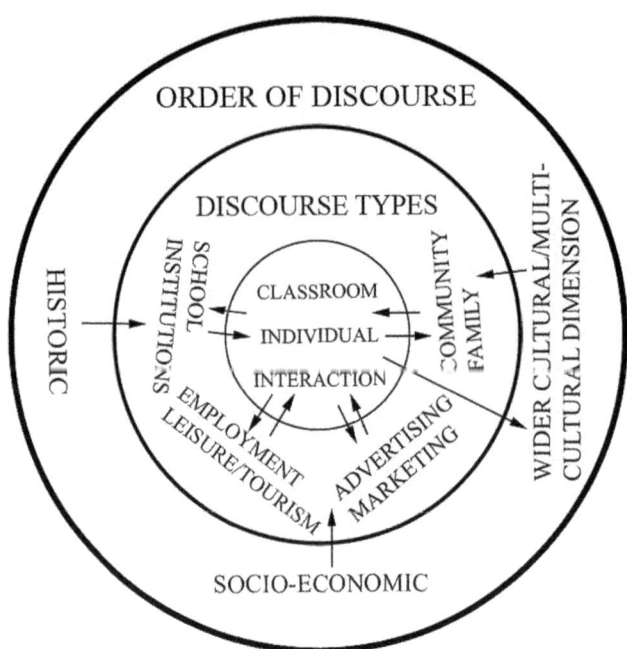

Figure 10.1 Based on Fairclough's (1989) socio-economic model of discourse.

as opposed to passive pupils and enabling students to take control of their own behaviour for learning. She further points out that classrooms are 'conceptualized as sites of cultural struggle where different modes of teaching and learning, different ways of thinking and being, and different versions of the world are battled over' (97). Gillette (1994) points out that, in spite of official teacher pedagogical and regulatory discourse, students learn for their own reasons as opposed to the stated aims of the lesson. Therefore within the same classroom and lesson some students may simply wish to conform to the teacher's demands, others resist and still others learn for much wider or different reasons from those that are officially stated. So, although in the diagram above, we see a representation of societal forces within the classroom, one also has to take into account student agency which in turn draws upon its own family and community discourses.

Gender as discourse within the classroom

Gender can be seen as an example of a dialectical interaction between the wider cultural influences of orders of discourse and the way in which students and others enact their gender in their daily interactional lives by perhaps not conforming to a powerful binary male-female gender model (Butler 1990). This can be seen as dialectical because the enactment of gender in daily interaction over time eventually acts back on the wider social orders of discourse that may have viewed gender as a binary construction. Eventually a different view of gender might emerge within the larger societal discourses. Creese et al. (2004), as an example of this, refer to masculinities and femininities in terms of gender as multiple rather than binary identities. They argue that gender identity is not a finished product but is continually being constructed and reconstructed in daily social interactions. Maleness and femaleness may therefore be seen along a continuum of multiple identities rather than a simple male-female binary. Baxter (2003) supports this view in arguing that she does not recognize gender meanings as fixed and unchanging, as subject identity is always constructed within discourse. Individuals should therefore be seen as negotiating their gendered learner identities within the classroom discourses themselves rather than shaped solely by wider social forces.

However in terms of these wider societal discourses, Pollman (2016: 9) refers to the current neoliberal hegemony in education which consigns less socioculturally dominant forms of cultural knowledge to institutional marginalization and 'curricular obliteration'.

In terms of foreign language education Pollman argues that, within MFL pedagogy, intercultural competence is not considered important and so very little MFL linguistic content in terms of vocabulary, grammar and syntax is deployed in favour of cultural understanding.

Learner identities

The classroom is then a contested ideological space containing a conflation of differing tensions at the intersection between different and often conflicting influences, the more powerful of which are shaped by wider orders of discourse.

Within classroom discursive spaces and interactions students construct their learner identities individually and in their own social groupings, shaped by the discourse of teacher pedagogy and, behind that, official school curriculum pedagogy. Kramsch (1993; 1998) takes the view that the individual is instrumental in shaping cultural learner identity through his/her own agency. She rejects the notion of a hegemonic socio-economic determinism in MFL learning and favours a position where the individual can challenge accepted normative cultural meanings, constructing alternative meanings for language learning in interaction with the language of the 'Other'. Kramsch's view of MFL learning leans towards the discovery of the language of the 'Other' and the community of the 'Other'. She maintains that students need to begin their exploration of the 'Other' from where they are at the present moment, since the act of using language is also the act of using culture in one's own situation. This is because, as Kramsch (1998) argues, culture is inscribed within language and therefore using language is also using culture. Van Lier (2000: 247) takes a similar position to Kramsch in terms of the cultural nature of learning by arguing for the 'ecological' nature of language where language is part of a sociocultural whole with which one interacts through one's use of the foreign language. Van Lier proposes the notion of 'Languaculture' where a new language contains new and different realities which amount to new ways of seeing the world and new possibilities for the learner's exploration of self and identity.

However Kramsch's (1993: 242) particular take on the student's use of the foreign language concerns the construction of a 'third culture' which represents a dialectical hybrid between the student's native culture and the target language culture. Therefore the cultural context for Kramsch is more than plagiarizing a foreign language culture but rather the self-empowerment of appropriating the culture for one's own needs not only in terms of language use but also for one's own critical cultural analysis. Kramsch's emphasis is on the way students construct culture as an ongoing process from where they are in the present. The 'third place' is an ongoing dialectical reconciliation between the student's subjective active interpretation of the foreign language-culture and the objectivity of the foreign language-culture as cultural product. The dialectic is therefore between culture as ongoing process and culture as an objective product. From the 'third place' the student can then move forward in his/her interaction with the language and culture and in doing so continually find new 'third places'. Kramsch (2009: 6) argues that, for example, the third space in learning English as a second language (ESL) is the 'right of non-native speakers to appropriate for themselves the English language and give it other meanings than native speakers would'. The notion of third place is then a subversive one and one of 'bricolage' (Kramsch 2009) where learners make do with the imposed meanings of others and so 'thirdness', as Kramsch argues, is 'speaking our meaning with their language' and 'reading against the grain'. This creates a third culture which is a hybrid one between the learner's own culture and the dominant culture of the foreign language. Furthermore because culture is fluid, third spaces are necessarily fluid and not located in a place but more a way of thinking and being.

Consequently, Kramsch now favours a notion of 'thirdness' rather than 'third place' to emphasize being rather than place.

Dornyei and Ushioda (2009) offer a more psychological paradigm for foreign language learning which is rooted in the individual as opposed to sociocultural context. Their model is weighted towards the future rather than the present in his notion of 'imagined future selves'. This looks towards the individual's potential future self-concept rather than the construction of culture in the present. Dornyei and Ushioda state that learning a foreign language is such a long-term activity that the learner needs to envision an ideal future self that combines the use of the language with how he/she would be in terms of self-concept having achieved mastery of the language. This positions future identity on the desire to integrate within a target language community. Their paradigm of identity is a psychological one rather than sociological and develops from earlier socio-psychological theories advanced by Gardner (1985) based on his notion of integrative motivation, defined as a desire to integrate to the target language community. This was differentiated from a purely instrumental motivation as purely 'end-on' socio-economic motivation in terms of passing exams or applying for jobs. Instrumental motivation was entirely extra-linguistic rather than internal to language. Dornyei's ideal future self model combines present and future states within the individual; however this is not a cultural model narrating an ongoing process, but rather a psychological and ideologically neutral model.

A more socio-economic paradigm for language learning is adopted by Norton (2000) is terms of learning a language as a 'cultural capital' which serves as a motivation because of a possible future socio-professional and economic return. In this 'social investment' paradigm cultural capital is analogous to economic capital and frames the learner as an integral member of a socio-economic community rather than just a linguistic community. This economic model of cultural capital advocated by Norton is drawn from the work of Bourdieu (1991) who refers to language as having a symbolic value which is the prestige value bestowed upon it by dominant socio-economic discourse.

In the light of the preceding lines of argumentation one could argue that socio-economic, intercultural and psychological future self-concept paradigms for learner identity are separately framed in opposition to each other rather than interacting with each other. This chapter proposes a methodological approach to learner identity, drawing upon ethnographic data which might come either to illuminate the relevance of the above theories, add to them or perhaps reconcile them acknowledging their interaction with each other.

Research study

In the following research conducted in Longmount Academy in the south of England, in a mixed methodology of interviews with secondary school students and lesson observations, we see student constructions of meanings for foreign language. The research participants were drawn from a year 9 Spanish class and consisted of fourteen students, seven male and seven female aged 14 years. The school, fictionalized as Longmount Academy, is a wide ability community school which became a 'converter' academy to gain independence from Local Authority control, and in terms of demographic profile is not dissimilar from others in the general locality. The year 9 Spanish class was a mixed ability class and the research participants were volunteers with parental consent to be interviewed and observed in lessons. All names of research participants have been fictionalized. As researcher, I had the support of the classroom teacher to undertake research on cultural discourses and learner identities in the classroom and also of the headteacher to undertake this research within the school.

An ethnographic style of observation was carried out twice a week over ten weeks and so there are in total twenty whole lessons, one-hour observations. Qualitative data of observations were recorded in my research diary during each observation from which extracts are used to illuminate learner identities.

There were fourteen semi-structured informant based interviews (Robson 1993) where students were asked about their ideas and attitudes relating to language learning. These interviews were recorded and extracts are used to highlight learner identities and triangulate against the observations for internal validity.

Interviews

The first student I interviewed was Georgina, a year 9 female student. Georgina expresses mixed motives in learner identity, partly socio-economic in terms of getting a job and partly intercultural appreciation.

Extract 1

(DE = researcher; G = Georgina)

1 **DE:** Is it important to learn a foreign language?
2 **G:** I think it is important to learn a foreign language because it can help
3 you like when you're older with getting jobs and when you go on holiday
4 there's more chance of being able to make friends and understand people

₅ and also it's fun to learn a language because you can learn about different
₆ people's way of lives and how they are in different countries.

Georgina's response draws upon different ideological discourses. The socio-economic one is in terms of employment – line 3. The leisure consumer one is about holidays in line 3 but then she expands on this with regard to getting to know and understand people in line 4. She thus widens the leisure holiday discourse into something of wider cultural interest. This becomes more than the functional language of ordering food and drink and would require a wider linguistic range. Much later in the interview when asked the question, 'What is culture in your opinion?', she responds by saying, 'Culture is a way of life and people's culture is important to them'. An interesting answer as not only does she say what culture is in her opinion but she also ascribes value to it.

This triangulates with the interview data in lines 5 and 6 where she says that it's fun to learn a language because you learn about different ways of life in different countries. The following extract refers to a reason as to why other cultures are to be valued.

Extract 2

₇ DE: D'you think it's an important thing to do (learning about cultures)
₈ G: Yeh because otherwise you just be kind of stuck to your way of life
₉ and think that everywhere is like how the U.K is. But different places
₁₀ have different cultures and things.

Georgina sees learning about different cultures as liberating in that you can break away from being 'stuck to your way of life' (line 8). She sees learning a foreign language and culture as emancipatory and the opposite of localized cultural confinement.

When asked about the connections between language and culture Georgina responds as shown in extract 3 from the interview.

Extract 3

₁₁ DE: D'you think that language and culture go together?
₁₂ G: yeh, coz your language kind of reflects your culture like some
₁₃ people use slang.
₁₄ DE: yeh
₁₅ G: and that reflects the way that they are and are brought up

This does not seem to reflect a socio-economic discourse but rather a wider cultural discourse in terms of the nature of language.

Similarly the interview with Lizzie and Aimee in the following extract shows that both girls have a keen cultural interest in Spanish.

Extract 4

(DE = Researcher; L = Lizzie; A = Aimee)

1 **DE:** what do you think are the main reasons for learning a foreign language?

2 **L:** there's loads of reasons

3 **DE:** give me all the reasons then

4 **A:** Holiday, because if you don't know a language you can't ask for things.

5 **L:** Employment cos you can get loads of jobs with languages.

6 **A:** and culture so you can learn what they do and what they eat and stuff like that.

7 **DE:** which of holidays, employment and culture are the most important reasons?

8 **A:** culture

9 **L:** employment and culture.

10 **DE:** why culture

11 **L:** Because it is important to know what people are like, to be different and stuff.

In the interview Aimee's priority is the cultural reason for learning a language whereas Lizzie combines employment and culture. In line 6 Aimee defines culture as the way people live their lives which would be of interest to her. In line 11 Lizzie also defines culture as the way people are and she also mentions difference. She says that it is important to know about this perhaps implying cultural exploration or discovery. In the next extract Lizzie expresses a view that we are all different because we say things in different ways and that the Spanish identity would be different from another national group due to the fact of speaking a different language (lines 13–17).

Extract 5

12 **DE:** Are the Spanish different from English people?

13 **L:** they will be different because we might speak in a different way to them-

14 it's the way we say things so they are bound to be different anyway and

15 their culture as well.

16 **DE:** is that caused by the different language?

17 **L:** Well not everything but it has a lot to do with the language.

In the next extract Aimee expresses the view that you have to appreciate the target culture to speak the language well. Lizzie concurs with this.

Extract 6

30 **DE:** Do you think that in order to speak Spanish or any language fluently, you've

$_{31}$ got to like the country and the people?

$_{32}$ **A:** if you don't like the culture, what they do and stuff like that, then there's

$_{33}$ no point learning the language, coz you're not going to go there because

$_{34}$ that's what you go there for, because of what it looks like and what's the

$_{35}$ food like and how people do stuff

$_{36}$ **L:** yeh, actually I agree with you Aimee

Aimee's viewpoint reflects her cultural identity as supporting the foreign language learning, because the foreign language expresses a cultural context. She says in lines 32–35 that the language is supported by the way of life and therefore one cannot learn the language well if one has no interest in the context. In line 36 Lizzie agrees with this.

As with Georgina, Lizzie displays a tentative awareness of some sort of connection between different languages and different cultural identities, transcending concepts of socio-economic necessity, while not denying the socio-economics of learning a language.

Shannen supports a wide cultural view of language learning in the following exchange

Extract 7

(DE = researcher; Sh = Shannen)

$_1$ **DE:** But would it be better if they (Spanish people) all spoke English and then you

$_2$ could go (Spain) and there'd be no problem?

$_3$ **Sh:** no because there'd be no excitement in learning a new language.

In this extract Shannen wants to learn a foreign language for the 'excitement' (line 3) of difference. In the following short exchange with another female student in the case study, Leah explains her need for cultural research.

Extract 8

(DE = researcher; Lh = Leah)

$_1$ **DE:** What do you understand by culture?

$_2$ **Lh:** like different sets of beliefs and things like that

$_3$ **DE:** are you interested in getting to know culture and beliefs?

$_4$ **Lh:** yeh before I go on holiday I usually look up the culture of the place I'm

$_5$ going to

Leah explains her cultural interest in lines 4 and 5 by researching the culture of her holiday destination before her departure.

The following interview extract with Alex, a male year 9 student, may be seen as a contrast to the cultural identity of Georgina, Lizzie and Amy and the other female students, because in the following extract, the cultural content for language learning is more instrumental in undertaking holiday transactions. While entirely legitimate as a reason for learning a foreign language, instrumental reasons may be seen as external to the language itself as opposed to reasons intrinsically contained within the language and its cultural expression.

In the following extract Alex views the MFL for its instrumental value.

Extract 9

(DE = researcher; A = Alex)

The following is an interview extract between Alex and the researcher.

1 **DE:** what importance do you see in learning a foreign language. Is it important and why?

2 **A:** yeh because you can go to other countries and ask for stuff

3 **DE:** right any other reason; is that the main reason?

4 **A:** that's the main reason

5 **DE:** right so what d'you think the attraction is for going to....

6 **A:** the weather

7 **DE:** The weather?

8 **A:** yeh

9 **DE:** ok have you been to Spain at all?

10 **A:** I went to Costa Brava

11 **DE:** ok and were you able to speak any Spanish?

12 **A:** I spoke to ask for crisps and a drink

Alex's view of the importance of MFL is instrumental in being able to buy food and drink.

Alex considers the connection between language and culture in the next extract.

Extract 10

22 **DE:** D'you think you need to know the culture well to speak the language well?

23 **A:** No

24 **DE:** So you think you could speak the language fairly well or very well without knowing the culture?

25 **A:** I think it would help to know it but it wouldn't make you speak

26 better Spanish I don't think.

As can be seen in lines 25 and 26 Alex does not consider that there is a close link between language and culture.

With regard to the interview participants it seemed to me that the two interviews were polar opposites in that the cultural resources which Alex and

Georgina draw upon for their meaning are completely different. Georgina understood that culture resided inside the language whereas for Alex culture and language seem to be separate from each other. Alex is however not interested in cultural difference at all as can be seen in the following extract.

Extract 11

[87] **DE:** Would you like to live and work in a foreign country?

[88] **A:** I think so yeh

[89] **DE:** what would be the advantage of this?

[90] **A:** Nice place to work

[91] **DE:** nice in what way?

[92] **A:** better weather

[93] **DE:** so what is important to you?

[94] **A:** sunny weather

[95] **DE:** are you interested in life and culture in other countries or is that

[96] not a big interest for you?

[97] **A:** it's not a big interest

[98] **DE:** thanks very much for taking part in this interview.

Alex's learner identity seems very different from that of Georgina. Although he enjoys Spanish and is developing his language skill, his cultural subject position is much narrower than Georgina and he does not as yet relate to the language as a way of life.

Fred shares a similar instrumental view of MFL to Alex as we can see in extract 12

Extract 12

(DE = Researcher; F = Fred)

[1] **DE:** so what are the main reasons for learning a language?

[2] **F:** cos if you know the language you can go to other countries like

[3] Brazil and other countries that speak Spanish instead of just Spain

[4] **DE:** yeh

[5] **F:** I mean if you learn you can ask for anything

[6] **DE:** so you think it's mainly for holidays or are there other reasons as well?

[7] **F:** well if you've got a job speaking Spanish down the telephone or

[8] something and if you go on holidays it would be helpful cos you can

[9] ask for stuff

[10] **DE:** are you interested in different ways of life and different ways in which people live their lives?

[11] **F:** you mean different routines of when they get up and that?

[12] **DE:** yeh, different cultures and ways of doing things

~13~ F: no not really to me but to other people that could be interesting-like
~14~ they want to know when a Spaniard gets up in the morning, what he
~15~ does, if he has breakfast in a different way or goes out. Some people
~16~ like that but I don't really mind how people do things. It's not really
~17~ interesting to know what people do.

Fred has a definition of culture and appreciates what this interest could mean for some people but he is frank when he says that this does not hold any interest for him at all.

The next interview I set up was with Sam, a male student. I was interested in finding a male student with a cultural interest in difference and cultural identity favourable to language learning. Although Sam does not speak the foreign language much in class, he does write it very well and has a sound grasp of word structure and grammar.

Extract 13

(DE = researcher; S = Sam, a male year 9 student)

~1~ **DE:** D'you find it important to learn M.F.L?

~2~ **S:** yeh, maybe if you want to move countries and speak their language. It's interesting as well to learn about it.

~3~ **DE:** right- what d'you think the main advantage would be?

~4~ **S:** maybe if you wanted to move countries for business and stuff

~5~ **DE:** d'you think it would be important to understand how other people live?

~6~ **S:** yeh it's important to learn other people's cultures

~7~ **DE:** why do you think that?

~8~ **S:** you've got to respect their culture

~9~ **DE:** right ok. Are you fascinated by the way people live?

~10~ **S:** yeh coz they live a lot differently to us, obviously bull-fighting and things like that

~11~ **DE:** So do you think Spanish people are different or the same as us?

~12~ **S:** They're a lot more different

Sam's answer to the following question later on in the interview, 'What is culture in your opinion? is that 'Culture is something people do which is different to us'. He sees culture therefore as difference rather than as the way we all live. However he clearly appreciates the sense of 'Other' in this difference. In the following extract he is excited by cultural difference.

~13~ **DE:** And do you like to know about this difference? Is difference important to you or should we all be the same?

~14~ **S:** difference is good cos then you can learn things off them. If we were all the same it would be boring wouldn't it, so it's exciting

~15~ DE: so you like the excitement of difference? Would you like to work in Spain?

~16~ S: yeh that's one of my ambitions, to move out to Spain and maybe start my own business or something like that.

~17~ So does that give you motivation for the language?

~18~ S: yeh

Sam seems to combine an interest in cultural difference with a desire to start a business. The following extract focuses on the relationship between language and culture.

~19~ DE: D'you think you can speak the language more fluently if you get to know the culture?

~20~ S: um

~21~ DE: or does it not matter?

~22~ S: No I don't think it matters really if you learn the culture or not. It's more enjoyable if

~23~ you do but I don't think you need to learn the culture to be able to speak it.

Sam likes to appreciate cultural difference but unlike Georgina, he does not make connections to language. Nevertheless he has an interest in Spanish culture and understands that cultural and economic reasons in learning a language make it attractive for him.

Cultural definitions

If teaching and learning a foreign language is a cultural event, then the cultural disposition an individual may have towards the language is important for progression in learning. Norton's (2000) 'social investment' model of motivation and Dornyei's 'imagined future selves' connect students like Georgina and Sam with the future, in that there is a future element of the possibilities of wider horizons lying within their present study of Spanish. For Sam it is the possibility of pursuing a business in Spain while for Georgina it involves an implied future of cultural difference and not being 'stuck to your way of life' as well as social investment (line 8 interview extract 2). Van Lier's (2002) notion of 'languaculture', where culture and language are learned together since culture is inscribed into language, is particularly relevant to Georgina's sense of the 'otherness' of foreign language. Lizzie, Aimie, Lauren, Louisa and Leah all support a learner identity focused on cultural difference and cultural meaning.

Alex and Fred show a far more instrumental learner identity in terms of learning a language to gain a material end result based on asking for consumer items.

Although much has been written on gender differences in foreign language learning and achievement, it would be unjustified, solely based on these interviews, to extrapolate Alex and Fred's more instrumental attitudes to learning Spanish to a general gender difference. For example, Sam's (a male student) stated learner identity is based on an appreciation of cultural 'otherness' and so it would be simplistic to attribute either instrumental learner identities on the one hand or culturally based learner identities on the other to a binary male-female gender. An enquiry into the meanings for gender as either a priori or socially associative characteristics and differences is beyond the scope of this chapter and so the most that could be stated, at this moment, would concern very loose associations based on observation. This could be, for example, that the majority but not all of male students exhibit a particular disposition or that the majority of females but not all, display another disposition. Any such differences should be acknowledged but not extrapolated to any generalized form of knowledge beyond the scope of this research.

It seems reasonable to say, from interview evidence, that there are two principal learner identities within the data. The main distinguishable identity that predominates among the female students is one that concerns an interest in knowing and exploring cultural difference. This identity is therefore internal to the notion of language-culture or the term used by Van Lier (2000; 2002) known as 'languaculture'. Within this, a further refinement can be discerned in the learner position of Georgina which is that of cultural difference within language itself, in terms of the notion that culture exists within language and not simply as a surrounding context. To contrast with Georgina, the interview with Sam shows that he is interested in the 'otherness' of culture but he does not see culture as being connected internally to language but rather to the external context of language. The other learner identity concerns Alex and Fred's language learner identities which are external to language-culture in that language is simply an instrument for an end result external to the language itself.

We should also take into account the students' own discourses in action within their own groups in the classroom in order to see them actively constructing culture. The best way to capture this and see how this impacts on the learning process is through ethnographic observation.

Observational fieldwork and analysis

The year 9 Spanish class was observed sixteen times over the space of six weeks or a half term. The students became used to my presence and, in gaining their permission and parental permission, I had explained the purpose of my research in general terms which was to research student learner identity in foreign language classes. I got to know the students and being a qualified foreign languages teacher in French and Spanish was able, on occasions, to help and advise them in their tasks. I had the full support of the teacher with the research and in interacting with the students.

The following is taken from my research diary notes which are an interaction involving male and female members of the class, between Fred and Alex on the one hand and Georgina on the other. We have already heard from these students in the interview data and have had some idea regarding the cultural positions they claim to occupy.

> Lesson starts with Latino music from Santana coming from the computer. There is a presentation on computer white board on preterite tense of 'er' and 'ir' verbs. Pupils have to copy down and make holiday diary using past tense activities. Fred and Alex seem 'hyped up' – taking Georgina's £1 coin. Georgina is trying to work. Fred makes as if to hand it back to her but drops it at the last moment. This leads to a commotion as Fred and Alex scramble about for it on the floor. (*End of observation*)

We can see a problematic encounter between two discourses, that of Fred and Alex, a pupils' discourse that is playful and not quite in line with the teacher-led discourse and that of Georgina who is following the official teacher-led discourse by trying to work.

In the following observation we see the classroom space dominated by a pupil discourse that is disengaged from the official teacher-led discourse. The girls are trying to work although Charlotte, a female pupil who does not feature in the interview data sample, is drawn into the boys' banter. The extract also contains participation from George, Mitchell and Adam, male students who do not feature in the interview data samples shown.

> The lesson starts with a presentation of the preterite tense. The teacher remonstrates with George for messing around with Charlotte. George lets go of Charlotte and turns to Fred laughing and joking about penis size. George starts to make monkey sounds and then puts up his hand to answer a question by the teacher about verb endings. Mitchell gets out of his chair and pretends to be an old man whilst bending down to pick up his pen. Alex, Fred and Adam are quiet, copying preterite verbs from the board. Fred is playing with coins on the table and turns round to Adam to play 'shove ha'penny'. Alex turns round to disturb Georgina who is quietly working. (*End of observation*)

The interesting thing to note here is the hybrid discourse of the boys who mix the teacher-led discourse with their own. Alex, Fred and Adam have spent quiet moments working, copying down preterite tense verbs but they rarely do this for any length of time without returning to their own discourse. George tries to draw Charlotte in to this discourse and nearly succeeds until the teacher intervenes. Georgina however remains faithful to the pedagogic discourse of the lesson.

The next classroom observation highlights this discourse hybridity in the lesson participation of George and Alex.

> How they would write 'Que hiciste ayer? = What did you do yesterday?' George comes to the board and writes 'Que' in minute letters that can hardly be seen even from close up let alone from the back of the room. Then in very big letters that take up most of the board space he writes 'hiciste' and then in normal letters writes 'ayer'. He knew the answer but did not have to present it this way except to evoke humour. Alex comes to the board and writes a correct answer in normal sized letters 'escuche musica' (I listened to music). (*End of observation*)

Here Alex decided to respond without acknowledging the call for humour. The dichotomy between the official lesson objective discourse and pupil discourse can be seen clearly at this moment whereas the two discourses are often intertwined and overlapping. In his write up on the board George sticks with pupil discourse to evoke humour and perhaps also to invoke a likeminded continuation from the next person to write on the board. I fully expected Alex to reciprocate. However to my surprise and relief, he conformed to teacher-led lesson discourse in his write-up.

Alex has a serious side in his work and the following is taken from my research diary

> We were revising the preterite tense and creating a powerpoint Easter holiday diary on laptops. Every student has a laptop computer for this type of activity and students become quickly absorbed within the creative possibilities that the computers are able to afford in terms of the graphics and varieties of text. At the end of the lesson Alex showed me the text he had quietly created in Spanish which was grammatically correct. (*End of observation*)

Although, from his interview in extract 11, Alex claims no 'intercultural' interest, he enjoys writing correct sentences in Spanish. He seems to enjoy the intellectual challenge of creating Spanish text and to show flexibility of movement between teacher-led discourse and pupil discourse. There are then male students who involve themselves in the teacher-led discourse but who still remain in the camp of pupil discourse, moving between the two.

Observation notes for another lesson once more show pupils constantly alternating between the different discourses. This is evident from the boys in the class because it is undisguised in terms of volume. There is also Natasha who was not part of the interview group because of irregular attendance at school. The notes are as follows:

> Presentation of 'Las Asignaturas' (school subjects) on powerpoint. Pupils write down vocabulary and repeat for pronunciation practice. Pupils start to get overly noisy in their repetitions and told to quieten down. Fred is using this as a cover to turn round and chat. Class now quieten and take part in question and answer session with teacher in Spanish on which subjects they study. George comes out to do the powerpoint presentation to the class. He presents a few frames then Shannon is invited to take over. Alex then goes up, has a change of mind, turns around then goes back again. George then starts arguing with Mitchell about whose turn it is to continue the presentation. Fred goes up to the whiteboard. While Fred presents, other pupils are talking amongst themselves – George, Alex, Natasha. (*End of observation*)

Initially it seems from the data that it is only the boys who are overtly constructing their own discourse within the teacher-led discourse of the class. Natasha however is particularly vocal when she is in the lesson. She is often absent but her presence is felt when she is there.

In the next observation we see the way the boys project their personalities into the social space while the girls are chatting quietly to each other. At one point I go up to join in a work group of girls.

> Class does me presento exercise (I introduce myself) in the text book Listos 3. The written work is undertaken quietly. This is followed by speaking dialogues-asking and answering questions about each other. Fred and Alex can't agree on who's asking the questions and so they both ask each other the same questions. They keep asking each other the same questions and neither is answering. They keep this going for some time and eventually Alex starts to answer and with each answer, he says 'Fred smells'. Georgina, Lizzie, Aimee and Shannen are doing the dialogues quietly in pairs. I go to sit next to Georgina and Leah to revise the preterite tense with them and ask Que hiciste el sabado pasado? What did you do last weekend? (*End of observation*)

In the next lesson the gap between the boys' pupil discourse and official teacher-led discourse seems to widen. Joel, a male member of the class who was not included in the interview samples, is present.

> Lizzie and Georgina are working on vocab asking the teacher how to say 'my parents are called' in Spanish? – reply from teacher 'mis padres se llaman'. Next question is 'How do you say they are divorced?' Aimee's hand is up, Shannen's

hand is up. At the back of the class George is playing with a football, bouncing it against a table. Mitchell is at the back talking to George and Adam and Fred are tying a white scarf around Mitchell's head. Towards the front on the left hand side Aimee, Shannen, Leah and Georgina are sitting around the table as a four. The talk is on personal issues as they work. Just in front of the back row on the right hand side Alex and Joel are arguing about a dictionary – Alex is trying to get it back from Joel and leaning over to prod him. Alex gets out of his seat and Fred leans over and puts his hand on the chair to prevent him from sitting back down. Adam is again bouncing his football against the table and Sam is now drawn into this. (*End of observation*)

A 'laddish' discourse type is taking over the back two rows of the class with normally well behaved male students getting drawn in such as Joel and Sam.

In the classroom observations so far, we can see the relationship between pupil and teacher-led discourses. The boys' pupil discourse seems to be a hybrid discourse which moves between the official teacher-led discourse and a 'laddish' discourse much as outlined by Sunderland (2004) in her notion of gender differences discourse. On occasions, we see a laddish discourse dominate the pupils discourse as some of the boys appear to completely disconnect from the teacher-led discourse. It must be acknowledged that the pupil discourse does not neatly map onto gender since, for example, Joel and Sam, two male pupils, remain within the teacher-led discourse most of the time whereas a female pupil, Natasha, often disconnects from it.

Findings: cultural identity and learner identity in interaction

An issue may arise here of whether cultural identity as a background feature accounts for learner identity or vice versa. Emphasis, in the classroom observations, has been on the agency of students to construct their own learning identities constituted within classroom discourse. They are thus able to create their own 'cultural capital'.

Two of the students however, Fred and Alex, do not see the foreign language as connected to intercultural awareness. This can impact upon learner identity in different ways. For example, Alex, at times, enjoys the creation of Spanish text even though he does not seem to have the cultural resources to connect the words he creates to wider meanings and discourses. The language is for him at present a classroom word game. The issue seems to be one of cultural learner identity and gender. Some of the boys do not evoke wider cultural awareness. By contrast all the girls interviewed and also, one of the boys expressed intercultural interest and awareness, although not to the sophisticated extent that Georgina and Lizzie make in connecting culture to the forms of language. Georgina connects language and culture from her own independent study interests and imagination even though she has never been to Spain.

Georgina's learner identity seems connected to her cultural involvement with Spanish and this feeds back into her language use. So this is more than just an instrumental motivation of learning Spanish to get a job. The cultural identity here should be seen as an active one where the student is engaged in the process of research and discovery for him/herself as opposed to culture as a finished product. This is therefore where culture as product interrelates with culture as a process. Culture as an active process seems to be a means of transporting one's identity from one place to another through language, much as in Kramsch's (2009) notion of third place.

Gendered identity

In this case study, the only students who saw learning Spanish solely in terms of functional uses with regard to holidays and jobs were male. Yet generally male/female gender difference in wider cultural awareness is often blurred. Gender can be seen as a continuum between characteristics deemed male at one end and female at the other. As mentioned previously in the chapter, Creese et sl. (2004) refer to masculinities and femininities in the plural where gender is not a finished product at any given time but is in a constant process of social construction. Natasha, a girl, has little cultural interest in the target language whereas Sam, a boy, is keen on the cultural aspects of the foreign language. There is no simple and clear-cut dichotomy with regard to male/female cultural identity but it seems here there are tendencies for female students to assume a greater cultural interest in the language than male students. From the data gathered there is more of a tendency for boys to see the end result of language learning in terms of gain rather than appreciate the process in terms of cultural enquiry.

Fred has a definition of culture and appreciates what this interest could mean for some people but he is frank when he says that this does not hold any interest for him at all (interview extract 12, lines 13–17). We have seen in the classroom observations that Fred remains very much on the outside of the language activities, engaging in the pupil discourse 'banter'.

Powerful socio-economic discourse often seems to supply the default for learning a foreign language in the absence of wider culture. Here Fairclough's (1989) notion of orders of discourse permeating down to the socio-economic discourse type at institutional level and then to interactional practice seems particularly relevant. If one is disinclined or unable to learn for intrinsic interest in language and culture and no other meanings seem available, one can always supply economic motivations of employment prospects, the need to sell to the Spanish in their own language or working in leisure and tourism. The problem here is that the focus on learning is geared towards the end result through acquiring linguistic transactional skills rather than a focus on the process of language acquisition. Metaphorically, it is the goal that counts rather than the beautiful game. MFL learning should be more than communication skills and, as Kramsch (1993) argues, the bland target language culture that MFL does communicate is portrayed as ideologically normative in terms of people's lives, families, interests, jobs and so on. It does not reflect ideological and discourse tensions that exist within the classroom space. Kramsch argues that the subject area must break out of its normative ideological stranglehold and it can 'no longer be the one-sided response to national and economic interests, and the pursuit of economic happiness; it must include the search for an understanding of cultural boundaries' (12).

Conclusion

In terms of the research study the data that emerges shows a conflation between cultural frameworks of interculturality/cultural understanding, psychological notions of identity, socio-economics and gender. The relationship between these cultural elements is complex and more often exists as an interrelationship rather than the categories standing alone.

The learner cultural identities for MFL in the research are recognizable in relation to the theoretical considerations at the beginning of the chapter although in practice they are mainly interrelated. Cultural/intercultural learner identities often interrelate with socio-economic considerations and notions of future identity and are divided between male and female students although not equally. From the findings, mainly the female students express cultural/ intercultural interest in the language learner and only a female student, Georgina, expresses the notion of culture residing within language. However it is only male students who express an instrumental learner identity, external to language-culture.

In the research we see student agency in the way students construct their identities in class. Yet we can also see that these identities are not constructed in isolation from the outside world but draw upon all the personal and ideological identity possibilities afforded by the larger discourses outside the classroom. Therefore gender is enacted from the repertoires available for male and female and pedagogical meanings are drawn from the cultural and socio-economic affordances in the wider structures of society and community. The balance therefore that we can see is between the freewill of agency and the determinism of structure which are played out in every classroom time and again.

In terms of the rationale of this book where both languages and language learning are a site of conflict between dominant economic capital and an intrinsic linguistic cultural capital which is often marginalized, we can see from the research study a balance between the two types of capital. At the edges this is exemplified in a gender divide but more often than not the two types of capital are interrelated where students learn a language for both intrinsic cultural reasons as well as economic reasons external to language itself. Ultimately however, from this small-scale research, we can see that although students may draw upon wider societal and institutional discourses, they interpret them according to their own learner identities in the classroom context. They exercise agency in enacting their own learner identities and consequently contributing to the construction of their own learning cultures.

However findings from a relatively small-scale research population can only express trends in a tentative manner based on necessarily unfinished interpretations. The findings are taken from a particular locality and not amenable for extrapolation to generalizable knowledge. Nevertheless they may point the way for further research into how learners construct and explore their identities, not just in terms of foreign language pedagogy but also the cultural contexts around and within language.

References

Bakhtin, M. (1981). *The Dialogic Imagination: Four Essays*. M. Holquist (ed.). Austin: University of Texas Press.

Baxter, J. (2003). *Positioning Gender in Discourse: A Feminist Methodology*. Basingstoke: Palgrave Macmillan.

Bourdieu, P. (1991). *Language and Symbolic Power*. J. P. Thompson (ed.). Cambridge: Harvard University Press.

Butler, J. (1990). *Gender Trouble: Feminism and the Subversion of Identity*. London: Routledge.

Creese, A., Leonard, D., Daniels, H., & Hey, V. (2004). 'Pedagogic Discourses, Learning and Gender Identification'. *Language and Education* 18.3: 191–206.

Dornyei, Z., & Ushioda, E. (2009). *Motivation, Language Identity and the L2 Self*. Clevedon: Multilingual Matters.

Fairclough, N. (1989). *Language and Power*. London/New York:. Longman.

Foucault, M. (1972). *The Archeology of Knowledge*. London: Routledge.

Gardner, R. (1985). *Social Psychology and Second Language Learning: The Role of Attitudes and Motivation*. London: Edward Arnold.

Gillette, B. (1994). 'The Role of Learner Goals in L2 Success'. In J. Lantolf and G. Appel, *Vygotskian Approaches to Second Language Research*. Norwood, NJ: Ablex Press.

Kramsch, C. (1993). *Context and Culture in Language Teaching*. Oxford: Oxford University Press.

Kramsch, C. (1998). *Language and Culture*. Oxford: Oxford University Press.

Kramsch, C. (2009). *The Multilingual Subject*. Oxford: Oxford University Press.

Lave, J., and Wenger, E. (1991). *Situated Learning: Legitimate Peripheral Participation*. New York: Cambridge University Press.

Norton, B. (2000). *Identity and Language Learning: Gender, Ethnicity and Educational Change*. London: Longman.

Oral, Y. (2013). ' "The Right Things Are What I Expect Them to Do"; Negotiation of Power Relations in an English Classroom'. *Journal of Language, Identity and Education* 12.4: 96–115.

Pollmann, A. (2016). 'Habitus, Reflexivity and the Realization of Intercultural Capital: The (Unfulfilled) Potential of Intercultural Education'. *Cogent Social Sciences* 2.

Robson, C. (1993). *Real World Research*. Oxford: Blackwell.

Sunderland, J. (2004). *Gendered Discourses*. Basingstoke: Palgrave Macmillan.

Van Lier, L. (2000). 'From Input to Affordance: Social Interactive Learning from an Ecological Perspective'. In J. P. Lantolf (ed.), *Sociocultural Theory and Second Language Learning*. Oxford: Oxford University Press.

Van Lier, L. (2002). *The Ecology of Language Learning and Sociocultural Theory*. Monterey Institute of International Studies.

Wertsche, J. V. (1991). *Voices of the Mind: A Sociocultural Approach to Mediated Action*. Cambridge, MA: Harvard University Press.

11

Teacher Development through Classroom Discourse Analysis: The Self-Evaluation of Teacher Talk Instrument Developed by Walsh

Karin Zotzmann

Introduction

Communication and interaction are essential for successful language learning, including, for instance, the negotiation of meaning, the modification of output and the exposure to a wide range of spoken and written genres (Ellis 1994; Swain 1995; van Lier 1996). Being able to create such a communication-rich learning environment requires sophisticated pedagogical and methodological competences on the part of the teacher. Effective pre-service, as well as in-service teacher training and development therefore often include opportunities to explore and reflect upon the discursive patterns of teachers' own classrooms. Awareness of the specificities of classroom discourse, that is, the relationship between communication and learning opportunities, is regarded as crucial if teachers want to facilitate their students' learning processes effectively and expand what Walsh (2006; 2011) calls their *classroom interactional competence.*

This chapter reports on a teacher development project with four in-service teachers of Spanish in Mexico who analysed a transcript of their own classes through a discourse analytical instrument developed by Walsh (2006; 2011). Discourse analysis (DA) is particularly interesting as it focuses on language *in context*, that is, communicative events are described, analysed and interpreted as they unfold over time in specific social situations, involving social actors with particular intentions and objectives. Walsh's discourse analytical instrument (Self-Evaluation of Teacher Talk, henceforth SETT) consists of a range of analytical concepts and procedures designed to foment the awareness of teachers about the language they use in class, the appropriateness of these discursive patterns to the pedagogic aims they pursue and the learning opportunities they thereby create for their students. SETT thus allows teachers to reflect upon their *own* classrooms. It responds to the call for attuning professional development to context-specific everyday practices (Wallace 1991; Gebhard and Oprandy 1999; Gebhard 1984).

In the professional development project I report on, four experienced teachers of Spanish were introduced to SETT, employed it in an analysis of their own classroom discourse and then reflected upon the experiences with this type of self-analysis in a semi-structured interview. Their respective class sizes ranged from five to twenty adult students either from the United States or Europe who had come to Mexico either to work, to do an internship or to study a semester abroad. Two of the four classes took place at a large private language institute, the other two at different private universities. The lessons, each of them fifty minutes long, were taped several weeks after the term had begun in order to ensure that students and teachers already knew each other and had established norms for and ways of working together.

Based on the interview data, transcripts and video-recordings of the respective classes, my initial aim was to find out whether the four participants experienced SETT as user-friendly, whether it indeed helped them to generate new insights about their own behaviour in the classroom and, conversely, whether or not the instrument constrained them in any way in their reflection. On a more theoretical plane, I thus wanted to explore the affordances and limitations of SETT, an instrument that was explicitly designed to make the link between classroom discourse, teaching objectives and context visible and accessible to teachers.

While all four participants pointed to a large number of benefits and a smaller amount of deficiencies of SETT, they also frequently referred to factors outside of the classroom that had influenced their decisions and reasons for specific communicative behaviour inside of this micro-institutional space. As individuals with specific identities and sense of agency, values (reasons) and abilities, they naturally differed in their interpretation of and responses to these multiple interlacing institutional and larger macro-level structures. By design, the SETT, however, focuses exclusively on classroom discourse and interaction as if teaching occurred in a social vacuum. Taking into consideration that a DA instrument needs to be practical and viable, I suggest that SETT might benefit from combining the micro-level discourse analysis with a broader account of the interplay between agency and structures as 'the enduring, affording and constraining influences of the social order' (Sealey and Carter 2004: xiii). To this end, I draw upon an ecological framework as proposed by van Lier (2000), Doyle (2006) and Kramsch (2003). In a first instance, though, I outline the concepts, theoretical foundations and procedures of SETT, explain the adaptations that the particular context of the investigation required and present evidence from interview data of how teachers reflected upon and explained their decisions and behaviour.

The Self-Evaluation of Teacher Talk developed by Walsh

The SETT instrument developed by Walsh (2006) consists of a range of analytical concepts and procedures that were designed to foment the awareness of teachers about the language they use in class, the appropriateness of these discursive patterns in relation to the pedagogic goals teachers pursue and the learning opportunities they thereby create for their students. The SETT is informed, in a first instance, by *Conversation Analysis* (CA) in that it emphasizes both the sequential and dynamic development of talk over time and the use of 'naturally' occurring classroom data. Similar to CA, the author also acknowledges that teachers have more power over turn taking patterns than students: They commonly begin, frame and end the interaction, hold the floor longer and select students to respond. In line with CA he assumes that in real-world classrooms the default option of discursive patterns still consists of a turn initiated by the teacher, a response by the student and feedback (IRF) (Sinclair and Coulthard 1975; 1992) or an evaluation of this response (IRE) (Mehan 1979) by the teacher.

While Walsh is sympathetic to CA, he also criticizes the framework for analysing instances of classroom discourse in isolation, that is, without establishing links to context and purposes. He argues that micro-linguistic behaviour such as *scaffolding, direct repair, content feedback, extended wait-time, referential questions, seeking clarification, extended learner turn, display questions* or *form-focused feedback* have to be interpreted in context, that is, in relation to the purpose a teacher pursues in this particular moment in class. Walsh calls these micro-contexts created by the teacher *modes* and differentiates between four empirically derived types: The *skills and systems mode* is characterized by a focus on language as a system constituted by, for example, lexical items and syntactical rules as well as learning strategies. While this could be regarded as one of the principal function of foreign language classes, teachers also have to organize students, check attendance lists, distribute them into groups for particular activities and ensure that they contribute to the class in a constructive manner. The author subsumes this type of activities under the *managerial mode* and sets it apart from the *materials mode*, where teachers direct the attention of students to any material employed for pedagogic purposes such as, for example, written texts or audio recordings. Instead of treating students exclusively in relation to their role in the classroom, teachers can also engage them in an integral and holistic manner, that is, as individuals with emotions, attitudes and opinions. The author calls this the *classroom context mode.*

The concept of mode allows Walsh to analyse classroom discourse with greater precision: Instead of classifying a sequence or even the totality of a lesson as 'missing authentic communication', the question is rather whether the intention the teacher pursues in a particular segment actually *requires* the holistic communicative involvement of students. The managerial mode, for instance, is usually teacher driven and includes mainly instructions. The communicative mode, in contrast, engages students as individual human beings and thus allows, at least potentially, for a broad variety of speech acts.

In terms of procedure, Walsh suggests that teachers audiotape between ten and fifteen minutes of their class, preferably a sequence with particularly intense interaction. Immediately after the lesson they are invited to listen to the recording several times, choose parts that appear interesting to them, transcribe these sections, decide which modes are operating in these transcribed sequences and evaluate the language they used in relation to their intentions. In a third step, they discuss this analysis with the teacher trainer or researcher in a post-observation dialogue. Since the procedure relies heavily on proactive teachers who can invest a considerable amount of time, several changes had to be made in the context of the project.

The context of the investigation and the need for changes in the procedure

The four participants worked, similar to as many foreign language teachers around the world, in somewhat precarious situations. Although experienced practitioners, they had always been employed on short-term contracts, that is, they were subjected to fluctuations in student demand. They worked long hours, sometimes in different institutions, and had little or no institutional support for professional development. As time was a scarce resource for them, I met the four teachers individually and provided extensive support to ensure continuing commitment throughout. Instead of them audiotaping their own classes, selecting interesting sections and transcribing these, as suggested by Walsh, I decided to videotape the classes and transcribe the entire lessons myself. Two further considerations influenced this decisions: In comparison with audiotapes, videos do not only offer richer data including information on body language, gestures and facial expressions, they also allow teachers to see the interaction from different angles and to, potentially, detect details which had escaped their attention while they were teaching. In addition to this, analysing a whole class instead of isolated passages seemed beneficial as sequences, key moments and points of transition came into focus. After teaching the class, they were asked to watch the videotape and write a short reflective text about students' participation and engagement during the class.

Since the four participating teachers had no experience in analysing their own classroom discourse and no previous exposure to individualized professional development, I anticipated that they needed more guidance in relation to the concepts and procedures of SETT. In order to know more about SETT and activate their knowledge the teachers were invited to explore their teaching philosophy beforehand through a semi-structured questionnaire, including, for instance, their attitudes towards the use of the L1 in the classroom, the role of grammar and interaction, the inclusion of cultural aspects and the nature of feedback and error treatment.

In order to facilitate the actual analysis via SETT, I designed a worksheet with three columns: The first column contained the transcription. In the second column, participants noted down the overriding mode or purpose of a specific phase of the lesson. In the third column they noted down the corresponding linguistic realization at the micro-linguistic level.

Transcription	Mode	Teacher talk
Teacher: . . . ok, let's begin . . .		

After having analysed the transcription of their classroom discourse and discussed it with me, teachers talked about their experiences with and their evaluation of the usefulness and viability of SETT. I explained to the participants that I did not favour any particular, positive or negative, evaluations but was interested in their truthful opinions. In addition to this, teachers were also invited to digress and explore any issues that they regarded as relevant in relation to their class and the analysis.

The utility of Walsh's model to foster reflexivity and awareness in teachers

All four teachers evaluated the experiences with SETT very positively and stressed that they had discovered new aspects about their own teaching practices and ways of communicating with students:

> I very much liked this project because . . . you are not aware of what you are doing in class. You often take it for granted that they [students] understand and that you are doing a magnificent job. (teacher D)

They found a variety of opportunities for improvement, for example, in relation to equitable participation, classroom management, choice of material, variation of activities, change of and transition between different modes, function of questions, length of pauses, quality of feedback and so on. Teacher A, for example, describes how she became aware of her tendency to respond to her own questions:

> For example, I make them . . . I asked them a question: 'So what can we see here in this picture?' And then immediately I myself respond to the question! Poor guys! I think they had not even understood the question. I did not give them time to reflect about what they wanted to answer and then immediately do I answer myself. And it seems to me that this is something that I do regularly in class . . . Maybe I do not ALWAYS answer to my own questions . . . but in this case where I can see the transcript over and over again I NOTICE it.

The same teacher realized that she tended to rely on the participation of stronger students and thus disadvantages learners who need more time to answer:

> I very much tend to . . . I don't know, to use the strongest in the class, for example when we introduce the forms. And then, I become too quick and probably do not give the others enough time.

Teacher D reported of a lack of transitions between different activities and modes:

> When I saw the transcription I really focused on the language: How do I manage the class? Do I give them an opportunity to speak or don't I? How do I make the transition from one phase to the next? Because what I also noticed is that I do not have a structure . . . I begin one thing . . . and then later I stop and then I begin something else . . . I do not link them or relate them to each other. As if I stopped and continued, stopped and continued.

After the analysis, she therefore tried to improve her teaching by signposting and explaining transitions to students. Similarly, teacher A reports of an immediate effect of her reflection on her teaching practice: 'Now every time I teach I think: Ok . . . slowly . . . Give them time! . . . Wait! . . . Let them reflect!'

While it would need a long-term empirical study to investigate the actual effects on teaching practices and routines of each individual teacher, the use of SETT generated an awareness in all four participants that learning opportunities are generated through the language employed. Teacher D, for instance, explains:

> When I watched myself in the video I thought: 'How lovely, nice and witty' but then I saw in the transcription: five lines teacher and then the student says: 'Aha.' Then again, four lines the teacher and the student says: 'Yes' . . . This is what I became aware of. It made me see that it is the student who should participate in class, not me.

Teacher B explains how the analysis changed her understanding of classroom communication:

> No, no, before I had never thought of how you can . . . guide a student through . . . these interventions that you do . . . I had never thought about how these can motivate or stop them . . . And that is also why it was so interesting for me to analyse the language.

The necessity to improve and complement the model

Although the evaluation of the instrument SETT was very positive in all four cases, some of the theoretical assumptions underpinning the model, above all the concept of mode, generated analytical difficulties for participants. For teacher D the concept was in a first instance very helpful:

> But it helps you really a lot because you say: Ah, and here I did this activity and then this sequence and then I changed the mode. Well, I think it helps you enormously in clarifying what you are doing in class, does not it?

At the same time, she mentions that the four modes seemed 'very general' to her and that it was difficult to categorize different phases of the class into different modes: 'Some of them just did not fit . . . they did not fit in any of them. So I said to myself: The closest one is probably this one.' She concludes that the four modes are insufficient and not clearly delimited, an opinion voiced by the other participants, as well. Teacher B thought that 'maybe there should be more [modes]. I do not know' while teacher A reported: 'In some cases, I just lost it. But then you told me that sometimes two purposes can be mixed and then I thought: Ah, that makes sense.'

One problem with the four modes is that although Walsh came to this categorization through empirical research the distinctions between them appear ambivalent. The material and the managerial mode, for instance, seem to merge as it is not always possible to distinguish an action that is oriented towards the organization of students in general and the organization of students in relation to specific tasks and materials. Furthermore, the separation between language (grammar, vocabulary and learning strategies) oriented sequences (*skills and systems mode*) and communication that involves students holistically as individuals (*classroom context mode*) replicate a commonly found phenomenon in traditional teacher centred classrooms. It does not take into account principles of communicative language teaching, task based teaching and learning and Content and Language Integrated Learning (CLIL) that combine the involvement of students with a focus on language as a meaning making resource in particular contexts.

Walsh himself emphasizes that modes have a process character and appear often in mixed forms. To this end, Walsh (2011: 129) introduced the concept of *mode switching* (movements between one mode and another), *mode side sequences* (movements between main and secondary modes) and *mode divergence* (interactional features and pedagogic goals do not coincide). In addition to this, the framework allows for other modes to be added, should they arise. Nevertheless, SETT is designed around four empirically derived modes and teachers tend to perceive them as predetermined or definite concepts, a view that can only be amended through further explanations.

The problems teachers in this professional development encountered are partly due to the fact that the concept of mode has little to offer in terms of analytical depth. In general terms mode designates the *form* or *condition* of a task or a *way* of performing it. It has been adopted in education, for instance, to differentiate between forms of interaction (*face-to-face* versus *blended learning*) or between different semiotic systems (*visual, verbal, written, oral, physical* or *musical*) and their 'multimodal' ensembles (Kress and van Leeuwen 2001). The notion of *genre*, in contrast, has been widely discussed in academia and increasingly refined. In a first instance, the term draws attention to the fact that people commonly attempt to standardize and stabilize recurring actions which have been successful in the past. These conventionalized forms of interaction or 'interactional genres' (Lefstein 2008; Hanks 2005; Rampton 2006) make behaviour relatively predictable without determining it. They are understood to be governed by specific purposes, similar to what Walsh aims to achieve with the concept of mode, although there is a widespread acceptance that 'communicative purpose' is a rather 'fuzzy and sometimes subjective' concept (Bhatia 2004: 113). The functional view of linguistic interaction as linked to and determined by specific intentions is hence regarded as too rigid, a concern that was voiced by the four participants. Since genres are semiotic resources based on previous experiences that people draw upon in specific social practices and in relation to their particular, often mixed and sometimes even contradictory purposes, they become actualized with differing degrees of variance. The degree of possible creativity and genre hybridity depends, however, on the openness or stability of the respective social situation and context. 'Participants always have the possibility of improvising, both within the bounds of generic expectations and also by stretching or breaking them, for example, by importing resources from other communicative genres, rejecting role expectations, or otherwise attempting to redefine the situation' (Lefstein 2008: 709). In particular *expert* members such as experienced teachers can employ and mix generic and discursive resources in order to integrate 'additional private intentions within the socially accepted and shared communicative purposes' (Bhatia 2004: 130). Instead of classifying different microcontexts as modes according to overriding purposes, a genre perspective might therefore achieve a balance between conventionalized forms of interaction and creativity and elevate hybridity to a normal feature of classroom discourse. It could function as a 'sensitizing' instead of a 'definite' concept. Sensitizing concepts, according to Charmaz (2003), might lack the security of fixed categories but provide clues about where to look for certain types of phenomena. This is particularly important in the context of the complex task the teacher trainer or researcher has to accomplish during the post-observation dialogue. While she has to provide and explain analytical concepts and instruments, scaffold their use and facilitate the construction of a narrative, she also needs to remain open to emergent themes so that teachers can explore topics and analytical avenues they find relevant and thereby become owners of their own professional development.

The case of teacher C is particularly telling in this context. While she had prepared the lesson, she seemed to be very flexible in changing the course of the classroom conversation according to students' needs, comments and questions. As a result, the lesson appeared fragmented and the analysis of the transcription displayed constant changes of modes. The teacher herself described it in the following way:

> If we look closely at the column for the modes, we can see that there is a dense mixture of modes. Apparently the dialogues between teacher and students, or between students, or between one student and the teacher, is good, fluid and

above all in Spanish. But if we talk in terms of Spanish as a foreign language class, the absence of a structure that includes appropriate management of time dedicated to modes, intentions, turns, activities, materials, state of mind of the students and classroom atmosphere is quite clear. This structure can be understood as a lack of a pedagogic discourse that is conscious and efficient. So, if you ask me to what extent the language and the pedagogic purpose coincide . . . and if we add the column with the language of the teacher, we can guess that there is a good intention, but nothing else. This means, there is dialogue and there is a class. But what is missing is an awareness that the mode and the language employed should be coherent instead of being a collage or disperse fragments of activities.

The use of the SETT instrument had clearly helped her to identify an apparent lack of classroom management and pedagogic purposes. At the same time, though, she points to the fact that the dialogues are 'good, fluid and above all in Spanish'. As a matter of fact, all students participated in her lesson; they appeared motivated and seemed confident in expressing ideas and doubts despite their beginners' level.

Encouraged to explore her reasons for communicating with students the way she did, the teacher explains that she wants 'to create a community', a culture or a 'fictitious atmosphere between us' 'having our own topics, for instance, . . . having our own secrets'. Through these shared moments and experiences they can speak about life: 'This has nothing to do with grammar . . . this has to do with life . . . with human life':

> I am trying to do something good . . . they are also human beings . . . and they are under pressure, pressure, pressure . . . you are worth as much as you produce . . . Well, that is how it is . . . this is the time we live in. I am not sure if this is good or bad but it is the reality. So that is why I think that . . . what we need are strategies of how to survive all this, without getting bitter . . . so I try to make people have a good time . . . if they have to let off steam, then let us do that, if they are angry then they should say it: 'Have you now let off steam?' 'Have we discussed this now? Ok, then let's continue with the class.' And what they like . . . they end up talking a lot about their family, about their private life.

Viewed through her eyes, the lack of order in class and the often abrupt topic changes appear only on some level as deficiencies as they are in accordance with her intention to prioritize the 'human element' through a flexible and spontaneous conversation. The ambivalence emerges further in the interview where she admits that it is this flexibility and apparent chaos that generates opportunities for students to talk:

I am not worried about the mess anymore because it already happened . . . so . . . but thinking the mess was very interesting because it helped me first of all to understand the . . . I knew the problem. And of course, I would like to solve it . . . and the other thing is not to lose the mess that makes them talk. This is like the challenge now.

What emerges here is ambivalence between order and disorder, planning and chaos, grammar and personalized communication which could not be neatly categorized in one of the four modes. In order to arrive at his reasoning it was important that both the researcher and the teacher felt comfortable to go beyond definite categories such as modes and explore the interactional genres she had co-created with her students in relation to her intentions.

While the notion of genre can remind us of the unavoidable hybridity of classroom discourse and sensitize us to the interactional work that is being done it also brings into view that classroom internal practices are shaped by classroom external factors.

The need to go beyond the classroom

Social groups do not develop patterned ways of interacting and communicating or interactional genres in a social vacuum. Each classroom is embedded in an institution and a sociocultural context with particular constrains and affordances. The fact that all three institutions the four participants worked in were private had an effect on the relations between teachers and students and by implication on the ways students were taught. The participants were, for instance, continuously being evaluated by students. Their re-employment and, in the case of the private language institute, the level of payment they received was dependent on the satisfaction of their 'clients'. Teacher A reports of the influence of her students on her income: 'but at the end of the year there is an evaluation and it depends on the feedback whether you get five pesos more or less, right?' As she explains the choice of modes has 'LOTS to do with the personality of the teacher' but likewise with the expectations of the students: 'the type of clients we have needs a lot of organization and structure.' She continues:

Yes, I think we are pretty influenced by working with Germans and for this reason our classes are shaped like this. It is because they like to have a structure: You begin one way and 'Now we are going to talk a bit, but then we are moving on to grammar'! 'Because I want to know the irregular forms of the indefinite.' So, they demand it from you . . . in an indirect way, right? They will never say: 'I want this' but . . . they do ask for it. They are very happy when they can write something about grammar in their notebook . . . this is what they want, what they expect, what the client asks for.

Teacher D who works in the same institution makes a similar comment: 'German students are terrible . . . They always ask for grammar.' She also feels obliged to comply with their clients' expectations although this is contrary to her belief: 'the problem is to learn the structures as rules. When they speak, it does not help them to search for rule No. 44 for the subjunctive, does it?'

Although teacher B designed her class herself, the syllabus was heavily adapted to the demands and goals set by the Spanish coordinator at the US-American University where students came from: 'Before they [the students] arrived, the coordinator got in contact and told me: "This is what I want them to do."' She was asked to concentrate on conversation and avoid giving grammatical explanations. This stirred a conflict in her as she felt the students needed grammar in order to converse adequately. Her solution of separating questions concerning grammar from the actual conversational part of the lesson caused further problems as she had to respond to students' questions about grammar in a decontextualized way. In addition to this, the conversation part itself did not flow either but for different rather macro contextual reasons: 'They do not speak, they do not react. And I give them topics and try to make them talk and . . . there is simply no answer.' She describes the motivation for learning Spanish as instrumental 'because learning a foreign language is obligatory. The foreign language for them is Spanish because the Latin population is increasing in the U.S.'

While all four teachers regarded contextual factors as crucial to the actual communication and interaction inside of the classroom, the SETT instrument itself does not provide a conceptual framework to account for these. This is partly due to the social-constructivist perspective Walsh adopts. Even though Walsh (2006: 60) acknowledges that L2 classroom are linked up with a series of social, political, cultural and historical contexts, classroom discourse remains an autonomous object of study which bears, neither theoretically nor analytically, any relation to the contexts it is embedded in. As a consequence the reflection through SETT can aim at a better understanding of the classroom discourse but falls short of indicating causality and explanations. Without a critical reflection on the institutional context it is difficult to gain a new perspective on what is actually possible, practical and desirable in particular institutions (Kumaravadivelu 1999)

To relate classroom discourse with the institutional and educational conditions that enable certain practices and limit or inhibit others, an ecological framework as proposed by van Lier (2000), Doyle (2006) and Kramsch (2003) might be fruitful. Kramsch (2003: 5) describes the ecology metaphor in the following way: '[T]he "ecology" metaphor is a convenient shorthand for the post-structuralist realization that learning is a nonlinear, relational human activity, co-constructed between humans and their environment, contingent upon their position in space and history, and a site of struggle for the control of social power and cultural memory.' Such a perspective would share similar assumptions as Walsh's model, namely, that the L2 class is guided by different pedagogical purposes which in turn influence the language used. Instead of limiting teaching and learning however to the interaction in the classroom, an ecological view would take into account the impact of wider social forces. Students, for instance, would come into view not only as learners but as agents with certain positions in particular societies who learn a language for specific reasons in accordance with their ambitions and the affordances this language offers to them. They come to the classroom with particular expectations and engage in interactional genres that are in turn shaped by the institutions and cultural traditions they are embedded in. Understanding classroom discourse from such a wider perspective would help teachers not only to function better in terms of being a more effective communicator; it would also help them to become aware of conflicts between their own values and views and institutional policies and practices.

Conclusion

The aim of this investigation was to evaluate the viability and utility of the SETT instrument for the professional development of foreign language teachers and to generate suggestions for improvement. In a first instance, several adjustments to the procedure had to be made for practical reasons, such as, for example, giving more support to teachers, both in terms of how to use the SETT and in terms of transcribing the lessons.

All four participants confirmed that the reflection about patterns of linguistic interaction through the transcript and the analytical instrument nurtured a new understanding of the communication that takes place in their classroom. They expressed that the awareness they gained had inspired them to change established routines and find new and more effective ways of communicating. At the same time, the participants reported of difficulties in assigning modes to different classroom sequences. I have argued that the concept of mode is analytically unhelpful as it suggest a predetermined concept that is imposed upon a rather complex and messy classroom reality in which purposes are not always clear and sometimes contested, where expectations of all participants intersect and communication evolves dynamically. In contrast, the notion of genre draws attention to both conventionalized forms of interaction and emergent meanings.

A discourse analytical instrument that helps teachers to achieve a closer understanding of how language use affects learning opportunities has to be fairly specific in order to generate a detailed and fruitful analysis. At the same time, it needs to be user-friendly for and comprehensible to practitioners who might come from diverse academic and professional backgrounds. This is a complicated balance to achieve and requires on the one hand predetermined, universal categories, and on the other an in-built context-sensitivity of the instrument itself. Walsh's great achievement is to have developed a procedure teachers can handle fairly easily. SETT offers a metalanguage that allows teachers and teacher trainers to exchange interpretations, ideas and experiences and to analyse the classroom discourse in a theoretically informed way. SETT thus generates new insights and knowledge which in turn might influence teaching practices. The viability and practicality is, however, achieved at the expense of specificity, that is, the instrument has no components which could capture the constraining or enabling effects particular contexts offer, such as, for example, teaching traditions, institutional preconditions related to the curricular, assessment and obligatory teaching material, the nexus between payment system and course evaluations of students, differences in socio-economic class and status of teachers and learners and so on. In this context, I have suggested that an ecological framework would be beneficial. Combined with a more critical view of classroom discourse it could ask for the reasons behind specific communication patterns and thereby help teachers not only to become more effective communicators but to become more responsible and conscious of their own values and choices.

References

Bathia, V. K. (2004). *Worlds of Written Discourse: A Genre-Based View*. London: Continuum.

Charmaz, K. (2003). 'Grounded Theory: Objectivist and Constructivist Methods'. In N. K. Denzin and Y. S. Lincoln (eds), *Strategies for Qualitative Inquiry*. 2nd ed. Thousand Oaks, CA: Sage. 249–91.

Doyle, W. (2006). 'Ecological Approaches to Classroom Management'. In C. M. Evertson and C. S. Weinstein (eds), *Handbook of Classroom Management. Research, Practice and Contemporary Issues*. New York: Routledge.

Ellis, R. (1994). *The Study of Second Language Acquisition*. Oxford: Blackwell.

Gebhard, J. G. (1984). 'Models of Supervision: Choices'. *TESOL Quarterly* 18: 501–14.

Gebhard, J. G., & Oprandy, R. (eds) (1999). *Language Teaching Awareness: A Guide to Exploring Beliefs and Practices*. Cambridge: Universidad de Cambridge.

Hanks, W. F. (1996). *Language and Communicative Practices*. Boulder: Westview.

Kramsch, C. (ed.) (2003) *Language Acquisition and Language Socialization: Ecological Perspectives*. London: Continuum.

Kress, G., & van Leeuwen, T. (2001). *Multimodal Discourse: The Modes and Media of Contemporary Communication*. Oxford, UK: Oxford University Press.

Kumaravadivelu, B. (1999). 'Critical Classroom Discourse Analysis'. *TESOL Quarterly* 33.3: 453–84.

Lefstein, A. (2008). 'Changing Classroom Practice through the English National Literacy Strategy: A Micro-interactional Perspective'. *American Educational Research Journal* 45.3: 701–37.

Mehan, H. (1979). *Learning Lessons: Social Organization in the Classroom*. Cambridge, MA: Harvard University Press.

Rampton, B. (2006). *Language in Late Modernity: Interaction in an Urban School*. Cambridge: Cambridge University Press.

Sealey, A., & Carter, B. (2004). *Applied Linguistics as Social Science*. London: Continuum.

Sinclair, J., & Coulthard, M. (1975). *Towards an Analysis of Discourse: The English Used by Teachers and Pupils*. Oxford: Oxford University Press.

Sinclair, J., & Coulthard, M. (1992). 'Towards an Analysis of Discourse'. In M. Coulthard (ed.), *Advances in Spoken Discourse Analysis*. London: Routledge. 1–34.

Swain, M. (1995). 'Three Functions of Output in Second Language Learning'. In: G. Cook and B. Seidelhofer (eds), *Principle and Practice in Applied Linguistics: Studies in Honour of H.G. Widdowson*. Oxford: Oxford University Press.

van Lier, L. (1996). *Interaction in the Language Curriculum: Awareness, Autonomy and Authenticity*. New York: Longman.

van Lier, L. (2000). *The Ecology and Semiotics of Language Learning: A Sociocultural Perspective*. Boston: Kluwer.

Wallace, M. J. (1991). *Training Foreign Language Teachers: A Reflective Approach*. Cambridge: Cambridge University Press.

Walsh, S. (2006). *Investigating Classroom Discourse*. London: Routledge.

Walsh, S. (2011). *Exploring Classroom Discourse: Language in Action*. London: Routledge.

12

Conclusion: A Pedagogy for Marginalized Language-Culture

David Evans

This concluding chapter sums up the key themes of marginalized language, discourse and culture from the case studies and then explores critical pedagogy as a resistant discourse and a means to revalorize marginalized language.

Bourdieu (2013) signals the way in which marginalization occurs in the relationship between symbolic and material value. He regards symbolic capital as being founded upon material economic capital. For him the Marxist analysis of material value comes first, which then generates symbolic value through notions of scarcity, demand, exclusivity and finally prestige. Material value and economic capital alone therefore do not tell the whole story of sociocultural hierarchy without the second layer of symbolic capital. This second layer tells a story of legitimacy of social properties which for Bourdieu can include phenomena such as lifestyle, clothing, interior design and also language. Bourdieu states as follows 'There is not a simple practice or property, . . . , characteristic of a particular manner of living that cannot be given a distinct value as a function of a socially determined principle of pertinence and therefore express a social position' (297). Of course language is a social property but it is also the means through which we represent other social phenomena to others and to ourselves in its linguistic structures. So language has an objective symbolic commodity value but also and more importantly a subjective value for the construction of social and cultural reality.

Bourdieu (2013) places emphasis on the distribution of social and material properties in his analysis of social inequality. Unequal distribution of material and social resources leads to exclusive and restricted access, subsequent demand and consequently a high symbolic value which needs to be maintained as exclusive in order to retain that value. Bourdieu argues that people who fail to see the social conferment of value on social goods as a result of unequal distribution are guilty of 'misrecognition' because they view these properties, including language, as containing inherent rather than conferred value. They see the inherent value of the properties such as standard language or 'Queen's English' as part of the natural order of the social world as opposed to an outcome of social conflict. Consequently prestige is viewed mistakenly as the inherent high value of a normative social order and not as a result of sociocultural domination and symbolic violence. Bourdieu states as follows, 'Any capital, whatever the form it assumes, exerts a 'symbolic violence' as soon as it is recognized, that is, misrecognized in its truth as capital and imposes itself as an authority calling for recognition' (299).

Social goods therefore which have been 'consecrated' (Bourdieu 2013: 299) into symbolic capital and highly valued due to unequal distribution are 'misrecognized' (299).

Consequently, a language or a language type becomes highly valued as a symbolic property through the symbolic power of 'King's/Queen's English' or socio-economic standing as world language but this is misrecognized value if considered to be inherent. Its value is conferred symbolically by dominant culture and to acknowledge it mistakenly as intrinsic by a marginalized culture is to conspire into one's own domination and submit to symbolic violence.

With regard to the symbolic violence suffered by marginalized language, Bourdieu (1989) makes the following comment about the domination subjected to the Creole of Guinea-Bissau by Portuguese, 'It is clear that throughout the period of colonial domination the colonialists pointed out to their colonial subjects that the only elegant and cultured language, capable of expressing beauty and scientific exactitude, was theirs, the colonialists. For them, their colonial subjects did not have a language, properly speaking' (117).

We have also witnessed a similar phenomenon currently taking place in Cameroon in Chapter 6 where Kum describes the historical development of Cameroon Pidgin English (CPE) in which indigenous Cameroonians interacted with their colonial rulers using a hybrid mixture of English followed by French on the one hand when the country united in 1961 and indigenous language on the other hand. Kum describes this hybrid language as a 'bridging language' because it is a unifying language understood across the country in tribal contexts as well institutions. Many Cameroonians would like CPE to be the official national language replacing French and English but although it is understood, its active use is discouraged in favour of French and English. CPE is considered to be a non-standard English and occupies an inferior linguistic status, not actively used in institution and not taught in schools or used as a medium for education. Kum points out that indeed there are notices in schools forbidding the use of CPE with strict sanctions for anyone caught speaking it. As we see in this chapter, Kum highlights the prestige of French as the language of knowledge and culture used in all levels of education as a language of prestige.

The language relations in Cameroon reflect similar hierarchical language power relations in the Uyghur province of northwest China. Sunuodola analyses the power relations between Mandarin Chinese spoken by the dominant Han majority in China and the regional Uyghur language. Sunuodola narrates the way in which Mandarin Chinese has gradually taken over socio-political and educational life in the Uyghur Xinjiang region to the point where the Uyghur language only officially exists now as a school subject. Although surveys show that students wish to speak Mandarin fluently and this is now the language medium of their education, they only want to do this for economic opportunity and not to enhance or maintain a civic bond with the dominant Han culture. Sunuodola refers to Bourdieu's analysis of language as a symbolic capital to show that the linguistic and cultural 'superiority' of the dominant Han language and culture is just a conferred one by dint of political power and contains no intrinsic value. To think otherwise is to engage in Bourdieu's concept of misrecognition (meconnaissance) and to conspire with domination. In this he demonstrates that state languages are simply social and ideological constructs.

In Chapter 4, in the southeast county of Kent, there is a parallel situation of cultural colonization where young entrepreneurial Londoners described by Anderson as expressing an alternative urban 'hipster' culture are migrating to Margate to establish an alternative metropolitan culture. This is perceived by locals as an incursion into their local culture by outsiders. The 'hipsters' see themselves according to a magazine article as culturally superior and in a position to transform the area.

Acknowledgement of such prestige culture, conferred value by a dominant culture, would be deemed 'misrecognition' according to Bourdieu and therefore an act of conspiring into one's own domination. This is not a phenomenon that just occurs across different languages with regard to perceived hierarchical value but also within an individual language, deemed to be a standard language or a language of prestige as opposed to that which is deemed to be a regional dialect.

Dalal (2016) refers to Bourdieu's notion of symbolic violence, in Dalal's definition, as the inculcation of meaning by the dominant group over the dominated through the education system. For Bourdieu, school is not an agent of liberation in itself but a means where the social order is reproduced by those in power. So school plays an important part in reproducing social divisions and classes through the construction of forms of symbolic and cultural capital. These different forms of capital are constructed within different forms of 'habitus' (Dalal 2016; Bourdieu 1977)

Habitus and field

Dalal (2016) points out that 'habitus' are the mental structures that one acquires in one's social milieu or 'Field' relating to ways of being, doing and thinking. Someone's habitus then comes to them as a natural way of being in the world but this could be radically different from another person's mental and cultural disposition. Bourdieu is criticized for his notion of habitus because it does not emphasize the agency of the individual and consequently has been regarded as deterministic. Dalal points out that in answering his critics, Bourdieu argues that it is necessary to first of all, gain knowledge of the constraining mechanisms of habitus and field in order to break free from such sociocultural positioning and consequent possible exploitation. If sociocultural lives are contained and constrained within fields leading to mental dispositions which adapt them to a particular social ecology as though natural, then other lives and language styles from other fields will seem alien or foreign. This may be the case in communities whose habitus is completely different and unique, where a particular valued sociocultural and linguistic capital would not have the equivalent value elsewhere; examples of this could be marginalized youth subcultures with styles of anti-establishment urban dialects such as rap and hip-hop.

Nonetheless as, Clark and Gieve (2006) point out, individuals are capable of multiple identities and therefore by extension, of speaking an urban dialect in one situation and a standard language in another. Consequently we should beware of framing language and culture as essentialistic by confining the individual to one sociocultural and linguistic place.

Bourdieu (1977) views the individual as being a re-enactment of history in his/her current life because his/her habitus is a product of history. He claims as follows, 'The "unconscious" is never anything other than the forgetting of history, which history itself produces by incorporating the objective structures it produces in the second natures of habitus' (79). He goes on to claim that '[t]hus, when we speak of class habitus, we are insisting, . . . that interpersonal relations are never, except in appearance individual-to-individual relationships and that the truth of the interaction is never entirely contained in the interaction' (81). Individuals are then framed here as products of history even as they remain unaware or unconscious of this and so they are the history that they have forgotten.

This raises philosophical questions of individual identity between a dichotomy of the individual and language-culture as product on the one hand and as a process, on the other. A post-structuralist account of language and culture would see the individual's identity rather as a process continually being constructed and also actively constructing itself over time. This means that the individual is not linguistically locked into an essentialistic habitus in terms of language and culture but can move between contexts adapting and changing language styles and discourse from situation to situation.

Post-structuralism

A post-structuralist approach to language, culture, meaning and identity is therefore orientated towards process rather than product. This is radically different from structuralism due to post-structuralist insistence on social phenomena being in flux and continually unfinished. Identity is unfinished because identity is existential rather than essential. This is because identity and language are not objective but ongoing social processes generated by social participants. As we have already seen, Bakhtin (1981) regards objectivity in language as an outcome of shared perception rather than materially grounded. In other words for post-structuralists language and meanings are actively constructed in social interactions and have no essentialistic grounding. This approach, as we have seen, is exemplified by Derrida (1978; 1997) who argues that meaning is iteratively constructed and reconstructed in an endless deferral. Foucault's (1972) position is that meanings, and knowledge therein, can only remain stable through power but then the configurations of power can change where meanings are framed differently. This contrasts with Bourdieu's version of power which ultimately is centred on the state as the main foundation.

With regard to culture, Bhabba (1990) distinguishes between cultural difference and cultural diversity. It is *impossible* to view cultures as different encompassing the notion of alterity or otherness if they are regarded as a part of the notion of diversity. This is because the idea of diversity results in a culture as being viewed not in itself but as being viewed from a dominant perspective. The latter would be more of a structuralist view where one particular language-culture is privileged from which one is able to survey all the surrounding language-cultures and therefore represents hegemony because all cultures are then defined through the dominant culture. Bhabba points out that this is cultural essentialism favouring a concept of diversity but not difference. By contrast cultural difference would involve Derrida's concept of deconstructing and decentring the dominant culture to be regarded as just one culture among others.

Language-culture as process rather than product

With regard to language itself, and from a sociolinguistic position, Creese and Blackledge (2015) argue that separate languages do not map directly onto separate identities or subject positions as fixed bounded units. Instead identities are performed through the linguistic resources at the disposal of participants in language use and we should therefore focus on the user and use of language to construct identity rather than focusing on the language itself. Creese and Blackledge support the view that languages conceptualized as separately mapped onto national borders is an ideological social construct. They point out as follows that 'it is now well established in contemporary sociolinguistics that one language does not straightforwardly index one subject position, and that speakers use linguistic resources in complex ways to perform a range of subject positions, sometimes simultaneously' (3). Therefore language users are able to perform their own identities within their own cultural processes of linguistic interaction rather than through the imposition of fixed cultural linguistic products.

We have seen that Bourdieu's view is that individuals are constrained by their own linguistic and cultural habitus often imposed upon them by a locus of power such as the state and the requirements of education and the exam system. This position does not always hold true in a more post-structural or social constructivist approach where power is less monolithic and more diffuse. Social groups and subcultures have their own locus of power and privilege which is not underpinned by state institutions and their subsets.

Bhabba (1990) argues for a cultural hybridity based upon language-culture as a continual process constructed in social interaction as opposed to a static fixed product. Consequently cultural borders are not fixed but fluid allowing for overlap and the formation of new cultural positions which Bhabba refers to as 'third space'. He states as follows, 'But for me the importance of hybridity is not to be able to trace two original moments from which the third emerges, rather hybridity to me 'is the third space' which enables other positions to emerge (211).

For these 'third spaces' to emerge the necessity, according to Bhabba (1990: 213), is for a decentring of the self leading to 'non-assimilationist claims of cultural difference'. Difference then is in terms of language-culture a result of fluid non-essentialistic identities. Languages therefore like the cultures they embody and generate are not pure and fixed but constituted by vocabularies imported from other languages over time. Most linguists not only know that English is constituted historically by other languages such as Latin, Norman French, Welsh, Saxon and so on but also contemporaneously by linguistic practices through heteroglossia, articulating the voices of others in one's own discourse (Bakhtin 1981). Metaphorically therefore language-culture is then more like a sea of currents and cross-currents than adjacent static plots of land. Bilingualism and biculturalism imply a notion of linguistic and cultural agency where users can use the languages at their disposal, exploiting the resources of language-culture as active ingredients to sociocultural exchanges.

Language-culture both as product and as process

Language and culture as product and as process reflect the interaction respectively between objectivity and subjectivity. A view of the world exclusively as objective or as constructed entirely subjectively could be conceived as reductionist. Objectively reductionist because it does not take into account lived experience or subjectively reductionist because it contains the world view solely in terms of the boundaries of individual subjective experience and perception.

In discussing the work of Michel de Certeau, Terdiman (2001: 407) states the following: '[N]o one formulation or monothetic conceptualization can ever be adequate to our complicated lives- a complication that arises not only on account of empirical profusion or plethora, of the multiplicity and scattering of facts, but from an authentic and multivalent diversity of interests that can never be subsumed, never to be reduced to a single hegemony.'

Terdiman explores the heterology of de Certeau in expressing the notion of meaning occurring in difference where difference lies at the edges and on the borders between something and something else. Terdiman (2001: 399) states, 'For meaning is the consequence of a limit, meaning is the effect of margins.' This acknowledges the objective existence of hegemony, of a dominant sameness of language among other things. National language, for example, is an objective reality, propped up by ideological power which Bourdieu would acknowledge as a reality. Bourdieu would have been fully aware that the French Academy polices the French language and allows some neologisms and foreign words in the public domain but prohibits others. Of course this doesn't affect the way people speak on the streets and anti-establishment languages such as 'le Verlan', an urban dialect, have appeared in the suburbs of French cities. However de Certeau would point out that these areas of street language are indeed at the margins of hegemony or as Bhabba would state as 'third spaces' where individuals and groups create their own social space to construct hybridity of language-culture. Meanings have been forced into the margins by hegemony of power as Terdiman (2001: 400) claims that 'marginalization inevitably embodies the cruel reality of power'. Again, we have seen this currently occurring in the Cameroonian case study of Chapter 6 where Cameroonian Pidgin English is a hybrid language-culture reflecting a national identity constructed as a bridging point by indigenous people to communicate with colonial rulers and yet it is pushed to the margins by the dominant sociocultural power arrangements. It is in fact a national language that is refused official state acknowledgement.

We also see marginalized language-culture pushed to the sidelines of mainstream life in the lived experiences of the 'dalits', otherwise known as the 'untouchables' in Indian society. In Chapter 8, Joseph narrates how dalits have developed a literature of resistance revealing their atrocious living conditions and exclusion. He analyses this exclusion defining it as an inclusion by exclusion so that dalits' inclusion acts as a way of being acknowledged as excluded and outsiders. A resistance to this has been the development of a dalit literature criticizing Hinduism for its endorsement of this system of exclusion and calling for a transformation of society. This literature therefore is not just descriptive of dalits' outrageously deprived conditions but is also generating a new consciousness of the need for transformation of society. Dalit literature is now gaining in cultural capital within mainstream India as a counter-culture. Chapter 8 is an example of de Certeau's thesis of looking for truth at the margins and this is indeed Derrida's purpose in deconstruction of the mainstream centre to reveal that which has been ignored.

Linguistic and cultural differences are consequently pushed to the sidelines and need therefore to be explored, valorized and foregrounded if meanings and forms of knowledge are not to be forever lost. Forms of knowledge then exist in the margins and power has to be claimed and handed over so that knowledge may resurface.

I believe that de Certeau adds a moral vision to the notion of difference expounded by Derrida, who is correct in saying that meaning is generated by difference since if all is the same and indistinguishable from anything else, then there are no meanings. Meaning proliferates under the conditions of difference, where many things differ from each other to the extent that the differing elements are named and to be named is to exist. Power is the element that perpetuates uniformity and sameness and with this, difference is pushed to one side. The moral argument of de Certeau is that the meanings at the margins need to be foregrounded and revalorized.

Hegemony of culture and language represent sameness and therefore the antithesis of difference whereas 'heterology' being de Certeau's theory of social differences represent the differences which have been marginalized and need to be empowered and resurfaced (Terdiman 2001).

Moreover, not only do the margins need to be empowered but also according to Saltmarsh (2015), spaces need to be opened up within hegemonic continuity for agency and cultural difference. The educational project of a pedagogy of marginalized language-culture would be to seek the voice of the other within hegemonic discourse through other languages, either foreign languages or indigenous native languages such as the Creole already cited in Guinea Bissau or the more established Celtic languages in the United Kingdom, Ireland and France. This has educational implications particularly in a UK system of education often predicated on socio-economics which promotes the economically marketable scientific and technological STEM subjects within the curriculum to the detriment of the arts and humanities subjects.

Post-structural agency in media discourse

The notion of discourse is important in the construction of identity since discourse concerns forms of communication in a much wider sense than the language based on internal features of grammar and lexis and internalized socio-political status from culturally conferred value. Discourse in then language use enacted in social context.

Discourse encompasses language types vis-à-vis social contexts and is language use in social action including other features of communication surrounding language such as gesture, dress, music, fashion, image and appearance much of which is now expressed through the social space afforded by the digital media of the new technologies. As Giardiello points out, 'In today's post-modern society the media has become as important as food and clothing' (p. 85 in this volume). In Chapter 5 she argues that the digital media provides a social space for the construction of youth identities, in giving youth its own voice. This can be construed as liberating in a situation where youth could be disempowered and marginalized by more powerful adult discourse. Social media does contribute to shaping identity although as Giardiello argues, this is part of an interactive process rather than a deterministic product. In her small-scale study at Millgate School, she shows how young people use media such as YouTube and Facebook to create their own space for the construction of identity and presentation of self. These social media platforms represent multiple areas where young people explore different possibilities for identity and even constructing not just one identity but multiple identities. Giardiello argues against the traditional notion of universal biological and psychological developmental stages of identity proposed by the American psychologist Granville Stanley Hall in the 1880s, who maintained that adolescence was a period of crisis or Storm and Stress imported from the notion of Storm und Drang within German literature. Giardiello argues for a notion of psychological development being shaped by culture and the Bourdieusian concept of 'habitus' that we have already mentioned in this chapter.

Digital media platforms offer possibilities, in the context of an active developmental pedagogy, for users to co-create spaces of habitus with fellow users where identities can be co-constructed and maintained in dialogues, experiments of presentation of self and the creativity of video production.

What emerges from Giardiello's study of youth media discourse is that today's youth, far from being marginalized, have a much wider array of media resources to explore identity resulting in a much lesser sense of deterministic identity than was experienced by previous generations of youth who did have television, radio, music and magazines but nonetheless had far less opportunity to actively contribute to their own identity construction.

We may conclude from this particular study that new technologies have the potential to liberate identities although at the same time also note the downside of the use of anonymity provided by virtual identity to bully and abuse others.

In this regard Anderson demonstrates how social media on the internet can become a site of conflict in the construction of regional identity. In Chapter 4, '"DFLs" versus "Locals"', Anderson shows how the struggle for regional identity in a Kent coastal town in southeast England became polarized when opposing cultural discourses competed over identities in Margate. Much like chapters in the international section 3 dealing with dominant languages seeking hegemony by marginalizing and colonizing minority language, we see in Chapter 4 how colonization operates at the level of discourses in an English setting. In this chapter, we see how young middle-class Londoners, many of whom Anderson defines as 'hipsters', are seeking to 'colonize' Margate by speculating on much lower property prices than in the capital and yet at the same time benefitting from the high speed train links allowing them to return to London in little over an hour. These 'hipsters' seek alternative urban lifestyles, working in the creative industries or in the arts themselves, and are looking to transform Margate which, as Anderson states, has suffered from massive deprivation since its Victorian heyday as a seaside holiday resort for working-class Londoners. The current discursive polemic revolves around a controversial article in an online lifestyle cultural magazine promoting Margate as a new cultural Phoenix emerging from the depths of deprivation with the locals being depicted in very derogatory terms as 'drunk', 'jobless', 'ill-educated', 'racist' and 'wasted' in opposition to the new young middle-class migrants who are 'cultured', 'well-heeled', 'creative' and 'avant-garde'. Such polarized identities are quickly established and circulated because of the communicative speed of the internet and then rapidly descend into an aggressive polemic of claim and counter-claim between the online magazine author and local middle-class residents who feel that they are being stereotyped and not represented. We witness then in this conflict a cultural power struggle over identity where in this local situation, much like in the international situations in the international section 3, a metropolitan powerful discourse seems to be attempting to marginalize a less powerful local discourse.

These are ethical issues of power that need to be researched and resolved in the area of abuse over the internet in terms of such unjust misrepresentation. Nevertheless new technologies of social media and the internet can provide an educative means of foregrounding and valorizing marginalized discourse as we see in the establishment of resistant discourse.

Pedagogy and the voice of alterity; empowering marginalized language-culture

Freire (1972: 46) views education as an emancipatory force for humanizing the voice of the other in a system which, contrary to the notion of emancipation, he describes as the 'banking' concept of education. The 'banking' system is an instrumental system of education orientated to socio-economics where the student is loaded up with knowledge and skill necessary to further economic prosperity for him/herself through performance rather than to question or challenge the ethics and justice of the system itself. Learning a language in this system would be learning an economically powerful language such as

French, German, Spanish and now Mandarin Chinese for national trade and development rather than cultural understanding in itself. Therefore the goals of education and language education are often economically extrinsic and not intrinsic. However, in terms of language as shaping intrinsic political identity in opposition to an externally dominant language-culture, we often see language as a powerful force in creating cohesion as an act of resistance.

In Montreal, for example, Bill 101 has bolstered the French language for employment and civic cohesion in a situation which was being dominated by the economic exigencies to speak English. Without this law, French may have become a marginalized language and so language use and value is not just cultural but also a socio-political issue of identity. This argument runs somewhat counter to the notion that language cannot be mapped on to national or political boundaries but used existentially as a readily available resource. We see that this might not be the case where languages and cultures are under threat and struggle then ensues for regional, national, linguistic and cultural identity all within the same package such as in the areas of Catalonia or the Basque country of Spain. Therefore whether one sees language as borderless, free from national and political ideology, or as part of a geographical identity may well depend on whether one occupies a marginalized socio-political position. In the example of Wales, without the Welsh government's support for the language in schools and political institutions as part of a national identity Welsh may also have become a language in danger of extinction.

Unfortunately in other areas of the world (see Chapter 6 for the Cameroon case study), where many languages are spoken in multilingual communities, the pupils' home language may well be ignored as teaching takes place in the hegemony of the dominant language-culture. Chapter 6 witnesses the marginalization of tribal languages in Cameroon such as Bamun, Fulfulde and Bulu which were not allowed to be used in education and where schools, which used these languages for teaching, were closed down. French was the required language for education, although English is now becoming more valued for its commercial global currency. This is echoed in Sunuodola's Chapter 9 where the Uyghur language in Xinjiang province of China is no longer the language medium for education and has been marginalized as a school subject by the dominant Han language and culture. In a similar way to French in Cameroon, Mandarin Chinese in the Uyghur province of China is the language of economic success as well as sociocultural recognition and symbolic cultural capital.

In Chapter 7, Kum narrates and analyses a situation where there is a complete loss of voice during and resulting from refugee journeys across national borders in their search for sanctuary. We see the loss of voice occurring due to economic and social powerlessness since they are uprooted and without a cultural and linguistic locus to act as a base for social capital. Their voice is consequently at the mercy of the hegemony of the host or transit nations and their media resources in transmitting derogatory and menacing labels and metaphors depicting images of invasion or incursion. An example of this is the *Daily Express* front page news headline as follows: 'Migrant summer chaos as thousands try to get into Britain, French official warns' (*Daily Express* 31 March 2017). This is an example of hegemony in language and communication where the other is objectivized by power through media.

In education, hegemony is expressed in Freire's notion of a 'banking' system where the dominant culture is inculcated rather than critiqued so that students concentrate on performance rather than analysis. According to Freire (1972: 45), 'Education thus becomes an act of depositing, in which the students are the depositaries and the teacher is the depositor.' Freire furthermore states that the teacher-pupils power imbalance reflects the inequalities in societies where the purpose of education is to possess and to acquire and where those who *have* set the cultural agenda both for themselves and for those who *have not*. The result of this is that pupils are authoritatively positioned to assimilate language and knowledge rather than develop critical awareness. As we recall, Bourdieu (1982) argues that this authoritarian process occurs through the imposition of standard language which is then monitored in the examination system.

To resist the 'banking' system, pupils need to become active student participants in education and this requires a change in the ontological perspective of social life. This changed perspective would be that reality is not a fixed given but instead that it is dynamic, in flux and co-constructed intersubjectively by all its participants, teachers and students alike. This is not to deny the existence of objective facts but to acknowledge that much of objectivity has already been socially constructed intersubjectively over time through historical processes and so students also in turn need to engage in a process which constructs and critiques facts intersubjectively rather to have them passively inculcated as pre-packaged knowledge. This means co-constructing knowledge through questioning and dialogue in the language of the learner rather than through the imposition of perceived dominant language alongside the imposition of facts. This also means engaging in textual critical analysis where headlines such as the *Daily Express* headline mentioned above are not just accepted as fact but questioned through the analysis of language and the effect it is intended to produce such as possible fear and/or outrage in the reference to 'migrant summer chaos'.

Freire's underlying rationale is that the world itself is an unfinished process where knowledge and identities are always working towards completion. This provides an underlying dynamic for education. Language is crucial therefore and is involved within the process of moving forward in the construction of identity and knowledge.

Bilingual education is then part of this process of learning within the language of the learner as part of an emancipatory construction of knowledge, free from the domination of a language-culture hegemony. This sort of pedagogic action would valorize or revalorize the marginalized language of the learner.

Bilingual education

Creese and Blackledge (2010) support a view that communication transcends the borders of languages as separate bounded units. Languages that come into contact with each other through their speakers, reciprocally drawing upon their linguistic resources and so consequently labelling them as separate, is an ideological act based upon geographical territory. Creese and Blackledge in their work on translanguaging, focus upon speakers in their use of linguistic resources rather than languages themselves as objective, bounded units. Garcia (2009: 44) defines translanguaging as follows, 'Translanguaging, or engaging in bilingual or multilingual discourse practices, is an approach to bilingualism that is centred not on languages, as has been often the case, but on the practices of bilinguals that are readily observable.' Indeed Garcia has initiated the use of the term 'languaging' (43) to refer to discursive practices as opposed to speaking languages and therefore translanguaging is an acknowledgement that in everyday interactions bilinguals move across their linguistic resources irrespective of language boundaries that can be viewed as politically ideological.

Therefore linguistic identity is not so much objectively imposed but rather subjectively and intersubjectively negotiated through language use by participants in linguistic interactions.

Languages are not hermetically sealed and even within a particular language, language users mix registers and discourses, as we have seen in the notion of heteroglossia as using the voices of others (Bakhtin 1981; Wertsch 1991).

Emphasis should therefore be placed upon what users are doing with language rather than languages themselves as separate entities since speakers are capable of drawing upon the totality of linguistic resources at their disposal.

Garcia (2009) maintains that translanguaging is a form of bilingual pedagogy that contrasts with separate bilingualism where two or more languages are acknowledged as distinct units between which occasional code switching occurs as participants select different languages to express different items.

However the aim here is not to focus systematically on a particular form of bilingualism, among the many that exist, due to a belief that the issue of bilingualism may well be shaped by the socio-political nature of the language and the socio-political position of user. In Quebec, for example, Blackledge (2005) points out that French is highly regarded by Anglophones and also, I may add, immigrants, as an affective civic and socio-political attachment to community. This seems to express a notion, in a bilingual society, of languages being spoken separately for different purposes and, in the case of Quebec, immigrants may also favour English for economic reasons as opposed to those of social cohesion and acceptance.

However in small-scale interactions, boundaries may well be fluid where language is used as a resource by bilingual users without linguistic borders. The aim of this chapter then is to focus on the way in which using both languages generally in bilingual education within a teaching and learning situation can revalorize and revitalize a marginalized language at the same time as maintaining the economic opportunity afforded by the dominant language.

Bilingualism for social justice

Asgharzadeh (2008) states Freire's position that social justice entails that education should take place in one's own language as opposed to a colonial language since this represents one's own voice. He points out that in multilingual societies, 'this voice cannot be that of the oppressor, the colonizer or the dominant' (350). For Freire the linguistic emancipation to use one's own voice is an integral and foundational aspect of sociocultural justice.

In the context of bilingual education, social and economic justice would be a goal by using the languages at the disposal of the learner to privilege the learner's position at the intersection between his/her own conceptual learner identity, the local community identity and opportunities afforded by the wider world. This may be by drawing upon his/her linguistic resources either consecutively or concurrently. Garcia (2009; 320) points out that the 'consecutive' or 'concurrent' debate depends on the language ideology and practice of the school and its sociolinguistic context but that the crucial matter is to value each language equally and respectfully and not to forbid the use of any of the languages in a learning situation, since 'an equitable pedagogy under no circumstances forbids a student to use either language'. Garcia acknowledges that traditional bilingual pedagogy separates languages where some curricula are taught in one language and some in another language but that this is not a natural way since languages are not naturally but ideologically divided. Garcia therefore states that 'a bilingual education that values only disconnected wholes and devalues the often loose parts, and insists on the strict separation of languages is not the only way to successfully educate children bilingually, although it is a widely conducted practice' (8).

Quite apart from the cultural discourses surrounding bilingualism, there are also other claims with regard to bilingual use of languages and these concern flexibility in thinking in being able to move easily between languages. There are claims that bilingual students are more likely to succeed at school academically as Christoffels et al. (2015) argue that bilinguals are able to switch between languages, resulting in the exercising of cognitive abilities. According to their research among Dutch students, their findings indicate that bilinguals outperform monolinguals even on non-linguistic tests of cognition and mental flexibility. This advantage includes those who learn a second language at school in the case of additive bilingualism since the crucial factor is not the age at which one learns the second language but the frequency with which one switches between language codes during the day. Christoffels et al. conclude as follows: '[O]ur results indicate that bilingual education may promote cognitive flexibility and a bias towards a more focused "scope" of attention' (377). Garcia (2009), who is a proponent of translanguaging, supports this view acknowledging the personal cognitive benefits of bilingual education due to the development of a greater metalinguistic awareness. This arises due to linguistic analytical effects derived from the process of switching between languages because children come to have a greater understanding of underlying linguistic structures. Garcia states, 'Bilingual children's ability to use two languages makes language structures more visible as children have to organize their two language systems' (95). They therefore gain an understanding in how language works in terms of underlying structures besides the ability to use the languages at their disposal.

It seems therefore that bilingual education can perform not only the role of social justice in foregrounding marginalized language so that learners use their own voice but also that code switching between languages gives them a greater cognitive advantage over monolinguals. Additionally, in using the language of economic opportunity which may be a global lingua franca as well as their own language, bilinguals gain in terms of community cohesion, cognitive flexibility as well as economic opportunity in the wider world.

Teacher professional agency in pedagogical discourse

In Chapter 11, Zotzmann addresses a methodological approach to teacher development in foreign language education called SETT – the self-evaluation of teacher talk where a group of teachers analyse their own classroom based interactions. They analyse this to understand their own styles of communication and its effectiveness. In this process of professional reflection, teachers take ownership of their own development and become aware of themselves in the classroom in such areas as how much time they allow their students to communicate, how they move from one topic to another and the extent to which their interactions are teacher centred or student centred. In the chapter, it becomes clear that teachers' pedagogy is more than classroom discourse since this itself is shaped by wider social discourses which place external expectations on teachers. Zotzmann concludes that this particular methodology of self-evaluation is empowering in providing teachers with a metalanguage to take theoretical ownership of pedagogical practice, yet still a more ecological context is also required for teachers to understand how their practice is also shaped by external social forces. This amounts to connecting micro classroom discourses with the exigencies of a wider sociocultural discourse. This chapter supports the professional agency of teachers who, like the students, in the preceding Chapter 10, are caught within the cross-currents of discourses and, without critical awareness or even a metalanguage, risk being at the mercy of powerful wider discourses. This would be then teachers and students at risk of losing voice and ownership within educational systems. Despite this Chapter 10 shows student agency where students formulate their own cultural motivations for learning a foreign language constructed from their own ways of seeing the world rather than that generated by official school discourse. This is because, in this particular case study, official school discourse embodied professionally by the teacher did not enjoy hegemony in the classroom but competed with other discourses embodied by the students which drew upon larger community and sociocultural discourses such as media. Consequently students were and, indeed, are able to construct their own motivations for learning from their own cultural resources (Gillette 1994).

Conclusion

This concluding chapter has proposed that a critical pedagogy, as proposed by Freire, is a process for redressing cultural and linguistic inequalities and for a revalorization of minority language and culture. Bilingual education, in terms of equal status for languages as opposed to dominant and subsidiary language-culture, is seen as a way of creating intercultural understanding where the minority language can operate in education alongside the dominant economically propitious language. The translanguaging model of bilingual education (Creese & Blackledge 2010; 2015) appears to exemplify this approach to pedagogy.

Even in areas deemed to be monolingual, a second language is necessary to gain a view of another language-culture as a valued other and a difference from one's own otherwise fixed point of view.

Students themselves, through creativity in the use of new technologies, can, as we have seen, empower their own voice and equally, as we have also seen, teachers can construct their own professional voice through their own language and metalanguage for their own autonomy and the benefit of students.

Pedagogy then as microcosm for society can also be seen as a model for society in an attempt to redress sociocultural power inequalities through a more process-led education, asking questions and constructing answers in dialogue rather than imposing prepackaged deposits of knowledge. Pedagogy needs to model a construction of knowledge as a process examining why things occur in such or such a way, as well as stating how things happen, therefore analysis as well as narrative, and process constituting product rather than just product alone.

References

Asgharzadeh, A. (2008). 'The Return of the Subaltern: International Education and Politics of Voice'. *Journal of Studies in International Education* 12.4: 334–63.

Bakhtin, M. (1981). *The Dialogic Imagination: Four Essays*. M. Hoquist (ed.). Austin: University of Texas Press.

Bhabba, H. (1990). 'The Third Space. Interview with Homi Bhabba'. In *Identity: Community, Culture, Difference*. London: Lawrence and Wishart. 2017–221.

Blackledge, A. (2005). *Discourse and Power in a Multilingual World*. Amsterdam/ Philadelphia: John Benjamins Publishing Company.

Bourdieu, P. (1977). *Outline of a Theory of Practice*. Cambridge: Cambridge University Press.

Bourdieu, P. (1982). *Langage et pouvoir symbolique*. Paris: Editions Fayard.

Bourdieu, P. (1989). 'Social Space and Symbolic Power'. *Sociological Theory* 7.1: 14–25.

Bourdieu, P. (2013). 'Symbolic Capital and Social Classes'. *Journal of Classical Sociology* 13.2: 292–302.

Christoffels, I. K., de Haan, A. M., Steenbergen, L. et al. (2015). 'Two Is Better Than One: Bilingual Education Promotes the Flexible Mind'. *Psychological Research* 79: 371.

Clark, R., & Gieve, S. N. (2006). 'On the Discursive Construction of the "Chinese learner"'. *Language, Culture and Curriculum* 9.1: 54–73.

Creese, A., & Blackledge, A. (2010). 'Translanguaging in the Bilingual Classroom: A Pedagogy for Learning and Teaching?' *The Modern Language Journal* 94: 103–15.

Creese, A., & Blackledge, A. (2015). 'Translanguaging and Identity in Educational Settings'. *Annual Review of Applied Linguistics* 35: 20–35.

Dalal, J. (2016). 'Pierre Bourdieu: The Sociologist of Education'. *Contemporary Education Dialogue* 13.2: 231–50.

Derrida, J. (1978). *Writing and Difference*. London. Routledge.

Derrida, J. (1997). *Of Grammatology*. London. The John Hopkins University Press.

Foucault, M. (1972). *The Archaeology of Knowledge*. London. Routledge.

Freire, P. (1972). *Pedagogy of the Oppressed*. London. Penguin Books.

Garcia, O. (2009). *Bilingual Education in the 21st Century: A Global Perspective*. Oxford: Wiley-Blackwell.

Gillette, B. (1994). 'The Role of Learner Goals in L2 Success'. In J. Lantolf and G. Appel, *Vygotskian Approaches to Second Language Research*. Norwood, NJ: Ablex Press.

Saltmarsh, S. (2015). 'Michel de Certeau, Everyday Life and Policy Cultures: The Case of Parent Engagement in Education Policy'. *Critical Studies in Education* 56.1: 38–54.

Terdiman, R. (2001). 'The Marginality of Michel de Certeau'. *The South Atlantic Quarterly* 100.2: 399–421.

Wertsch, J. V. (1991). *Voices of the Mind. A Sociocultural Approach to Mediated Action*. Cambridge, MA: Harvard University Press.

Newspaper- Daily Express newspaper front page headline- 31-03-2017.

Contributors

Christopher Anderson is senior lecturer in applied linguistics and communication at Canterbury Christchurch University, United Kingdom. His research interests cover discourse analysis, intercultural communication and qualitative research methods. In specific terms, he is interested in the intercultural dimensions of social media use and in epistemological and ethical questions in applied linguistics.

David Evans is fellow in education at Liverpool Hope University, United Kingdom. His research interests are in language and identity within education and pedagogy. Wider research interests are in marginalized language-culture and multilingualism for social justice and opportunity. He is co-author and editor of *Language and Identity: Discourse in the World* (2014).

Patricia Giardiello is lecturer in childhood and youth studies at Manchester Metropolitan University, United Kingdom. Formally a senior lecturer at Liverpool Hope University, Patricia is now working part time to allow more time for academic writing and pursuing her research interests around children's and young people's voice, rights and participation. Wider research interests include empowering early childhood educators, international pedagogies and intergenerational learning.

Henry Kum lectures in education studies at Liverpool Hope University, United Kingdom. He has taught in schools and universities in Cameroon, France, Scotland and England. His research interests include voice and inclusivity of marginalized children; the intersectionality of class, race and gender; post-conflict education and the education of refugee communities. His wider focus is on issues around inequality and equality in schooling and education.

Mamtimyn Sunuodula teaches Asian politics and international relations in the School of Government and International Affairs at Durham University, United Kingdom. His research interests include language and identity in multi-ethnic and multilingual political entities; language, power and social equality; and language-in-education policies.

Joseph Mundananikkal Thomas is assistant professor in the Sociology Department at the University of Mumbai, India. His abiding research interests, among others, are centred on life worlds of dalits in contemporary India, with particular reference to the state of Maharashtra.

Karin Zotzmann is lecturer in applied linguistics at Southampton University, United Kingdom. Her research interests include the ways in which socio-economic, political and institutional factors and processes impact upon the teaching and learning of foreign languages. She has also published widely in the field of intercultural learning and education

Index

Lightning Source UK Ltd.
Milton Keynes UK
UKHW020708020120
356167UK00004BA/63/P